AF477678

# Art for Equality

# ART FOR EQUALITY

## The NAACP's Cultural Campaign for Civil Rights

JENNY WOODLEY

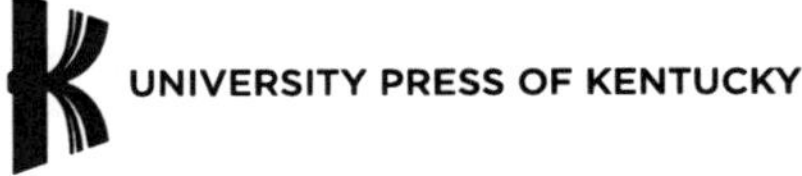

UNIVERSITY PRESS OF KENTUCKY

Copyright © 2014 by The University Press of Kentucky

Scholarly publisher for the Commonwealth,
serving Bellarmine University, Berea College, Centre College of Kentucky, Eastern
Kentucky University, The Filson Historical Society, Georgetown College, Kentucky
Historical Society, Kentucky State University, Morehead State University, Murray
State University, Northern Kentucky University, Transylvania University, University of
Kentucky, University of Louisville,
and Western Kentucky University.
All rights reserved.

*Editorial and Sales Offices:* The University Press of Kentucky
663 South Limestone Street, Lexington, Kentucky 40508-4008
www.kentuckypress.com

Library of Congress Cataloging-in-Publication Data

Woodley, Jenny, 1980-
  Art for equality : the NAACP's cultural campaign for civil rights / Jenny Woodley.
    pages cm. — (Civil rights and the struggle for Black equality in the twentieth
century)
  Includes bibliographical references and index.
  ISBN 978-0-8131-4516-7 (hardcover : acid-free paper) — ISBN 978-0-8131-4518-1 (PDF) —
ISBN 978-0-8131-4517-4 (ePub)
  1. National Association for the Advancement of Colored People—History—20th century.
2. Arts—Political aspects—United States—History—20th century. 3. Anti-racism
—United States—History—20th century. 4. African Americans—Civil rights—United
States—History—20th century. 5. Civil rights movements—United States—History—
20th century. 6. African American artists—History—20th century. 7. African Americans
in art—History—20th century. 8. African Americans—Intellectual life—20th century.
9. United States—Intellectual life—20th century. 10. United States—Race relations—
History—20th century. I. Title.
  E185.5.N276W66 2014
  323.1196'073--dc23                                          2014003473

This book is printed on acid-free paper meeting the requirements of the American
National Standard for Permanence in Paper for Printed Library Materials.

Manufactured in the United States of America.

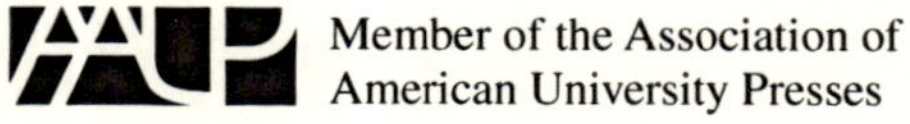

Member of the Association of
American University Presses

For Niamh,
who arrived when this book was in its final stages
and who is the most wonderful distraction.

# Contents


Introduction: "The national mental attitude"    1
1.  The Birth of a Cultural Strategy    11
2.  Representing the New Negro    35
3.  Du Bois's *Crisis* and the Black Image on the Page    63
4.  "A union of art and propaganda"    97
5.  White in Hollywood    127
6.  Blacks, Reds, White    159
Conclusion: "The true picture of America"    191
Acknowledgments    205
Notes    207
Bibliography    227
Index    241

Introduction

# "The national mental attitude"

In 1926 W. E. B. Du Bois was addressing an audience in Chicago when he rhetorically asked of the National Association for the Advancement of Colored People (NAACP), "how is it that an organization of this kind can turn aside to talk about Art?" Why was it that an organization more commonly associated with courtroom battles and political lobbying should spend time, money, and effort encouraging, publishing, challenging, protesting, and creating poems, novels, short stories, plays, artwork, exhibitions, and films? The beginnings of an answer can be found in an article written by James Weldon Johnson, the NAACP's first black executive secretary, in 1928. He set out what had been done to try to solve the "Negro problem." The approaches to date had been "religious, educational, political, industrial, ethical, economic, sociological." There had been some success, but, he argued, the time had come for a new approach. It was one that "requires a minimum of pleas, or propaganda, or philanthropy. It depends more upon what the Negro himself does than upon what someone does for him." Johnson's idea was "the approach along the line of intellectual and artistic achievement by Negroes, and may be called the art approach to the Negro problem." Johnson was writing during the Harlem Renaissance and so believed that there was already evidence of its success. The effect of black artistic achievement for the African American could be seen on "his condition and status as a man and citizen." Johnson, reasserting a claim he had made earlier in the decade in his *Book of American Negro Poetry,* argued that "the 'race problem' is fast reaching the stage of being more a question of national mental attitudes toward the Negro than a question of his actual condition." It was "becoming less a matter of dealing with what he is and more a matter of dealing with what America thinks he is." It was necessary, Johnson argued, to challenge racial stereotypes; in this way, the national mental attitude would be altered, and its consequence—racial inequality—would be defeated. This idea, though sometimes modified, formed the core of the NAACP's engagement with culture during its first half century.[1]

The NAACP launched a number of cultural campaigns between 1910 and the 1960s that included publishing art and literature in its magazine, the *Crisis,* and becoming involved with the Harlem Renaissance; using the arts to change white attitudes toward lynching; and protesting degrading images in film and television and lobbying for more positive depictions. These were not just random excursions followed on a whim or fancy but were driven by a specific strategy. This strategy was to use representations of African Americans in the arts and popular culture to challenge race prejudice. The NAACP believed that racial inequality was caused by the attitudes of white Americans toward blacks. The association hoped that if it could change those views, then it would open the way for greater civil rights. Prejudices were reflected in and reinforced by stereotypical depictions of African Americans. Therefore, the NAACP believed it needed to challenge these representations, enforce their removal, and replace them with more positive images. This would alter white attitudes about African Americans and deliver a blow to race prejudice. Following this logic, the NAACP hoped that cultural forms could influence opinions about specific issues and be used to bring about political change. Furthermore, the NAACP argued that, in some cases, the very creation of the arts should be celebrated and that black talent would provide proof of the race's status. Its cultural work, therefore, was directly linked to its legal and legislative efforts. These ideas shaped its attitude toward and involvement with a whole range of cultural media and art forms for half a century.

The way in which the NAACP conceived of the race problem was central to its development of a cultural strategy. It believed that racial inequality was the result of "race prejudice." In other words, African Americans suffered political, social, and economic discrimination because of the attitudes of white Americans toward the race. To the NAACP leadership, racism existed as an ideology or doctrine rather than in the structures of society. This reflected discourses about race during this period. As early as the 1850s, Frederick Douglass defined racism as the "diseased imagination." George Frederickson traces the historiography of racism and finds that scholars at the beginning of the twentieth century were concerned with "the history of ideas rather than with the social and political applications of prejudiced beliefs and attitudes." Indeed, the very term *race prejudice* suggests an emphasis on thoughts rather than action. Nevertheless, the NAACP did recognize the practical and structural implications, and implementations, of racism. It spent the majority of its time fighting educational inequality, segregation in public facilities and housing, disenfranchisement, and inequality before the law. However, it saw these problems as manifestations of prejudicial beliefs and argued that if these attitudes could be changed, then the practical applications of racism would also end.[2]

In 1910 W. E. B. Du Bois argued that much of race prejudice "is born of ignorance and misapprehension, honest mistake and misguided zeal." The NAACP would, therefore, "fight the wrong of race prejudice" by "doing away with the excuses for prejudice," by "showing the unreasonableness of prejudice," and by "exposing the evils of prejudice." The NAACP saw racism as something that could be eradicated through exposure, education, and persuasion. It wanted to show whites the true nature and real achievements of African Americans and hoped that this would convince them to treat blacks as equal citizens. The NAACP needed to change the way white America thought about blacks. As Moorfield Storey said, "We want to make race prejudice . . . as unfashionable as it is now fashionable." If racism existed in the minds of white America, then public opinion would be a key tool in the NAACP's battle for civil rights.[3]

Racism as an ideology did not fully emerge in America until the nineteenth century. It was not until abolitionists began their sustained attack on slavery that whites needed a coherent argument to defend America's "peculiar institution." The process of defining blackness (and therefore whiteness) in the United States began with slavery but accelerated in the post–Civil War era. Race, Grace Elizabeth Hale suggests, became the "crucial means of ordering the newly enlarged meaning of America." White supremacy was an ideology that grew in strength as blacks won greater freedoms and threatened whites' way of life and their sense of identity. Anti-black prejudice varied in degree, but most racist whites shared common ground. The central tenet was that blacks were physically, intellectually, and morally different from whites. Furthermore, they were inherently inferior to whites. The differences between the races either were permanent or would only change very slowly, and therefore an integrated society was virtually impossible.[4]

The ideology of racism was perpetuated and reinforced through American culture and more specifically through the representation of African Americans within that culture. There is a long history of derogatory depictions of blacks in America, which began in the antebellum period but persisted and developed after the Civil War, as racism grew in strength.

African Americans were depicted in art and literature, in songs and on sheet music, in cartoons, in advertising, as collectibles and on household goods, on stage and in films. White creators of these depictions followed a prescribed pattern of looks, speech, actions, and traits. Some of the stereotypes had names—"Sambo," "Mammy," "Uncle Tom," "Aunt Jemima," "Jim Crow," and "Zip Coon"—while others were nameless caricatures.[5] These cultural representations provided a way for whites to work through issues about race and to enforce the ideology of racism. For example, images of contented slaves and loyal ex-slaves, which were so common in early twentieth-century American culture, absolved the South of blame for slavery and the North of any responsibility for America's blacks. African Americans also appeared in more threatening guises as the black beast, which showed the black man freed from the restraints of slavery and reverting to his "natural" savagery. Such depictions were used to justify the repressive treatment of African Americans, particularly through mob violence. Cultural products could spread the message of black inferiority to a wide audience. In those areas where there was little contact between the races, cultural representations shaped people's opinions about blacks. In others, like the South, they not only confirmed existing prejudices but also increased hostility. Deriding and mocking the race helped keep blacks in their place. American culture thus taught both whites and blacks the "acceptable" boundaries of behavior and interaction.

The NAACP believed that the way in which African Americans were represented culturally affected how they were treated socially and politically. Race prejudice worked by suggesting that African Americans were as dim-witted, docile, or depraved as their cultural image and therefore that white America was correct to treat them as such (never mind that such depictions often contradicted each other): blacks were stupid and so could not be trusted with the franchise; they were lazy, and therefore education would make no difference; they were content with their lives, so philanthropy was misguided; they were immoral and violent, so they must be segregated from white society; and they were licentious and needed to be controlled. The NAACP was convinced that it had to change this perception of African Americans in order to open the door for such advancements as the franchise, desegregated education, and, ultimately, full civil rights. It sought to remove these damaging images from the culture; to encourage the introduction of what it considered "positive" depictions of African Americans and black life; and to educate Americans about black talent and achievements. It believed that if it could alter the cultural representation of African Americans, then it would be one step closer to eradicating racism.

The NAACP's cultural strategy worked in a number of ways. It wanted to change the way African Americans were portrayed in a wide range of media, from literature and art to advertisements, songs, and greetings cards. It focused particular attention on images of blacks in visual mass culture: first motion pictures and then television. At times, it was concerned with simply removing the offending images or preventing their distribution, which led it to advocate the controversial and limiting tactic of censorship. At others, the association lobbied for the inclusion of what it considered to be positive images. The NAACP's cultural strategy also involved the development and promotion of black literary and artistic talent. The association encouraged black authors, poets, painters, playwrights, and other creative individuals. These artists were to be shining examples of what the race could achieve and would prove to whites that African Americans were "civilized" and therefore deserved equal rights. According to August Meier, the "striving for literary and intellectual accomplishment was connected with the idea that it would be the intellectuals" who would "lead the race into achieving higher culture and civilization." Du Bois had predicted that the intellectual, educated, and professional blacks, what he called the "Talented Tenth," would save the race. "Was there ever a nation on God's fair earth civilized from the bottom upward?" he asked. "Never; it is, ever was and ever will be from the top downward that culture filters. The Talented Tenth rises and pulls all that are worth the saving up to their vantage ground."[6]

The emphasis on cultural attainment began with the formation of the NAACP's official magazine, the *Crisis,* in 1910 and led to the association's involvement in the Harlem Renaissance in the 1920s. The NAACP also used the arts to change public opinion on specific issues, most notably lynching. It hoped to turn public apathy and approval of mob violence into condemnation by exposing the true nature of lynching. Furthermore, it wanted to challenge the white story of lynching—the way lynching was remembered and explained—and the arts allowed African Americans to create an alternative to the dominant white narrative. This reflects its broader desire to challenge America's historical memory, an issue that took on great significance when it came to the Civil War and Reconstruction. The NAACP's objection to such films as *The Birth of a Nation* (1915) was based, in part, on its depiction of this important period of American, and black, history. The final element of the NAACP's cultural strategy focused not on white attitudes, but on those of African Americans. The creation of black culture and the projection of positive black images were intended to raise black pride and to forge a sense of collective African American identity. This self-esteem and collectivism were crucial in the struggle for civil rights. These different strands can be seen weaving their way throughout all the NAACP's cultural campaigns during its first fifty years. Underpinning them all was the principle that the arts and popular culture could be used to shape opinions about African Americans.

For many years the NAACP had a reputation for being controlled by whites and for being assimilationist, middle class, and conservative. Some of these charges, such as the first, have been challenged by historians; others remain.[7] This study is not an attempt to either defend or criticize the NAACP, but rather to try to understand its approach. It asks why the association followed the tactic of a cultural strategy, what it hoped to achieve, and how it responded to and used different forms of culture. I examine what these campaigns reveal about the NAACP as an organization and how it approached questions of assimilation, cultural pluralism, class bias, cultural elitism, censorship, and propaganda. Furthermore, consideration is given to the impact of this work on the organization. I evaluate whether adopting a cultural agenda was an overly cautious approach to the civil rights struggle or a necessarily pragmatic tactic, given the racial situation in which the NAACP operated. In so doing, I place the cultural campaigns within their historical context and alongside the association's other work.

The NAACP's approach to fighting racial inequality reflected its origins and the ideologies of its founding members. The association's immediate beginnings lay in the horrified reaction of liberal whites to the violence meted out against African Americans. On August 14, 1908, in Springfield, Illinois, the hometown of Abraham Lincoln, a race riot broke out during which six African Americans were shot, two were lynched, over fifty were wounded, and thousands fled from their homes. The following month, William English Walling, a wealthy southerner, reformer, and socialist, published a scathing report on events in the *Independent*. "Race War in the North" warned of dire consequences if America let such violence pass without action. Summoning the spirit of abolitionism, Walling called for action to assist America's black populace, asking, "what large and powerful body of citizens is ready to come to their aid?" Mary White Ovington, a settlement house worker already interested in the plight of African Americans, responded to Walling's call. Along with the journalist

Charles Edward Russell and Dr. Henry Moskowitz, a social worker, they vowed to form such a body. Their first meeting was held at Walling's New York apartment in January 1909. The group soon expanded to include, among others, Oswald Garrison Villard, the grandson of the abolitionist William Lloyd Garrison; Lillian Wald and Florence Kelley, who were both leading settlement house workers; and two black ministers, Bishop Alexander Walters and Reverend William Brooks. They issued a call for a conference "for the discussion of present evils, the voicing of protests and the renewal of the struggle for civil and political liberty."[8]

The National Negro Conference was held in New York on May 31 and June 1, 1909, and was attended by three hundred men and women of both races. During the keynote speech William Hayes Ward, editor of the *Independent,* declared that the purpose of the new organization was "to re-emphasize in word, and so far as possible, in act, the principle that equal justice should be done to man as man, and particularly to the Negro, without regard to race, color or previous condition of servitude." The delegates called for a campaign to educate America about the achievements of the race, for a legal bureau, and for a political and civil rights bureau to secure the enforcement of the Fourteenth and Fifteenth Amendments. A Committee of Forty to establish a permanent organization was chosen, and the group passed a series of resolutions demanding equal civil and educational rights; the right to work; and protection against violence, murder, and intimidation. The organization's second annual conference was held a year later, again in New York. After some wrangling the organization adopted its new name, and the National Association for the Advancement of Colored People was formed.[9]

In its earliest years the NAACP's leadership positions were dominated by whites. To begin with, the association could not afford to pay most of its leaders and therefore relied on the pro bono services of wealthy whites.[10] Moorfield Storey, a Boston lawyer, was the first president, and Walling became chairman of the Board of Directors. Joel E. Spingarn, a wealthy professor of literature, held both these positions in the following decades. His brother, Arthur Spingarn, was responsible for much of the NAACP's early legal work. Ovington held a number of positions during the many years of her involvement, including secretary and chair. Another woman, May Childs Nerney, was executive secretary from 1912 until 1916. Villard was chairman and treasurer. Initially the exception to this white dominance was W. E. B. Du Bois, who was appointed director of publicity and research. He was the only African American in a salaried position until

James Weldon Johnson first became field secretary and then replaced John Shillady as executive secretary in 1920. By the time Johnson was replaced by Walter White in 1931, blacks had taken control of much of the day-to-day running of the association. Jessie Fauset was Du Bois's assistant editor, and Robert Bagnall, who became director of branches, and William Pickens, field secretary, did a good deal to increase the NAACP's presence in black communities throughout the country. The Board of Directors was almost evenly split along race lines. Perhaps most significantly, by 1919 it was estimated that nine-tenths of the NAACP's members were black.[11]

W. E. B. Du Bois, James Weldon Johnson, and Walter White had very different personalities and contrasting ideas and methods. Nevertheless, their "strengths meshed together so as to diminish each individual's weaknesses." Johnson, in particular, was a steadying influence between the clashing egos of Du Bois and White.[12] These three men developed and instigated much of the NAACP's work during its first forty years, and they were especially influential when it came to its cultural work. Indeed, the association's cultural campaigns were shaped by the ideas, preferences, and talents of these leaders. It is significant that, even during the early years of white domination, the association's black personnel led this work. Du Bois and his literary editor, Jessie Fauset, set the cultural agenda for the *Crisis,* and Johnson and White were heavily involved with the Harlem Renaissance. White also spearheaded the association's work in Hollywood. The exception to this rule was the fight against *The Birth of a Nation,* which was led in the national office by white secretary May Child Nerney. However, this protest also provides another exception, in that much of the initial impetus came from African Americans in the local branches, and much of the work was done by these city and state chapters. Most of the other cultural projects were initiated and implemented by national staff members, and there were very few national campaigns that required assistance from local branches. It is important to note that there was not just one cultural strategy. The NAACP's approach to culture changed over time and across different forms. There were disagreements and debates between leaders, between branches and the national office, and between salaried officers and members.

Historians have examined many areas of the NAACP's work, from its fight against lynching and segregation, to its battles in court and lobbying of Congress, to the struggle for black enfranchisement. Much of this research has focused on the association's legal and legislative campaigns and often on the national organization. While there has been some broadening in this historiographical approach in recent years, there have been no full-length studies that focus solely on the NAACP's cultural work. A number of studies do explore *specific* aspects of the NAACP's cultural work, and these are discussed in subsequent chapters. Many of these scholars recognize that the NAACP was involved in cultural activities during the first half of the century, but no previous attempt has been made to place this aspect of its work at the center of the research, nor do any of the existing studies compare the association's treatment of different cultural forms. Research into the NAACP, an organization that was founded in the first decade of the twentieth century, provides evidence for a "long civil rights movement," a now widely accepted recognition that the movement was not confined to the "classical" phase between *Brown v. Board of Education* in 1954 and the Voting Rights Act of 1965. This study fits within that historiography by focusing predominantly on the period before 1955 and by demonstrating how the seeds for its relationship with culture were sewn in the early years of the NAACP. [13]

Scholars have done much important work on the intersections between civil rights and culture. This has included studies of the Black Arts Movement of the 1960s and 1970s. While I focus on a different era and consider different participants, I share with these scholars an interest in considering the political aspects of culture in order to more fully understand the black activism of our respective periods. Two of the most useful monographs on an earlier era are Barbara Savage's study of African Americans and radio during the Second World War and Lauren Rebecca Sklaroff's examination of black culture and the New Deal. Both Savage and Sklaroff use an approach similar to that adopted in this study: they show how African Americans thought about culture and how they attempted to use it, and they consider how this cultural production needs to be understood in its historical context and the ways it was shaped by outside forces. Finally, and perhaps most important, Savage and Sklaroff demonstrate that the way the NAACP conceived of culture and its relationship to civil rights was shared by others. Sklaroff argues that while African Americans realized positive racial images or black cultural production were not a substitute for political and economic rights, they nonetheless "understood culture as central in procuring civil rights." Savage explains black efforts to engage with radio in a similar manner. She also reminds us of why it is important to study culture. It is, she warns, too easy to dismiss protests about representations or efforts to increase black control "simply as efforts to find ways of presenting idealized positive racial imagery." In fact, attempts to alter representations in the mass media and popular culture "can reveal a keen and sophisticated appreciation of the relationship between popular images, political symbolism, public opinion and public policy." It is a similar appreciation by the NAACP, albeit one that was sometimes flawed or problematic, that I examine in the following chapters.[14]

This study of the NAACP's cultural campaigns begins with the association's fight against *The Birth of a Nation,* a struggle that established many of the key principles of its cultural strategy. Chapters 2 and 3 consider how, between 1910 and 1934, the NAACP used African American art and literature to advance the race. Chapter 2 examines its involvement with the Harlem Renaissance and attempts to establish the NAACP's model of African American culture. Chapter 3 looks at the association's magazine, the *Crisis.* During the twenty-four years of his editorship, Du Bois used African Americans' creative work to challenge stereotypes, encourage racial pride, and forge a sense of black collective identity. In Chapter 4, I evaluate the NAACP's strategy of using the arts to change opinions about a specific example of racial discrimination: lynching. The deployment of plays, poems, and paintings with an overt political message in the antilynching fight provides one of the clearest examples of the NAACP's fusing of art and propaganda. Chapter 5 assesses Walter White's attempts to change the portrayal of blacks in motion pictures during the Second World War. The final chapter investigates the NAACP's cultural strategy between 1945 and 1955. It considers the signs of improvement in movies at the same time that a new medium—television—forced the association to resort to former tactics. In the conclusion I examine the continuation and modification of the NAACP's cultural strategy from the mid-1950s until the late 1960s. Stretching the project over half a century allows a comparison among different contexts, attitudes, and media. In so doing, I hope to answer the question that Du Bois put before his audience in Chicago in 1926.

# 1

# The Birth of a Cultural Strategy

This book begins, perhaps inevitably given the nature and scale of the struggle, with the NAACP's fight against *The Birth of a Nation.* The campaign against D. W. Griffith's film remains the best-known and most widely discussed of all the examples of the NAACP's attempts to challenge offensive depictions of the race in popular culture. It marks the first time the association spent considerable effort on such a cause. The campaign tells us much about the NAACP's attitude toward culture as it established paradigms central to the ways in which the organization would try to influence the depiction of African Americans. The NAACP's response to stereotyped representations of blacks, the tactics it used to challenge the film, and the issues it encountered in this campaign would all be repeated during the NAACP's first half century.

As a film that made cinematic history, *The Birth of a Nation* has received much scholarly attention. The most complete account of the film, its reception, and the NAACP's campaign against it is by Melvyn Stokes. While Stokes's focus is broader than just the NAACP, he considers the reasons for the protests, arguing that the association understood the dangerous power of film and thus saw *Birth* as a racist attack on African Americans. Stokes also explores the effects of the struggle on the organization and, by taking a long view, finds them to be, on balance, largely positive. Stephen Weinberger also reflects on the ways in which the campaign helped to shape the NAACP and concludes that, despite its limitations, the fight "elevated the association to a position of national stature and indeed preeminence in the struggle for civil rights in America." Significantly, the organization had to change its methods when dealing with *Birth:* it couldn't use the courts and instead was forced to turn to censorship. Weinberger also argues that, "for better or worse, the association felt it had no choice but to respond" to the movie. While the campaign was reactive rather than proactive, the NAACP did in fact have a choice about whether to respond;

it made a conscious decision to launch a full-scale attack, and that decision reflected, in part, its approach to cultural representations of African Americans. This chapter, then, aims to build on the existing scholarship by placing the NAACP and its ideas about culture at the center of the discussion. It considers why most in the NAACP were so vehemently opposed to the film, what the resulting struggle tells us about its beliefs about culture and about the NAACP as an organization, and how this fitted within the context of the wider struggle for civil rights.[1]

D. W. Griffith's film ran across twelve reels and lasted three hours. It remains one of the most popular, profitable, and certainly "most controversial" motion pictures of all time.[2] It was largely based on Thomas Dixon's novel *The Clansman* (1905), which had previously appeared as a stage play. It is a historical epic, told through the lives of the northern Stoneman and southern Cameron families. It incorporates plantation nostalgia and the reconciliatory narrative of the Civil War as a conflict in which North and South fought with a shared heroism and pain. The film paints Reconstruction as a time when blacks ran wild and only the formation of the Ku Klux Klan could restore order. The NAACP was extremely worried about the effect the portrayal of the race in *Birth* would have on white people's attitude toward African Americans. It believed negative images of the race confirmed and reinforced white people's negative perceptions. The images in *The Birth of a Nation* went beyond "negative": they reinforced every prejudice white America held against blacks. Du Bois complained that the film represented the Negro as an "ignorant fool, a vicious rapist, a venal and unscrupulous politician, or a faithful but doddering idiot." The NAACP feared that it would inflame racial hatred. In a letter to the mayor of New York, the NAACP's Board of Directors protested, "One only has to watch the emotional effect upon the audience and to listen to their comments to realize what the ultimate effect of this must be upon the masses." According to the letter, a "prominent Southern woman who saw the play yesterday said that on leaving the theatre the young man who accompanied her remarked, 'I should like to kill every nigger I know.'" The story, probably apocryphal but often recounted in NAACP correspondence, highlights campaigners' fears that *Birth* would lead to racial violence or, at the very least, be used to justify it.[3]

The association's objections to the film were summarized in a letter from the Los Angeles branch to the city council. They claimed the film "serves to revive the differences and the causes of differences between the North and the South which led to the Civil War." The "Negro is made to look hideous and is invested with most repulsive habits and depraved passions." They objected in particular to the "questionable scene suggesting illicit relations" between northern congressman Austin Stoneman and his mulatto housekeeper, Lydia, claiming it is "unfit for a public performance." The conflict between the Camerons' eldest son, Ben, and "the Negro soldiery" is "calculated to inspire bitterness and to suggest the solution of violence for the petty differences which might arise between members of the opposite races," while the meeting between Cameron and Silas Lynch, Stoneman's mulatto protégé, is a "diabolical piece of art" that is "calculated to excite feelings of animosity between the races." They concluded that the production is "historically inaccurate" and claimed that "with subtle genius" it is "designed to palliate and excuse the lynching and other deeds of violence committed against the Negro" and "to make him in the public mind a hideous monster."[4] The NAACP objected to the film because it painted the race not only in an unflattering and historically inaccurate light but also in a way that was provocative and dangerous. It worried about the effect of this depiction on race relations and argued it would be used to excuse violence and discrimination against African Americans. The NAACP knew it could not let such a depiction go unchallenged.

The widely acknowledged artistic merits of the film were also a cause for concern. The members of the Los Angeles branch recognized that the film displayed "some artistic qualities," and E. Ceruti, the branch secretary, admitted that Griffith's film "is a masterpiece of his art and, from an artistic point of view, the finest thing of its kind I have ever witnessed." Furthermore, Walter White, fifteen years after its release, wrote that "'The Birth of a Nation,' by its very excellence of photography and staging . . . make it to my mind a most vicious and dangerous thing." The NAACP recognized that Griffith's skill as a filmmaker only made his film's message all the more powerful. It attracted not only critical adoration but also huge audience numbers.[5]

From the opening scene to the closing image, Griffith used his "subtle genius" to create what might remain the most virulently anti-black film ever made. The film is a white supremacist tract that demonizes African Americans. Much of its racist ideology came from the source material and its creator, Thomas Dixon, but Griffith also added his own prejudices to the mix. Their views, however, were not anomalies; they reflected the prevailing racial attitudes of their time. As Dixon boasted, *Birth* "expresses the passionate faith of the entire white population of the South. If I am wrong, they are wrong."[6] The racist imagery that filled the screen was not simply the creation of Dixon and Griffith. They drew on at least a hundred years of American culture for their inspiration. Throughout the film African Americans are portrayed in a derogatory manner, using almost every stereotype of the race in American culture. There are happy, loyal slaves (complete with "Mammy" and "Uncle Tom"); foolish comics; watermelon-eating, banjo-playing "darkies"; oversexed, lustful, and power-hungry mulattos (male and female); dandified, ridiculous upstarts; and vicious and savage black brutes. These images have their precedent in decades of American culture, from minstrel shows through popular literature and song to the earliest films. The power of *Birth* came from its ability to reflect a racist imagery that was widely accepted by the American public. The circulation of these images and ideas in the broader culture facilitated *Birth*'s production and created the circumstances for its popular reception. The NAACP was all too aware that Griffith's film drew on a century's worth of cultural representation of African Americans. Indeed, it targeted *Birth* as an example, a symbol, of this cultural hegemony. It believed that in attacking *Birth* it could strike a blow against the racist culture and racist ideology that it elucidated and reinforced.

Griffith's film incorporated a range of offensive stereotypes of African Americans, all of which were of concern for the NAACP. In the antebellum section of the film the slaves are shown as content and conditions are almost idyllic, with what the intertitle describes as the "two-hour interval given for dinner, out of their working day from six till six." When the Camerons show the visiting Stonemans around the plantation, the slaves perform for their masters and guests. They dance and clap, bow and scrape, with the grin of the "happy darkie" on their faces. Even during the war and in its aftermath the slaves stay loyal to their masters, as represented by the Camerons' faithful servants, who include an overweight, headscarf-wearing Mammy. Griffith and Dixon cited these loyal servant characters in defense of their racial attitudes (they could not be anti-Negro when they created such "positive" images). They are a classic example of the "plantation myth" in action: the slaves were so content with their position they remained with their masters rather than choose freedom. This is presented as absolving the South of blame for the institution of slavery and both the North and the South for their neglect of the race after the war.

Blacks provide comic relief throughout the film. In an early scene some black children, "pickanninies," fall from the back of a wagon. Later, an old black man registering to vote says, "Ef I doan' get my franchise to fill mah bucket, I doan' want it nohow." Such scenes present blacks as nonthreatening and childlike. They reflect a paternalistic attitude, a sense of white southerners needing to "care" for their black charges. Griffith said the claim that he was anti-Negro "is like saying I am against children, as they were our children, whom we loved and cared for all our lives."[7] There is a more serious message behind a scene such as the one above: if the black voter is so foolish he does not know what to do with his vote, then his race cannot be trusted with the franchise. The NAACP was aware that such depictions undermined its fight for black voting rights, an issue that was high on the agenda from the association's inception. Indeed, in the same year as *Birth*'s release, the Supreme Court struck down the "grandfather clause" as a tool to disenfranchise voters in *Guinn v. the United States,* a case in which the NAACP filed *amicus curiae.*

It is no coincidence that two of the most important, named black characters in *Birth* are mulattos, a figure common in nineteenth- and early twentieth-century American culture. Lydia, Stoneman's housekeeper, and Silas Lynch, Stoneman's henchman, reflect a white distaste for and fear of racial mixing. They incorporate many of the supposed qualities of the mulatto: fiery temper, lasciviousness, and a desire for power. Lydia is introduced in a scene that shows her reacting to a white senator slighting her by throwing herself to the ground, grabbing her breast, staring wild-eyed, and, in an overtly sexual gesture, licking the back of her hand. The impression is animalistic, sexual, and wild. Lynch has more of a veneer of respectability, but from the outset it is obvious that he is driven by both his lust for power and his lust for white women, more specifically for Stoneman's daughter, Elsie. Toward the end of the film Lynch has kept Elsie captive in his room and proposes marriage. When Lynch shows her the scene of black triumph on the street outside, Griffith equates black freedom and power with what he considers the real desire of black men: to "marry" white women.

The Lynch and Elsie storyline betrays one of the great obsessions of both Griffith and Dixon, as well as many white southerners: interracial sex. Southerners were convinced that black men wanted to use any new-found freedom or power to instigate sexual relations with white women, and American culture from this period was full of examples to prove it. In a scene from *Birth* showing an election rally, a white carpetbagger is holding a sign that reads, "Equality: Equal rights. Equal politics. Equal marriage." In another, the black-controlled South Carolina House of Representatives celebrates the passage of a bill "providing for the intermarriage of blacks and whites." The film's creators used fear of racial intermixing to attack the NAACP. Dixon claimed the "Negro Intermarriage Society," as he dubbed the organization, "hates 'The Birth of a Nation' for one reason only—it opposes marriage of blacks to whites." Griffith, in a letter to a newspaper defending his film, launched an astonishing attack against "this prointermarriage organization," in which he pointed out the ways in which it had attacked "anti-intermarriage legislation." Incredulous, he clarified for his readers what this meant: "they successfully opposed bills which were framed to prohibit the marriage of Negroes to whites." The NAACP did indeed protest against the attempts to introduce miscegenation laws in a number of northern states between 1913 and 1927. However, it was not "prointermarriage." As Peggy Pascoe has shown, the association, all too aware that it was a contentious issue among both black and white Americans, was careful not to endorse interracial marriage. This, she writes, put it in the "awkward, almost contradictory, position of wholeheartedly opposing laws that banned a practice it refused to defend." Yet this stance was "based on astute political calculations," and it had considerable success in halting proposed legislation in the North.[8]

The intertitle immediately after the scene in the House of Representatives reads, "Later. The grim reaping begins" and there are the first shots of Gus, Flora Cameron's attacker, lurking in the shadows. Griffith thus makes a direct link between black political equality and black rape of white women. Gus is a "black brute," the freed black man who has regressed to his primitive, savage state and is driven by his lust for white women. This figure became increasingly common in later nineteenth- and early twentieth-century culture, reflecting white fears about a "New" Negro unleashed from the controls of slavery. The black brute was used to justify the lynching of black men, under the premise of protecting white women from assault. Dixon and Griffith certainly make this link (among the freed black man, rape of whites, and lynching) explicit in their story. Gus chases Flora, declaring his desire to "marry." Here again, marriage is synonymous with rape. This must partly be a matter of early twentieth-century sensibilities; an overt rape scene would not have been appropriate for the audience or the censors. It also reflects contemporary racial prejudices by suggesting that black men did not want to marry white women but rather wanted to have sexual relations with them. Such a message was worrying for the NAACP, which, conscious of the dangers of black men calling for free choice in whom to marry, had to walk a tight line when protesting against interracial marriage laws. Countering claims that black men were motivated by a sexual desire for white women, it argued that, in fact, southern miscegenation laws "protected White men from having to take social and economic responsibility for their continuing sexual activity with Black women." These laws "provided incentives for race-mixing by promoting illicit sex." In this way, Pascoe concludes, the NAACP "turned the logic of the miscegenation law"—a logic that argued that it protected white women from black men—"against itself."[9] Thus the organization's campaign against *Birth* can be understood in the context of its broader challenges to the legal restrictions facing African Americans.

In the film, the consequence for Gus for his transgressions, as for many African Americans (including, as was often the case, those not guilty of rape), is lynching. Gus is hunted down and put on "trial" before the Ku Klux Klan. According to Seymour Stern, the original film included a castration scene, an act common in actual lynchings.[10] The remaining scene fades out as the Klan members move to inflict their judgment on Gus. His dead body is dumped on the steps of Lynch's house, as, according to the intertitle, an "answer to the blacks and carpetbaggers." *The Birth of a Nation* offers a visual representation of the justification of lynching so common in white discourses about the phenomenon. The NAACP was particularly disturbed by this element of the film as it was in the midst of a campaign against mob violence. This battle was a growing priority in the 1910s; it used a range of methods, including investigating and publicizing incidents, pushing for federal intervention, and lobbying for legislation. One key element centered on trying to turn white Americans against the phenomenon; the film, its critics feared, could undo this work and stimulate support for lynching. Denouncing Griffith's glorification of mob violence was therefore part of the NAACP's wider antilynching struggle.

Not only were freed blacks consumed by their desire for white women in Griffith's narrative, but they also abused their power in other ways. A scene in the first half of the film shows black soldiers attacking the peaceful town of Piedmont, assaulting and killing whites and looting their houses. The scenes in the South Carolina House of Representatives show the "negro party in control." One of the politicians is eating chicken, another sits drinking, and a further man takes his shoes off and puts his feet on the desk. The picture is one of black incompetence and was designed to send a chill through the heart of watching whites. Indeed, the whole film is calculated to inspire hatred of African Americans. Griffith brought white fears to life; he made them real. *The Birth of a Nation* is a horror story of black freedom and power. It is only through violence, in the form of the Ku

Klux Klan, that order (racial, social, and political) is restored. The NAACP believed that such images would indeed inspire hatred of the race. It was convinced that the way in which African Americans were represented in American culture would affect how they were treated in American society.

The NAACP had only been in existence for six years when Griffith's film was released in 1915. In many ways the battle against the movie was a testing ground, not just for its attitude toward culture but also for the structure, reach, and influence of the association itself. In January of that year the Los Angeles branch initiated what turned out to be a decades-long campaign against *The Birth of a Nation.* Using tactics that would be adopted by branches all over the country, it first tried to get the city censor board to ban the movie. When that failed, it appealed to the mayor and chief of police, but both claimed they were "without authority to stop the pictures," that they were "powerless." When his attempts were unsuccessful, branch secretary E. Ceruti suggested to national secretary May Childs Nerney that she put pressure on the National Board of Censorship (which was based in New York). He argued that "as this is a larger question and concerns the whole country," this tactic "would seem to have great advantage over the waging of local fights wherever the 'Clansman' is introduced."[11]

The National Board of Censorship of Motion Pictures and the NAACP were formed in the same year, and the establishment of both organizations can be understood in the context of the Progressive era. Many of the founders of the NAACP were Progressives (a term used to refer to concerned citizens and professionals who believed intervention could improve the social, economic, and political environment). The white members in particular "fit the Progressive profile perfectly": they were affluent and college-educated, "old stock" Americans, Protestants, Republicans, and Socialists, and they lived in the big cities of New York, Boston, and Philadelphia. They shared the reformist mentality: they believed in "investigation and exposure" and the "importance of laws and of the state as a guarantor of social order." They brought the tactics of Progressivism to the NAACP: they carried out investigations and circulated their findings, held rallies and conferences, lobbied and litigated. Like the Progressives, the association did not call for a radical overhaul of society. It believed that the Constitution, if properly applied, would grant African Americans full equality. The National Board of Censorship was sponsored by the People's Institute, a Progressive reform organization in New York. Progressives were concerned about the potentially harmful effects of motion pictures, particularly on immigrants and children, though many believed that the right type of movie could have important educational value. The motion picture industry (that is, the exhibitors and then the manufacturers) responded to pressure from reformers. As Nancy Rosenbloom explains, they saw a "tactical advantage" in forming such an alliance. The film industry advocated voluntary censorship in an effort to stave off legal or federal censorship. While there was no legal compulsion for filmmakers to submit their movies for review, the National Board had considerable influence on whether films were shown across the country. Therefore an appeal to the board was the obvious next step for the NAACP.[12]

The association first had to try to persuade the National Board of Censorship to revoke its earlier approval of the film. Nerney approached its chairman, Frederic Howe, who called a special screening at the beginning of March. Howe managed to convince himself and the NAACP that the board had changed its mind and now condemned the film. However, after a subsequent meeting with the film's producers, during which they promised to make cuts to their picture, the board voted to approve the film. Again, the NAACP switched tactics and appealed to the mayor of New York. In many cities mayors acted as film censors, as they could revoke, or threaten to revoke, a theater's license.[13] Over five hundred people were present at the hearing to listen to speakers including Howe, Du Bois, and Oswald Villard of the NAACP; Fred Moore, editor of the *New York Age;* and president of the Brooklyn Citizens' Club George Wibecan. The NAACP, as this meeting suggests, was not the only organization concerned about the vicious representation of African Americans in *Birth.* The example of New York, however, demonstrates that not all was the picture of cooperation. Indeed, the delegation was surprised to learn that the week before their meeting Charles W. Anderson, a close associate of Booker T. Washington, had already spoken to Mayor John Mitchel, who, on Anderson's advice, had seen the film and decided that there should be cuts. Some small cuts were made, but the most offensive scenes, including the Gus chase scene and Lynch's attempt to force marriage on Elsie Stoneman, remained.[14]

The next site of NAACP protest was Boston, and again activists appealed to the mayor for action on the film. At the hearing before Mayor James Curley, on April 7, speakers included the NAACP's Mary White Ovington and Moorfield Storey (whose evidence was dismissed because, incredibly, he had not seen the film) and William Monroe Trotter, the editor of the *Boston Guardian.* Trotter was an outspoken and—from the NAACP's perspective—unpredictable and potentially embarrassing ally in the fight. Trotter reminded Curley that, as mayor, he needed black political support and warned him that black voters would be paying attention to how he responded to the film. Despite these warnings, the mayor claimed he had no power to stop the motion picture in his city. The few cuts he promised did little to appease the campaigners, and on April 17, a week after the film opened in Boston, Trotter led a group of African Americans to the Tremont Theater. They were denied tickets to see *Birth,* and when the group refused to leave the lobby, they were removed by police. Trotter and ten others were arrested and charged with disturbing the peace. This was the first example of direct action against the film, and it provides a contrast with the NAACP's approach of lobbying and persuasion at this time. These were the tactics with which the NAACP felt most comfortable. Although it too would later organize direct action against theaters, it remained wary of any form of mass public protest.

Instead the NAACP took its protest to Governor David Walsh. He promised prosecution of the Tremont Theater for showing the film, but, yet again, the pledge came to nothing but a few cuts. More promising was the introduction of a censorship bill by the state legislature. By the mid-1910s state censorship boards were being established in a number of areas. The NAACP helped put together a bipartisan coalition, and when it had secured enough support, it lobbied members of the legislature to support its amendment that the new board of censorship only needed a majority decision rather than unanimity. The act was signed into law on May 21, but the new censorship board voted to approve the film. This incident shows how political pressure on certain constituencies could prove effective, particularly when African Americans worked together, as they did in Boston. It also shows the limits of this approach, as the NAACP was instrumental in establishing a censorship board but then could do nothing to control its decisions. Furthermore, the different provisions for censorship across states and cities (in some places it was the responsibility of the police department, in others the mayor) made it difficult for the NAACP to establish a pattern for action.[15]

As events in Boston demonstrated, opponents of the film faced a formidable foe, not least because *The Birth of a Nation*'s producers and backers were at least as active in supporting their film as the activists were in campaigning against it. They challenged every attempt to have the film cut or banned. In Chicago, Mayor William Thompson, after an appeal by the local NAACP, was persuaded to rescind the license for the film. Immediately lawyers for *The Birth of a Nation* got an injunction passed that overturned the mayor's decision. Chicago was just one of many instances of the film's supporters securing injunctions to stop mayors from acting against their interests. This is not to say that the NAACP campaign was entirely without success. In Ohio, the Cleveland branch, with the support of Nerney and the national office, successfully used pressure from allies in high places, including the governor, to persuade the censorship board to reject the film in the state. It was banned, albeit usually only temporarily, in a host of cities, including Gary, Indiana; St. Louis, Missouri; Atlantic City, New Jersey; New Haven, Connecticut; Providence, Rhode Island; Springfield, Massachusetts; and Minneapolis, Minnesota.[16]

The fact that in some places, even if the measures were only temporary and had little effect on the popularity of the film, campaigners were able to exert pressure on mayors, governors, and other elected officials reflects the growing number and political significance of African Americans in the North. This period saw the beginning of the "Great Migration" of African Americans from southern rural areas to the cities of the North and Midwest.[17] The NAACP benefited from these demographic changes in a number of ways. Its own membership grew as African Americans poured into urban areas, where it was strongest. Furthermore, as Stokes has shown, it attempted to use the presence of increasing numbers of African Americans in cities to convince officials to ban *The Birth of a Nation*. It deliberately played on the concerns of the civic authorities about racial tension, warning that screenings could lead to race riots and civil unrest. It also pointed out the increasing importance of the black vote to many of these elected officials. It warned them that African American voters would use their response to the film as a measure of their concern for the race. Thus the campaign against *The Birth of a Nation* was also a mechanism for rallying the black community and for bringing the concerns of African Americans to the attention of the public and politicians. NAACP leaders quickly realized it could have beneficial consequences for their organization and for their wider struggle for equality. It mobilized African Americans behind a common cause and provided a national issue that raised the profile of the NAACP and the black community more generally. This was particularly important because the NAACP was still a new organization that was finding its feet and trying to achieve a national profile and secure a solid base within the black community. According to Patricia Sullivan, NAACP officials discovered that it was "difficult to keep a branch alive if there were not some type of protest or agitation to keep people engaged." Of course, this was not the only activity with which the organization was occupied. On a national level it campaigned against federal segregation and opposed discriminatory legislation; on a local level it responded to cases of police brutality, wrongful arrest, and lynching. Many efforts were made to build its membership; for example, NAACP officers Joel Spingarn and W. E. B. Du Bois went on tours of the country, spreading the association's message and encouraging the formation of new branches. Nevertheless, many of the NAACP's goals were long term and required a gradual and cumulative campaign. Fights such as the one against *Birth* were important, therefore, because when successful they allowed people to see the immediate effect of protest in their local area.[18]

By May 1915 the NAACP had developed a strategy for fighting *The Birth of a Nation.* Most of these campaigns were carried out at the state level, with support and coordination from the national office; this meant that most of those carrying out the day-to-day work against the film were African Americans but that the campaign was led by white officers at the top. Replying to a query about challenging the film in Indianapolis, May Childs Nerney suggested asking a lawyer to see whether an ordinance already existed in the city that could be interpreted in order to keep it out (this was usually one that invoked concerns about public disorder). If so, she argued, "it will probably be easy to suppress the picture under that authority." If not, then "two courses are open"; these were "to get an ordinance introduced into the Common Council which will cover it, or to build up such public opinion that the play cannot be shown." In Nerney's opinion the "first procedure will be very difficult. The second's practical but means hard work. . . . You should immediately interest the local clergy, colored and white, civic organizations, welfare societies, secret societies, women's clubs etc." Letters from these groups and individuals "should be sent to the Police Commissioner, License Commissioner and Mayor protesting against the play on the ground that it endangers public morals and may lead to a breach of the peace."[19] Nerney's letter set out the limited options open to opponents of the film. Their only real chance was to try to persuade the authorities that the film caused unrest.

America's entry into the First World War allowed the NAACP to develop a new angle to its campaign. Although it still involved persuasion, world events allowed it to strengthen its attack. Using a strategy that would be repeated and developed during the Second World War, the association's leaders argued that the film would be detrimental to morale and could disrupt the war effort. John Shillady, who had replaced Nerney as national secretary, warned that at a time "when colored people are performing their full share of patriotic service both in the fighting forces of the nation in the battle fields of Europe and at home, and when national unity and not race antagonisms should be accentuated, it is important to the national morale that all diverse influence be subordinated to the common good." The NAACP summoned arguments of black patriotism to challenge the racist premise of the film. It had some success with this approach as, for example, *Birth* was banned in West Virginia for the duration of the war. In October 1918 the NAACP launched a nationwide campaign to persuade state governors and state councils of defense to ban the film; the governors of Oregon, Minnesota, and Rhode Island promised the film would not be shown in their states.[20] This was important because it suggests that the tactic of lobbying could be successful in areas without a significant black population, especially when the organization could tap into the national patriotic discourse.

After a few years of relative inactivity with regard to *The Birth of a Nation,* the NAACP sprang into action once again in 1921. In one of the few examples of the association using tactics of direct action during this period, it challenged the film's screening in New York by protesting to the civic authorities and by organizing a demonstration outside the Capitol Theater. The protest outside the cinema was carried out by "colored veterans of the world war and others" in order "to register a peaceable protest against what is planning propaganda for the Ku Klux Klan." According to NAACP press releases, five people were arrested and convicted for distributing leaflets. The symbolism of African Americans who had fought for their country objecting to the film was stressed by the NAACP. Equally important was that the association had begun to combine its fight against *The Birth of a Nation* with the fight against the Ku Klux Klan. It made the link again when protesting a new run of the film in Boston the same year, and this time, unlike in New York, the organization and William Trotter were successful in getting the film banned.[21]

When it heard about a showing in Kansas two years later, the NAACP sent a telegram to the governor reminding him that "this dangerous film in its deliberate distortion of known historical facts and its glorification of the infamous KKK has caused numerous racial clashes and is largely responsible for [the] present day revival of [the] Klan." Walter White's suggestions to the chairman of the Kansas City branch of the NAACP for ways to fight the film included the "political angle." He pointed out that Governor Davis would know he might antagonize black voters, and "with anything like a close election, Negroes can swing any election in the state." White also suggested getting Catholic, Jewish, and labor groups on board.[22] Melvyn Stokes suggests that the NAACP's campaign in the first half of the 1920s was relatively effective. This was largely because it combined an assault on *The Birth of a Nation* with an attack on the revived Ku Klux Klan: that is to say, because "the Klan was no longer just anti-black, the NAACP began to find new allies among those whom the Klan attacked."[23] The NAACP, it seemed, was most successful when it could tap into national discourses (patriotism and unease about the revival of the Klan) and if it could secure allies outside the black community. The NAACP files reveal that these were tactics that the NAACP would repeat both in its fight against racist white culture and in its broader struggle. However, this reliance on outside forces serves to highlight the fact that when fighting *The Birth of a Nation* by themselves and on their own terms, African Americans' options were severely limited.

In its fight against *The Birth of a Nation,* the NAACP used a variety of methods, but its aim was consistent: to have the film banned outright and, if this was not possible, to have it cut beyond recognition. The goal of censorship proved to be its greatest challenge and, according to some scholars, the underlying reason for its failure. By 1915 censorship was becoming an increasingly contentious issue. As Thomas Cripps notes, "In intellectual circles cinema was beginning to take on serious aesthetic overtones that precluded the use of censorship as a tactic." Melvyn Stokes suggests that these changes had a direct impact on the NAACP because liberals were caught between their hatred for *The Birth of a Nation* and their hatred for censorship. The NAACP board was divided over *Birth;* some felt the film was not the great danger to the race that others supposed, and many were strongly opposed to any form of censorship. The NAACP leadership were aware that their call for censorship was contentious and that it lost them supporters. They were uneasy about the principle but decided that the alternative—to do nothing and let Griffith's film go unchallenged—was worse. In a letter to the branches, for example, Nerney conceded that "all forms of censorship are dangerous to the free expression of art," but, wherever a censor board existed, "it was our right and our duty to see that this body acted with fairness and justice." Du Bois later acknowledged that "we are aware now as then that it is dangerous to limit expression." However, he went on, "without some limitations civilization could not endure." Jane Gaines reminds us that "when the call to censor is simultaneously a struggle for social equality and a campaign for racial consciousness and against marginalization, we have to consider how censorship empowers those groups who have no claim on power." In other words, African Americans had few other options when trying to exert some control over how they were depicted in white culture.[24]

In February 1915, in the case of *Mutual Film Corp v. Industrial Commission of Ohio,* the Supreme Court had ruled that motion pictures were a commercial product and not protected speech under the First Amendment. It found that the "exhibition of motion pictures is a business, pure and simple, originated and conducted for profit like other spectacles." This, in theory, should have made the NAACP's task easier. At the very least it might have made its fight against a motion picture easier to defend. Furthermore, Louis Menand argues that during the Progressive era rights were actually understood to be inherently conservative. They were invoked by business to claim protection from regulation or public intervention. It was not until the fight for the right to speak out against America's involvement in the First World War that Progressives began to champion the First Amendment. Therefore, it is not as incongruous at it may first appear for a civil rights organization such as the NAACP to subsume a constitutional right to an argument about public order.[25] In fact, sources from the period suggest that even in 1915 the NAACP was uneasy about championing censorship but saw it as a necessary step to prevent a greater evil.

As might be expected, the film's supporters framed their arguments in terms of free speech. Griffith, for one, was incensed by the Supreme Court ruling. He published a pamphlet, "The Rise and Fall of Free Speech," in which he described cinema as the "laboring man's university" and motion pictures as "the pictorial press." He warned that if people "muzzle the 'movies'" they will "defeat the educational purpose of this graphic art," for "censorship demands of the picture makers a sugar-coated and false version of life's truths." The NAACP knew that for many white liberals, and indeed black ones too, the demand for censorship was a slippery slope. If the NAACP wanted to ban pictures that showed African Americans in a negative light, what was to stop people from banning films that showed the race in positive ways? Both Cripps and Stokes identify white liberal uneasiness about censorship as an explanation for the NAACP's failure in its campaign. Cripps goes so far as to argue that "in the final battle censorship was a rearguard action rather than a direct assault on racism in American life."[26] However, while the campaign was reactive rather than proactive, the NAACP still saw it as a "direct assault" on racial prejudice. The film did more than just show racism on the screen: it was racism; it caused it and was an example of it. So to attack the film was to attack racism. Unfortunately for the association, one of the few ways in which it could attack the film was through censorship. It was to be an issue that would haunt the NAACP's fight against *The Birth of a Nation* for as long as the campaign continued.

Censorship became the main course of action because there were so few others available to the NAACP when *The Birth of a Nation* was released in 1915. One that did emerge was to produce alternative images on film to counteract the negative impact of Griffith's depiction. This approach would prove to be equally, if not more, fraught than that of censorship. Nickie Fleener lists the difficulties in using films to produce positive images to challenge *The Birth of a Nation:* this course "required money, technical expertise, equipment and access to motion picture distribution channels."[27] For African Americans at the start of the century, all of the above were in short supply. Nevertheless, steps were taken in this direction, with limited success.

A short epilogue, called "The New Era" and since then commonly referred to as the "Hampton Epilogue," was added to *The Birth of a Nation* and first shown at Boston's Tremont Theater on April 16, 1915. Little is known about how precisely this addition came about or of what exactly it consisted. The intention was to show the "progress" of blacks since Reconstruction, and it was made up of scenes filmed on the campus of the Hampton Institute (a historically black center of education training). The epilogue reflects the argument frequently made by the film's producers that *Birth* was a comment on blacks during Reconstruction and not a reflection of African Americans since that period, used to deflect criticism of the film as racist. The NAACP was highly critical of the epilogue; Nerney said it was simply "adding insult to injury." From the NAACP's perspective it was a cynical attempt by the filmmakers to get around restrictions on the film and to legitimize their production.[28]

Around the same time that the Hampton Epilogue made its debut, the NAACP became involved in plans to make its own contribution to the world of motion pictures. The idea for *Lincoln's Dream,* as this production was to be called, seems to have originated with the Universal Film Manufacturing Company. Elaine Sterne, a screenwriter with Universal, approached the NAACP about a possible film. According to Mary White Ovington, after seeing *The Birth of a Nation,* Sterne felt "impelled" to write a story as an alternative. She wanted to "treat the periods of slavery, Civil War and Reconstruction with dignity and historic accuracy" and to "show the important and often heroic part that the Negro played during these difficult times." Universal would raise $150,000 of the capital needed to make the film if the NAACP could raise the remaining $50,000. In a letter to raise funds, Nerney reminded supporters that the "effect of this play on the public cannot be overestimated. If it goes unchallenged it will take years to overcome the harm it is doing. The entire country will acquiesce in the Southern program of segregation, disenfranchisement and lynching." She suggested that "if we do challenge" the film, "it must be done in some telling way, that is, by a spectacular photo-play." The NAACP's national leadership could see the advantages of such a film, but they knew that they did not have the resources needed to fund such a venture. Soon, Universal became aware of this too, and the idea sank from view.[29] The incident serves to show the restrictions that African Americans and their supporters faced in 1915. They did not have the resources to create anything like a viable alternative to Griffith's accomplished and successful production. This is not to say that the NAACP dismissed the idea of creating positive images of the race. Rather, as will be seen in the following two chapters, it realized that this would have to be done elsewhere, using different media.

*The Birth of a Nation,* from the NAACP's perspective, had such a powerful effect on racial prejudice because of its claims of historical accuracy. It purported to tell the true story of the Civil War and Reconstruction. In this historical narrative slaves were content with their position in the South, the Civil War was fought over states' rights, and Reconstruction was a grave mistake that allowed corrupt northerners to exact revenge on the South and gave blacks power that they abused in a wanton display of brutishness and destruction. One of the chief architects of this horror was the Radical congressman Thaddeus Stevens, who appears in the film as Austin Stoneman, complete with club foot and mulatto housekeeper. The film purports to be an accurate "history" in a number of ways: historical figures, such as Lincoln, or characters closely based on historical figures appear throughout, and the central story—that of the Cameron and Stoneman families—is set within the context of historical events.

African American historian John Hope Franklin blames the historical propaganda of *The Birth of a Nation* on Thomas Dixon, and much of the material discussed above comes from Dixon's novels, particularly the second half of the film, which deals with Reconstruction and the rise of the Klan. However, while Griffith used Dixon for his inspiration and his interpretation of history, much of the film's claim to historical accuracy was created by the filmmaker and his staging and technique. This, for the NAACP, was part of Griffith's "subtle genius." He quoted from historical sources in the intertitles and created "historical facsimiles," which were scenes introduced by titles that cited published sources and were "staged to produce the effect of a line drawing coming to life." Both Dixon and Griffith continually defended the film as an accurate portrayal of events. In response to an attack on the film by the *New York Globe,* Griffith claimed his film was "based upon the authenticated history of the period" and to d "a story which is based upon truth in every vital detail." The film's producers could demonstrate that it was based on "authenticated history" by citing scholarly writing from the period that shared *Birth*'s interpretation of events. An application by the distributors in 1925 to overturn a ban in Ohio included an annotated bibliography that listed eight major sources for its version of Reconstruction along with excerpts from these histories. The sources in the lawyers' application included Woodrow Wilson's *History of the American People* (1902), *Documentary History of Reconstruction* (1906–7) by Walter Fleming, and James S. Pike's *The Prostrate South. South Carolina under Negro Rule* (1873).[30]

The consensus in academic and popular history at the beginning of the twentieth century was that Reconstruction had been at best a mistake and at worst the cruel and vindictive punishment of the South, during which freed blacks and corrupt northerners exploited the defenseless region (and its women).[31] Just as it drew on decades of derogatory imagery of blacks in popular culture, so *The Birth of a Nation* drew part of its strength from this historical consensus. The NAACP strongly objected to the film's representation of history and its claims of accuracy because they made its task all the more difficult. In fighting Griffith's film the association was also fighting a wider discourse on race in American memory. Indeed, this was one of the very reasons it mounted such a campaign against *The Birth of a Nation;* it deliberately wanted to challenge this historical and cultural consensus. *The Birth of a Nation* was a symbolic target for America's acceptance of this interpretation of history.

Moorfield Storey wrote to the editor of the *Boston Herald* to challenge the argument that the film was a presentation of "history." He quoted some basic facts about Reconstruction in order to show "how absolutely false is the view of history presented by this play." Storey explained the motivation for and effect of such a distortion: "It is an effort to mislead the people of this country who are ignorant of these facts, to excite a strong feeling against the colored people already suffering everywhere from race prejudice, and to strengthen the hands of those who would deny them their equal rights as citizens." When, during a meeting in Boston, Griffith offered to give ten thousand dollars to charity if Storey could find a single incident in the film that was not historically accurate, the NAACP president asked whether "it was historic that a lieutenant had held a white woman in a room . . . and demanded a forced marriage." Griffith had no reply, and when he went to shake Storey's hand, the NAACP man refused.[32]

Storey and his colleagues knew that history was important, that perceptions of the past shape the way the present is understood, and that whoever controls the historical narrative wields great power. The old cliché that history is written by the victor must have rung painfully true for the NAACP. Dixon and Griffith could protest all they liked that the film was merely a comment on blacks in the last century; indeed, Dixon argued, "I am not attacking the Negro of today. I am recording faithfully the history of fifty years ago."[33] But the NAACP knew that it reflected on African Americans in 1915. So-called evidence that blacks abused freedom and were corrupted by political power was clearly harmful to a race struggling for full enfranchisement and equality.

Few people were more acutely aware of the importance of history in the battle for civil rights than Du Bois. Throughout his life he was engaged, in the words of David Blight, in a "struggle for American historical memory." Du Bois "appreciated the political and social stakes of historical debates; he understood the power of historical images in shaping social policy and human interactions." There had been some earlier challenges to the prevailing consensus on the Reconstruction era, including one by Du Bois himself, but the groundbreaking work that dismantled the arguments of Dunningite historians was his *Black Reconstruction in America* (1935).[34] In his book Du Bois challenged the "Old South" myth of slavery as an idyllic and paternalistic institution; he argued that slavery was a central cause of the Civil War and stressed the important role of abolitionists and blacks in the period. He celebrated the achievements of Radical Reconstruction and mourned the dismantling of black gains. *Black Reconstruction* did more than provide an alternative history; it provided an alternative way of thinking about history and, with that, of thinking about race.

*Black Reconstruction* may not have been a direct answer to Griffith's film—Du Bois was more concerned with challenging historiography than popular culture—but it certainly stands as one of the best refutations of the film's historical narrative. It was not, however, Du Bois's only alternative construction of black history. The motion picture industry was all but closed to African Americans, so Du Bois used another medium, one more readily accessible: theater or, more specifically, historical pageantry. *The*

*Star of Ethiopia,* Du Bois's grand pageant, "was to be the most thoughtful, ambitious response to Dixon and Griffith's racist epic."[35] Written in 1911 and first performed in 1913, it preceded *The Birth of a Nation* by a number of years. Nevertheless, Du Bois had anticipated the tone and message of the motion picture because *The Birth of a Nation* fitted within a wider discourse that undermined black history and culture. When the film was released Du Bois already had his answer to hand, and the 1915 production in Washington must have been staged with *The Birth of a Nation* in mind.

*The Star of Ethiopia* was an ambitious project carried out on a grand scale. The first production in New York was followed by three more, in Washington, DC (1915), Philadelphia (1916), and Los Angeles (1925). According to Du Bois, 350 actors were used in the first production, and a thousand appeared when it was performed in Washington. The pageant, wrote a reviewer in a black newspaper, "covers a period of 10,000 years and more in the mythology, history and development of our race. It vividly tells the story of its work, its suffering, triumphs and hopes as an integral part of the human family." It consisted of five scenes: "The Gift of Iron," "The Dream of Egypt," "The Glory of Ethiopia," "The Valley of Humiliation," and "The Vision Everlasting." Using music, dance, and tableau, representations of black history flowed across the stage. The early peoples of Africa were followed by the great civilizations of Ethiopia and Egypt. The horrors of slavery, as well as the efforts of abolitionists and insurrectionists, were shown. Next came the Civil War to free the race from bondage. These freed slaves developed professions and culture but came under attack from discrimination and violence. Despite these setbacks the pageant finished with a message of hope as the gifts of "Knowledge," "Labor," "Science," "Justice," and "Love" were assembled to create the "Tower of Light."[36]

Du Bois, according to Stokes, had "grown increasingly doubtful of the value of political protest in connection with *Birth*" and so saw his pageant as a "cultural weapon." Rather than lobbying and boycotting, African Americans could fight culture with culture. This, Du Bois thought, might be a more effective way to challenge the historical narrative. The pageant was created and performed as an explicit contribution to the nation's historical memory; it made its debut during the "National Emancipation Exposition" in New York to commemorate fifty years since the Emancipation Proclamation. Du Bois's pageant reminded its audience that the Civil War was fought over the issue of slavery and that African Americans had played and would continue to play an important role in the nation's history. Du Bois's intentions for his work stretched even further. He wrote that the pageant aimed to "get people interested in the development of Negro drama," to teach "colored people themselves the meaning of their history and their rich emotional life through a new theatre," and "to reveal the Negro to the white world as a human, feeling thing."[37] Broadly speaking, these goals were to shape much of the NAACP's cultural strategy during the early decades of the twentieth century. During the Harlem Renaissance and through the *Crisis,* the NAACP sought to highlight the culture and history of the race and instill racial pride among African Americans. At the same time, it hoped to prove to whites that blacks were the product of great civilization and the producers of great art and therefore were entitled to full citizenship and equal rights.[38]

The campaign against *The Birth of a Nation* between 1915 and 1923 brought mixed results for the NAACP. It failed in its efforts to get the film banned in most places for any substantial period of time, and although some cuts were made, the film's basic message of white supremacy remained intact. Melvyn Stokes concludes that the NAACP campaigns in 1915 and 1916 had "essentially failed." The organization faced many difficulties, including "widespread indifference" on the part of some blacks and "deep-seated opposition to censorship" on the part of many whites. However, its later campaign in the 1920s was more successful. Thomas Cripps, who focuses on the earlier period of activism, finds that the black campaign against *The Birth of a Nation* failed because of internal divisions among African Americans (for example, the opposing forces of the NAACP, the Tuskegee machine, and William Trotter), the lack of a coherent plan, and the alienation of potential white allies because of the issue of censorship.[39]

The NAACP not only failed to stop the film, but its campaign may even have been counterproductive. The publicity surrounding the many battles only increased the notoriety of the film and therefore the public's interest. In fact, Du Bois recognized that they "probably succeeded in advertising it even beyond its admittedly notable merits." Every time the NAACP organized a public hearing or staged a boycott or printed an article about *Birth,* it risked raising the profile of the film. Even more damaging, according to Jane Gaines, was that the focus on Griffith's film came at the expense of films made by African Americans, such as the work of Oscar Micheaux. Indeed, the NAACP seemed closed off to the possibilities of black filmmaking and would remain that way for the following four decades. Of greater concern, from the NAACP's perspective, was the conclusion that white film producers suppressed black roles as a result of the aggressive campaign against *The Birth of a Nation.* Cripps reports that rather than having to alter roles to fit campaigners' demands or risk a fight, filmmakers began to cut black parts altogether.[40]

The consequences of the fight were not all negative, however. Perhaps most significantly for the NAACP, it helped to raise the profile of the organization. This was the first campaign that really brought the fledgling association to the nation's attention. Melvyn Stokes measures the impact in terms of the NAACP's membership figures. At the beginning of 1915 it had five thousand members, by early May membership had grown to over seven thousand, and by December there were almost ten thousand. However, as Stephen Weinberger has shown, the NAACP's membership was already growing steadily before *Birth* was released. Furthermore, it is difficult to judge the extent to which the growth in the organization's size was caused by this one campaign or whether other factors, such as the migration of African Americans northward and into cities (which increased with the outbreak of war, as did the membership rolls), played an equally important role. Nevertheless, the campaign against *Birth* also gave African Americans a cause to rally behind. The Report of the Chairman in January 1916 concluded that "nothing has so helped to unloosen the energy and to stimulate the cooperative support of the colored people of this country as this attack on their character and their place in history." The campaign raised racial consciousness and gave African Americans a voice when they were so often denied one. Furthermore, if the NAACP believed that racial prejudice was African Americans' worst enemy and that it was shaped by representations in American culture, the campaign against *The Birth of a Nation* provided it with the perfect opportunity to illustrate this to others. Indeed, Gaines finds that "in the end" the NAACP "won the publicity war, evidence of which is the fact that the 1915 public interpretation of the film as viciously racist has remained the dominant interpretation." The NAACP might not have been able to convince the public authorities to ban the film in 1915, but it was able to persuade future generations of Americans of the dangerous and offensive message of Griffith's film.[41]

The campaign against *The Birth of a Nation* tells us much about the NAACP's approach to culture, both through what it achieved in the fight and through what it failed to accomplish. The basic premise behind all the association's cultural campaigns was that inequality was caused by racial prejudice and that this mental attitude was largely shaped by images of African Americans that appeared in the arts and popular culture. Therefore, to alter racial prejudice, African Americans and their allies had to alter those images. During the campaign against *Birth* this consisted primarily of a negative fight to censor the representation of race in the film. Censorship proved problematic for the NAACP, not least because of its piecemeal provision and changing legal status. It also exposed fault lines within the NAACP; it showed that the board and the wider membership were not always united in their attitude toward culture. Nevertheless, this tactic was not discarded by the leadership. It would continue to call for *Birth* to be banned in the 1930s, and it had the same aim in the battle against *Amos 'n' Andy* in the 1950s.

Other tactics, in their broader sense, proved both more successful and more appealing. Lobbying and persuasion were often the preferred approach of the NAACP. National and branch leaders had some, albeit often temporary, success when they appealed to city mayors and state governors. Their appeals for action were especially effective when they could invoke the national discourse of patriotism and morale, as they could during the First World War. This was a lesson well learned, and by the Second World War it had become an important tactic. When Walter White went to Hollywood during these years, he used the tactics of lobbying and persuasion, albeit on a more personal level, and made similar appeals to morality, patriotism, and national unity. White and his organization seemed to have learned an important lesson by the 1940s: they could not wait until a film had been made (when they could only resort to censorship); they must try and influence the filmmaking process itself.

Another lesson learned from *Birth* was how to conduct a campaign. Most of the battles against the film were instigated and carried out at a local level, with the national office offering advice and attempting to coordinate these various actions. This piecemeal, branch-led approach ultimately proved ineffective. From then on any cultural campaign was devised and directed by the national office. Even more significantly, the fight against *Birth* marked the first and only time that whites would lead the national office's involvement with art and culture. By the time the NAACP renewed its fight against *Birth* in the 1930s, African Americans would be spearheading the campaign to influence how their race appeared in American culture.

The NAACP has been criticized for focusing too much attention on Griffith's film. Weinberger argues that it "drained much of the association's energies and very limited finances from the struggle against the more tangible forms of racism affecting black people throughout America."[42] However, the organization was, despite its relatively meager resources, still able to engage in other activities during its early decades. These included campaigning against miscegenation laws; fighting disenfranchise-ment; and responding to racial injustices and violence, such as lynching. Indeed, while it might have diverted time and effort, the NAACP leader-ship saw the protest against the movie as helping these other causes. After all, to attack the film was to attack racism; it was to challenge the racial attitudes that made anti-black legislation, disenfranchisement, and mob violence possible. More broadly, then, this protest demonstrates the ways the NAACP's cultural work could operate alongside its other campaigns.

The protest was not just a battle against one film; it was also a struggle over the national cultural and historical consensus. The NAACP deliber-ately targeted *Birth* because it was a symbol of white culture's excoriation of the race. In the end, focusing on one film was a misguided tactic. The NAACP became obsessed with the film, to the extent that it was blinded to almost all other cultural representations of African Americans during these years. To the association, stopping *Birth* became an end in itself rather than a means to an end. For a while the film's importance became grossly exaggerated; the NAACP lost sight of the fact that this was just one ex-ample in a racist culture. Furthermore, after the protracted and ultimately unsuccessful war against *Birth,* the NAACP became disillusioned by its lack of influence on white culture. It continued to engage in tussles with Griffith's film, but it would be the end of the 1930s before it felt it could take on the white film industry again.

The association recognized the need to create alternative images that showed the race in a more accurate and positive light. Even before the release of *The Birth of a Nation* the NAACP had been engaged with other types of culture. It realized that there were forms—fine art, poetry, fic-tion, drama—that, while they might not have the popular appeal or reach of film, offered other advantages. African Americans could not only use these forms of "high" culture to produce positive images of black life, but the very act of creation would also demonstrate their talent and culture; they could instill in African Americans a real pride in their race and forge a sense of black collective identity. If the campaign against *Birth* was re-active and negative, this would be a positive celebration of black life and culture. It began with the first publication of the *Crisis* magazine in 1910 and would come to fruition with the unprecedented cultural outpouring of the Harlem Renaissance. The art exhibitions and book publications; the lauded black artists; the pictures and stories of talented, successful, and respectable African Americans: it would all add up to an exuberant black riposte to Griffith's film.

# 2

# Representing the New Negro

In 1925, James Weldon Johnson, literary critic, author, mentor, songwriter, poet, and first black executive secretary of the NAACP, published the *Book of American Negro Spirituals* with his brother, Rosamond. This collection showed some of the many sides to this (Harlem) Renaissance man. Johnson had a long-standing interest in the arts, particularly in spirituals and what he saw as black American art forms. The book also complemented his work as a civil rights leader because it reflected his belief that by showing the world the achievements of his race he was helping to break down racial prejudice. As he wrote in the introduction to the anthology, there is "a change of attitude going on with regard to the Negro. . . . America is beginning to see the Negro in a new light, or, rather, to see something new in the Negro." Furthermore, "this change of attitude with regard to the Negro which is taking place is directly related to the Negro's change of attitude with regard to himself. It is new, and it is tremendously significant."[1]

The change to which Johnson was referring was part of the Harlem Renaissance of the interwar years. The 1920s was an important decade for the association; it was a period when it was, in the words of W. E. B. Du Bois, laying "foundations." It was still a new organization, one that was finding its place in the black community and in America at large. This process of development included establishing an interest in culture—not just responding to white representations, as it had with *Birth of a Nation*, but also concerning itself with the creation of culture by members of the race. Johnson, along with Du Bois, was one of the NAACP's most important figures at this time, and the two men, with many of their colleagues, contributed to a debate about the nature and purpose of culture. It was a discussion that was often contentious and that exposed differences of opinion both within and outside the association. It was also a debate that demonstrates some of the ways in which, according to the NAACP's leadership, the arts could play a significant role in securing civil rights. Thus, conversations on whether culture should be "Negro" or "American" and arguments about the relationship between propaganda and art can tell us much about the NAACP's model of African American culture and the relationship of this model to the struggle for racial equality.[2]

The Harlem Renaissance lasted from around 1919 until the middle of the 1930s. This was a period when many intellectuals and artists debated what was meant by "Negro art." In the 1920s Harlem, New York, became the center, psychologically and physically, for an outpouring of African American culture. This concentration of poets, novelists, artists, dancers, and musicians was, in part, a product of the massive migration of African Americans out of the South to the cities of the North and Midwest. During the 1920s nearly a million blacks moved from the rural South to the cities. Men and women were drawn to Harlem because of the promise of jobs and the bright lights of city life. James Weldon Johnson called Harlem "the Negro capital of the world."[3]

The Renaissance marked the emergence of what contemporaries termed the "New Negro." Alain Locke, editor of a key text of the Renaissance, *The New Negro* (1925), identified a psychological change in African Americans and the growing assertion of a racial identity—a "renewed self-respect and self-dependence." These New Negroes were the writers, painters, musicians, and others who were, according to James Weldon Johnson, "zealous to be racial, or to put it better, determined to be true to themselves, to look for the art material within rather than without." The Renaissance, he wrote in 1926, is "a movement which embodies self-sufficiency, self-confidence and self-expression, and which is lacking in the old group sensitiveness to the approbation or opinion of its white environment."[4] As discussed later in the chapter, there was debate about the extent to which the art produced should be "Negro," rather than "American." Indeed, there were considerable differences among the types, aesthetics, and philosophies of work produced during the Harlem Renaissance. What united the participants, however, was the sense of being part of a movement.

A number of NAACP officials played an important role in encouraging and shaping that movement, including Walter White, Joel Spingarn and his wife, Amy, and Jessie Fauset. The most significant figures from the association were W. E. B. Du Bois and James Weldon Johnson. Both men were authors, but their real influence came from their position as two of the leading black intellectuals of the period. They frequently expressed their ideas about the style, content, or purpose of the work being produced by African Americans, ideas that developed over time. In this way they he ped to shape what might be seen as an NAACP "model" of African American culture in the 1910s and 1920s. That is not to say that everyone within the association, or even within its leadership, subscribed to every aspect of this model. Indeed, Johnson and Du Bois disagreed with each other over some issues. Nevertheless, both, in their different ways, were important in supporting and influencing the New Negro movement. These two figures increasingly dominated the NAACP during this period. Du Bois was editor of the NAACP's official magazine, the *Crisis* (a position discussed in the next chapter), and when Johnson was made executive secretary in 1920, it marked the transition of power from white to black within the NAACP; the white board relinquished control to the black secretariat.[5] This involvement with the Harlem Renaissance is particularly significant because it marked, to a large extent, an African American strategy.

Of course, art and literature were not the NAACP's primary concerns during the postwar years. The beginning of the Harlem Renaissance coincided with the "Red Summer" of 1919, which saw outbreaks of racial violence throughout the country; there were riots in Chicago, Washington, DC, and Longview, Texas. This upheaval continued throughout the 1920s. When a group of black sharecroppers in Phillips County, Arkansas, were accused of planning an "insurrection," dozens were shot and killed and the remainder arrested. Walter White went to investigate and reported that the accusation of a plot to massacre whites was a pretext to halt the sharecroppers' challenge to the inequities of peonage. The NAACP organized the defense of the imprisoned men and after a four-year fight secured their acquittal in the Supreme Court. This response reflected the NAACP's strategy: investigation, exposure, and, if there was a case to be argued, court action. According to historian Patricia Sullivan, "By the mid-1920s, the NAACP's leadership had concluded that the courts offered the most promising avenue for advancing the association's goals."[6]

It was not, however, the only avenue, and NAACP leaders made a concerted effort to incorporate culture into their work. During the 1920s a cultural strategy formed a specific part of the association's agenda: a press release regarding the association's activities for 1925 listed the "Cultural and Artistic development of the Negro," alongside campaigns against segregation, lynching, and discrimination.[7] The association hoped that the production of art and literature by African Americans would change white attitudes toward the race and undermine the prejudice that underpinned racial inequality. It encouraged and celebrated black artists as examples of black achievement and proof of "civilization." These artists were to create the forms of "high" culture that the NAACP believed middle-class white Americans valued and admired. The hope was that this demonstration of culture would convince whites that African Americans deserved and were capable of achieving full equality. The creation of culture was thus a political act. Furthermore, there were those within the NAACP who believed that the content of that culture should be political, that art and literature could advance the race by showing positive images of African Americans that challenged racist white assumptions. In addition, this "Negro" culture would be both "black" and "American": it would celebrate distinctive racial characteristics at the same time that it was integrated into a wider American culture.

In 1923 James Weldon Johnson wrote to Walter White, "It has long been a cherished belief of mine that the development of Negro Art in the United States will not only mean a great deal for the Negro himself, but will provide the easiest and most effective approach to that whole question called the race question. It is the approach that offers the least friction." Johnson, and many of his NAACP colleagues, believed that the arts could have an ameliorating effect on racial prejudice. This belief was grounded in the notion that the creation of "high" art, in particular, was seen as a signifier of a group's status. Amy Kirschke writes that "Americans saw high culture as a measure of their greatness and level of civilization." Johnson explored this idea in his preface to an anthology of black poetry, a book that itself offered proof of black artistic talent. "The world does not know that a people is great until that people produces great literature and art. No people that has produced great literature and art has ever been looked upon by the world as distinctly inferior," Johnson wrote. "Nothing will do more" to change the "mental attitude" toward the Negro and to "raise his status than a demonstration of intellectual parity" through "the production of literature and art." Johnson hoped that if the white public saw blacks producing novels, poetry, and paintings, then they would have to accept that African Americans deserved equal rights.[8]

The NAACP was not alone in hoping that the arts could improve race relations. A number of historians have argued that many of those involved in the Renaissance believed a demonstration of artistic talent could challenge white ignorance and help break down racial barriers.[9] Black intellectuals such as Alain Locke, a professor of philosophy at Howard University, and Charles S. Johnson, the director of research at the National Urban League and the editor of its magazine, *Opportunity,* saw the creation of art as important for the black race. In 1925 Locke wrote that the "immediate hope" for the race "rests in the revaluation by white and black alike of the Negro in terms of his artistic endowments and cultural contributions, past and prospective." Charles Johnson, much like the NAACP's Johnson, believed that black artists and their work could help change the self-image of blacks, freeing them from feelings of inferiority, and could affect white attitudes toward the race. "There is," he editorialized, "an extreme usefulness for the cause of inter-racial good-will . . . in interpreting the life and longings and emotional experiences of the Negro people to their shrinking and spiritually alien neighbors; of flushing old festers of hate and disgruntlement by becoming triumphantly articulate; of forcing the interest and kindred feeling of the rest of the world by sheer force of the humanness and beauty of one's own story." Johnson's magazine, as well as the Brotherhood of Sleeping Car Porters' *Messenger* and Marcus Garvey's *Negro World,* all published examples of and discussions about black literature and art. A piece in the latter celebrated the "new crop of literary people of the Negro race." In an echo of James Weldon Johnson's statement of two years earlier, the article went on, "No people can get very far in their own estimation or that of their neighbors who do not write their own history, their own prose and verse, who do not have their own philosophers and scientists."[10] This is not to say, however, that there was a consensus on the nature and purpose of black culture. As will be discussed later in the chapter, some of Du Bois's ideas about propaganda put him at odds with many of the artists of the Renaissance. Some of those from what was considered the "younger" generation, such as Langston Hughes and Wallace Thurman, thought men like Du Bois were too controlling. Nevertheless, they did often look to the NAACP and its leaders (including Johnson, Walter White, Jessie Fauset, and even Du Bois himself) for support. Furthermore, it was often these very debates about the arts, as well as the work itself, that helped give the Renaissance its vitality and lasting importance.

James Weldon Johnson was the NAACP's most articulate advocate for engaging with the arts during this period. He had developed his ideas over many years in his fiction, poetry, and literary criticism. Johnson wanted African Americans' achievements as creators of culture to be acknowledged and celebrated. Their accomplishments, he believed, proved their status, and thus the very act of creating art could aid the civil rights struggle. As his narrator states in *Autobiography of an Ex-Colored Man,* "the colored people of this country have done four things which refute the oft advanced theory that they are an absolutely inferior race, which demonstrate that

they have originality and artistic conception." These four things were the
Uncle Remus stories, the spirituals or slave songs, the cakewalk, and ragtime. They "are the greatest proof which the race has yet brought against
the common charge of inferiority, because they are not the work of one or
two gifted individuals but of the race as a whole. They are a demonstration
that the Negro is a creator, a creator of that which has the power of universal appeal. They show that from his own inner consciousness the Negro
can evolve that which will move and influence the world. And that is proof
of inherent power." Thus Johnson saw culture as an important weapon
because it could change the way white Americans thought about African
Americans as a group. Furthermore, music, in particular spirituals, could
help end racial antagonism by touching people emotionally. The "gift"
of music "is the touchstone, . . . the magic thing." Through it "the Negro
can bridge all chasms. No persons, however hostile, can listen to Negroes
singing this wonderful music without having their hostility melted down."
Much of the NAACP's cultural strategy as it related to the Harlem Renaissance was built around the hope that whites would appreciate black talent
on an intellectual level; here Johnson hoped it would affect them on an
emotional level as well.[11]

The NAACP leadership more broadly had an uneasy relationship with
black music. Popular music evoked what were, to the NAACP, uncomfortable associations with minstrelsy and the "entertainer" stereotype. For decades, minstrel shows had used music and dance to belittle the race. When
black people were portrayed as singers, dancers, and jesters, it made them
appear unthreatening and contented with their unequal status. "Popular"
entertainers, in contrast to "high" artists, did not offer an image of the
race that would improve white attitudes. Furthermore, music such as jazz
came from the bottom up (in other words, it was created and popularized
by the working classes). The NAACP was more comfortable with the top-
down forms of culture produced by its own leaders and members. Indeed,
the black performers whose careers the NAACP most loudly celebrated
were Roland Hayes and Marian Anderson, who included classical music
in their repertoires. Walter White helped to organize Anderson's famous
Lincoln Memorial concert in 1939, and that same year she was awarded
the NAACP's Spingarn medal in recognition of "her special achievement
in the field of music" and "her magnificent dignity as a human being."
Singers such as Anderson and Hayes were performers of whom African
Americans should be proud, and their success reflected glory onto the
race. As the medal committee reported, "Her unassuming manner . . . has

added to the esteem not only of Marian Anderson as an individual but of the race to which she belongs."[12]

Nevertheless, the national leaders did, at least on some level, recognize the importance of popular black music. Benefits were organized starring performers such as Duke Ellington, Ella Fitzgerald, Cab Calloway, and Bill "Bojangles" Robinson. Furthermore, they did not shun all forms of "black" music. Hayes, for example, was known for his singing of spirituals. Johnson, for one, proclaimed the importance of both spirituals and ragtime. He defended ragtime from those who were concerned by its association with the seamier side of black life. He had been criticized by the music critic H. E. Krehbiel for discussing what Krehbiel called "vulgar music." In a letter to the editor of the *Chicago Tribune,* in whose pages the critic's complaint appeared, Johnson argued, "I do not see that the fact that ragtime music originated in, as Mr. Krehbiel puts it, 'houses whose character is not a fit subject for description' has anything to do with the consideration of it as music. That it did originate in such houses is merely incidental. The contention that ragtime should not be studied or even mentioned because of its vulgar origin strikes me as a most absurd standard of criticism." However, Johnson's discussion of ragtime was not a break with the NAACP strategy but rather an affirmation of it. He finished his letter by expressing his hope that "this creative genius which has been hitherto exercised in what may be called lower forms of art will some day be expressed in the higher forms, especially in literature."[13] Johnson's greatest hopes still rested in "high" culture.

For Johnson, the most important fact about ragtime was its status as an "American" art form. It was, he claimed, "the one artistic production by which America is known the world over." Ragtime "has not only influenced American music, it has influenced American life; indeed, it has saturated American life. It has become the popular medium of our national expression musically." It had become American, "national rather than racial," as Johnson put it, but its origins were black, and Johnson stressed this fact. Like the spirituals, ragtime had been created by blacks within the United States and was shaped by their experiences. Johnson, when discussing black artistic achievements more broadly, applauded the "power of the Negro to suck up the national spirit from the soil and create something artistic and original, which at the same time, possesses the note of universal appeal." A similar idea was expressed some years later by Du Bois, who argued that "American Negro art was built in the sorrow and strain inherent in American slavery, on the difficulties that sprang from Emancipation, on the feelings of revenge, despair, aspirations, and hatred which arose as the Negro struggled and fought his way upward." He celebrated the unique racial qualities of black culture; it was specific to African Americans and came out of the particular experiences and heritage of race. But it was also influenced by its American context.[14]

These ideas reflect an adherence to cultural pluralism that shaped the NAACP's strategy, a belief that culture could be both "Negro" and "American" simultaneously. The literary critic George Hutchinson, in a discussion of the *Crisis* that could be applied to the NAACP's cultural work more broadly, argues that the magazine's "idea of assimilation entailed the 'blackening' of national culture." At the same time, "the magazine consistently argued that the American Negro was thoroughly a product of American experience and institutions."[15] The NAACP celebrated the uniqueness of "Negro" art but at the same time saw it as fitting in to the broader American (white) culture. It did not want to create a separate black culture, but nor did it want to lose the sense of race within its culture. The NAACP wanted black culture to infiltrate and change white culture without losing its own distinctive qualities, until it too was accepted as "American."

This pluralism also reflects the dual aspects of the NAACP's engagement with culture during the 1910 and 1920s: it wanted to change white attitudes, but at the same time it hoped to encourage racial pride among African Americans. This could be seen most clearly in the material published in the *Crisis,* which is discussed in chapter 3. Johnson believed that when the African American turned his gaze "inward upon his own art material, upon his own cultural resources," it would create "a change in attitude of the Negro toward himself," a new "race consciousness." This "cultural awakening," as Johnson called it, was part of a larger stirring within the race. In a speech in 1922, the NAACP secretary said his organization's mission was "to awaken the Negro," to "instill a determination" to get that to which he was entitled. African Americans themselves, it was argued, needed to be aware of their achievements and contributions, in this case in the cultural sphere; the arts could help show them that they deserved their rights. Thus, although the emphasis was often on the potential effect of cultural representations on whites, many of the NAACP's leaders were aware too of the psychological impact of the arts on the race itself.[16]

The debate about African Americans and culture was waged beyond the confines of the NAACP. One of the most provocative contributions to the discussion was by journalist and author George S. Schuyler. In a piece published in the *Nation,* Schuyler denied there was any such thing as African American art. He wrote, "Negro art there has been, is, and will be among the numerous black nations of Africa; but to suggest the possibility of any such development in this republic is self-evident foolishness." He argued that there was no difference between "the literature, painting and sculpture of Aframericans" and that of white Americans. Indeed, he went further and denied there existed any differences between the races: "It is sheer nonsense to talk about 'racial differences' as between the American black man and the American white man." According to Schuyler, "The Aframerican is merely a lampblacked Anglo-Saxon."[17] This opinion was antithetical to the beliefs of many African Americans, including those in the NAACP. During a period when race consciousness was being encouraged and race achievement vaunted, the denial of a uniquely "Negro" art was offensive to many.

A week later Langston Hughes published a passionate and eloquent rebuttal to Schuyler's piece. He lamented the "mountain" that was the "urge within the race towards whiteness" and that stood in the way of "any true Negro art in America." He complained that artists wanted to be "as little Negro and as much American as possible." It was the duty of the black artist to inspire race pride, to "change through force of his art that old whispering, 'I want to be white,' hidden in the aspirations of his people, to 'Why should I want to be white? I am a Negro—and beautiful.'" Although he stressed the importance of art in shaping race consciousness, Hughes concluded that ultimately the artist was answerable to no one but himself: "We younger Negro artists who create now intend to express our individual dark-skinned selves without fear or shame. If white people are pleased we are glad. If they are not, it doesn't matter. . . . If colored people are pleased we are glad. If they are not, their displeasure doesn't matter either. We build our temples for tomorrow, strong as we know how, and we stand on top of the mountain, free within ourselves."[18] Hughes not only rejected Schuyler's argument but also the position of the NAACP. He believed that the artist should have to please neither whites nor blacks but should be free to do as he chose.

Alongside James Weldon Johnson, W. E. B. Du Bois played a central role in shaping the NAACP's model of culture during the Harlem Renaissance. Du Bois was at the heart of one of the most contentious debates during the Renaissance, that of art versus what Du Bois termed "propaganda." This dispute is significant for what it tells us about not only Du Bois and his NAACP colleagues' ideas about the nature and role of culture but also the views of others in the artistic and intellectual circles of Harlem. The

*Crisis* editor grew increasingly out of step with the direction of the Renaissance. In the early 1920s, Du Bois had a relatively relaxed attitude toward the type of work produced by and featuring African Americans. He celebrated the "younger literary movement" and the work of as diverse a group as Jessie Fauset, Jean Toomer, Langston Hughes, Countee Cullen, Georgia Johnson, and Claude McKay, among others. He actually accused the race of being "tremendously sensitive" about its depiction in the arts. He recognized that a history of cultural stereotyping had led to suspicion among African Americans: "Any mention of Negro blood or Negro life in America for a century has been occasion for an ugly picture, a dirty allusion, a nasty comment or a pessimistic forecast." However, he warned that this was limiting and would have dangerous consequences for the development of black culture. Du Bois argued that black artists had a responsibility to be truthful and to portray black life as it happened. "Negro art is today plowing a difficult row, chiefly because we shrink at the portrayal of the truth about ourselves," he wrote. "We want everything that is said about us to tell the best and highest and noblest in us." He warned, "We insist that our Art and Propaganda be one. This is wrong and in the end it is harmful." Du Bois recognized that there were good reasons for this insistence, because artists were afraid that any negative portrayal would be seen as racial stereotyping and be seized upon by those advocating racial inequality: "We fear that evil in us will be called racial, while in others it is viewed as individual." This fear meant that the white artist, "if he be wise and discerning," might be better placed to see "the beauty, tragedy and comedy more truly" than African Americans themselves. Du Bois was optimistic about blacks' position in society; he felt they could cope with truthful portrayals: "We stand today secure enough in our accomplishment and self-confidence to lend the whole stern human truth about ourselves to the transforming hand and seeing eye of the artist." He saw beauty in truth. Du Bois believed art should be truthful; he wanted to encourage "the Eternal Beauty that shines through all Truth." Du Bois's ideas about what this "truth" should be, however, would begin to take shape as the Renaissance progressed.[19]

By the middle of the decade, Du Bois was becoming increasingly disillusioned with the direction in which the movement was heading. In the 1926 call for entries for the Amy Spingarn Prize he began to test his ideas about the need for propaganda. He wrote that he did not "believe in any art simply for art's sake." It must have some other purpose, although he was not yet ready to pronounce what this should be. What he did know was that he was less concerned with aesthetics than with message: "We want the earth beautiful but we are primarily interested in the earth. We want Negro writers to produce beautiful things but we stress the things rather than the beauty. It is Life and Truth that are important and Beauty comes to make their importance visible and tolerable." At this stage, however, Du Bois was just testing the water, and he provided a disclaimer: "Even this as we say it is not altogether true." He instructed the entrants to his competition to write "about things as you know them: be honest and sincere." Betraying his displeasure at some of the work coming out of the Renaissance, he promised that in his magazine "you do not have to confine your writings to the portrayal of beggars, scoundrels and prostitutes; you can write about ordinary decent colored people if you want." However, he counseled, "do not fear the Truth. Plumb the depths. If you want to paint Crime and Destitution and Evil paint it. Do not try to be simply respectable, smug, conventional." He was not yet ready to insist on propaganda and told his writers to "use [it] if you want. Discard it and laugh if you will." All he asked was that they "be true, be sincere, be thorough, and do a beautiful job."[20]

Five months later he was ready to speak more forcefully on the subject of art and propaganda. At the NAACP annual conference in Chicago Du Bois laid out his "Criteria of Negro Art." For Du Bois, "Beauty," "Truth," and "Right" were "unseparated and inseparable." He reiterated his concern that the perceived need to please white publishers and a white audience damaged black writing. Whites "want Uncle Toms, Topsies, good 'darkies' and clowns." Black writers needed to break away from the constraints imposed on them by white America. It was their duty to begin the "great work of the creation of Beauty," using the tools of "Truth" and "Goodness." Du Bois then made his most infamous statement about black literature: "All Art is propaganda and ever must be, despite the wailing of the purists. I stand in utter shamelessness and say that whatever art I have for writing has been used always for propaganda for gaining the right of black folk to love and enjoy. I do not care a damn for any art that is not propaganda. But I do care when propaganda is confined to one side while the other is stripped and silent." He was not arguing that there could be no pro-white propaganda, but rather that blacks were denied positive propaganda. He explained that "it is not the positive propaganda of people who believe white blood divine" to which he objected, but "the denial of a similar right of propaganda to those who believe black blood human, lovable and inspired with new ideals for the world." The white public demands "racial pre-judgement which deliberately distorts Truth and Justice, as far as colored races are concerned." There also needed to be a change in how blacks themselves viewed art. "We are ashamed of sex and we lower our eyes when people talk of it. Our religion holds us in superstition," Du Bois complained. "Our worst side has been so shamelessly emphasized that we are denying that we have or ever had a worst side." He argued, "We are hemmed in and our new young artists have got to fight their way to freedom." In order to achieve change, African Americans had to set a new standard for their art themselves. "The ultimate judge has got to be you," he told his audience of (predominantly middle-class) African Americans; "you have got to build yourselves up into that wide judgement, that catholicity of temper which is going to enable the artist to have his widest chance for freedom."[21]

Du Bois's statement on propaganda has often been taken out of the context of the rest of the speech and understood as a demand for art to be made completely subservient to propaganda. In fact, his ideas are more complex that that interpretation. As Keith Byerman notes, he did not reject artistic freedom.[22] He wanted African Americans to be free from the constraints imposed on them by white America. Freedom meant African Americans, rather than whites, being the judge of black culture. He did, however, want art to be put to good use. Art did not need to be aesthetically beautiful, for "beauty" meant "truth." The "truth" is the most important element of art, if that truth helps the fight for racial justice.

Du Bois might have spoken of artistic freedom, but that did not stop him from attacking those authors and novels to which he objected. The first book to really raise his ire was Carl Van Vechten's *Nigger Heaven* (1926). A boy-meets-girl (or rather girls) story, it begins and ends with the exotic and savage side of Harlem, but for the most part it is set in the well-to-do homes of the city. The novel divided opinion: on the whole it was hated by blacks, many of whom could, literally, not get past the novel's offensive title (which was supposedly a reference to a segregated balcony in a Harlem theater), and it was loved by whites. Du Bois wrote a damning review in the *Crisis*. He called it "a blow in the face." "It is an affront to the hospitality of black people and the intelligence of white," he complained, referring to Van Vechten's appearance at many of Harlem's social gatherings and his friendship with African Americans. "I find this novel neither truthful nor artistic," he wrote. "It is a caricature." He admitted that at "some time and somewhere in Harlem every incident of the book has happened," but Van Vechten's focus on these events, he stressed, was a distortion. There was too much emphasis on the seedy side of Harlem, which Du Bois argued was not representative of black life there. According to the *Crisis* editor, the average black man in Harlem was a laborer who went to church, lodge, and movies and was as "conservative and conventional" as all working people. There was something "racial, something distinctively Negroid," in Harlem, but "it is expressed by subtle, almost delicate nuance," not by the "wildly, barbaric drunken orgy" of this book. "There is laughter, color and spontaneity at Harlem's core," but it would not be found in cabarets, most of which were financed and supported by whites and so were not genuine expressions of black culture. What was more, the book was poorly written and did not entertain. He compared Van Vechten's and Langston Hughes's depictions of Harlem, quoting Hughes's "Cabaret": "One said he heard the jazz band sob / When the little dawn was grey." (Actually it was a "she" who heard the jazz band in Hughes's original poem.) Van Vechten "never heard a sob in a cabaret"; he only heard "noise and brawling." Du Bois argued that Hughes, the black poet, was able to capture the depth and soul of black culture in his poem, whereas Van Vechten, as Du Bois wrote, only "slops about" in the "surface mud." This comparison suggests that it was not so much the material to which Du Bois objected, but rather the way in which that material was used. It was the message behind it that he interpreted as offensive to his race.[23]

There were many African Americans who agreed with Du Bois, but not all. James Weldon Johnson, a personal friend of Van Vechten, defended the white author. He claimed Van Vechten was not antagonistic toward the race, but rather a great admirer of it. Johnson understood why people objected to *Nigger Heaven,* but he maintained that they were wrong. Van Vechten was the "first well-known American novelist to include in a story a cultured Negro class without making it burlesque or without implying reservations and apologies." If Du Bois had focused on the debauchery of the novel in his review, Johnson emphasized the "High Harlem" that appeared in its pages. Furthermore, he argued that "Mr Van Vechten has paid the Negro this tribute in 'Nigger Heaven,' he has written of them as people—and as he would of any other people—as he has often written of white people. He has sketched them in every phase of life." Wallace Thurman also praised the book, although he liked it for different reasons than Johnson. He was critical of the propaganda elements and instead praised what he saw, with a dig at George Schuyler, as its racial flavor: "Once the characters cease discussing the 'Negro problem,' once they cease spouting racial equality epigrams, and anti-racial discrimination platitudes, the novel begins to move—begins to pulsate with some genuine rhythms peculiar (objections from G. S. Schuyler) to Harlem alone, and, thereupon holds the reader rapt until he reaches the dramatic climax."[24]

Du Bois was aggrieved by a white man's portrayal of Harlem, but he was dismayed when it was not only repeated but to his mind made worse by an African American. Claude McKay's *Home to Harlem* (1928) features Jake, a deserter from the army who returns to Harlem and finds a life of cabarets, brothels, gambling, and loose women. Du Bois wrote that it "for the most part nauseates me, and after dirtier parts of its filth I feel distinctly like taking a bath." He acknowledged in his review that there were parts that were "beautiful and fascinating." Perhaps unsurprisingly, he liked Ray, the educated intellectual of the novel. However, he asserted, "McKay has set out to cater for that prurient demand on the part of white folk for a portrayal in Negroes of that utter licentiousness which conventional civilization holds white folk back from enjoying." Du Bois believed he "used every art and emphasis to paint drunkenness, fighting, lascivious sexual promiscuity and utter absence of restraint in as bold and as bright colors as he can." "If this had been done in the course of a well-conceived plot or with any artistic unity," Du Bois claimed, "it might have been understood if not excused." But *Home to Harlem* was "padded" with a weak plot. Furthermore, Du Bois concluded, as "a picture of Harlem life or of Negro life anywhere, it is, of course, nonsense." As with *Nigger Heaven*, this distortion came not so much from its "facts" but "on account of its emphasis and glaring colors."[25] The *Crisis* editor was worried about the harm such novels could cause; he saw them as perpetuating the negative stereotypes that helped oppress the race.

Not everyone, even within his own organization, entirely agreed with Du Bois's views on art and propaganda. The editor knew this only too well because before he made his speech in Chicago, he had initiated a symposium to spark debate about the issue. A list of seven questions was sent out to black and white publishers, writers, and critics on the subject of the "Negro in Art." Du Bois wanted to know if white or black artists were under any "obligations or limitations as to the sort of character he will portray." He asked whether authors could be criticized "for painting the worst or the best characters of a group" and whether publishers could be criticized "for refusing to handle novels that portray Negroes of education and accomplishment, on the ground that these characters are no different from white folk and therefore not interesting." "What," he wondered, "are Negroes to do when they are continually painted at their worst and judged by the public as they are painted?" The next question asked whether the "situation of the educated Negro in America with its pathos, humiliation and tragedy" did not call for "sincere and sympathetic" artistic treatment: "Is not the continual portrayal of the sordid, foolish and criminal among Negroes convincing the world that this and this alone is really and essentially Negroid?" Finally Du Bois asked if there was "a real danger that young colored writers will be tempted to follow the popular trend in portraying Negro characters in the underworld rather than seeking to paint the truth about themselves and their own social class."[26]

Over the next eight months responses were printed in the *Crisis* that demonstrated wide-ranging opinion on these issues. Du Bois would not exactly have been comforted by many of the responses from his white acquaintances. Carl Van Vechten replied that the "squalor of Negro life, the vice of Negro life, offer a wealth of novel, exotic, picturesque material to the artist," whereas "there is very little difference between the life of a wealthy or cultured Negro and that of a white man of the same class." This type of comment confirmed Du Bois's worst suspicions about white attitudes toward African Americans in literature. Alfred Knopf dismissed the question about publishers refusing to handle novels that portrayed educated Negroes as "senseless." H. L. Mencken suggested that in order to counteract the derogatory portrayal of African Americans, black artists should "depict the white man at his worst." He provided the example of Walter White, who had done this "very effectively," presumably by representing a white character as a barbarous lyncher in *The Fire in the Flint*.[27]

Of the African Americans who took part in the debate, Countee Cullen's views most closely reflected those suggested by his future father-in-law's questions. He argued that if publishers rejected books about middle-class blacks because they were too much like whites, "they should reject those about lower class Negroes for the avowed reason that they do not differ essentially from white folk of the same sort." Black authors, like all authors, had the right to cover whatever topics they chose, but he warned that "the Negro has not yet built up a large enough body of sound, healthy race literature" for only books about the lower classes to be written, in case they were taken to be "truly legitimate" by white America. He argued that authors "must create types that are truly representative of us as a people." Langston Hughes, on the other hand, dismissed the premise of the debate, asking, "What's the use of saying anything—the true literary artist is going to write about what he chooses anyway regardless of outside opinions."[28]

Although he did not respond directly to the questionnaire, Charles

Johnson wrote an editorial in August 1926 in response to the Schuyler-versus-Hughes debate. He made a plea for artistic freedom. He wrote that what was most important was that "these black artists should be free, not merely to express anything they feel, but to feel the pulsations and rhythms of their own life, philosophy be hanged." This was not to say that Johnson rejected the social and political role of art, but rather that he dismissed overt propaganda. He could not agree with Du Bois's insistence on art always showing the "best" of black life; he believed that African Americans had to be true to their own experience, whatever that might be. Alain Locke also objected to Du Bois's stance, although he approached the question from a different perspective. Locke emphasized aesthetics and beauty; his was an art-for-art's-sake mentality. In a piece published a couple of years after Du Bois's symposium, he explained that his "chief objection to propaganda, apart from its besetting sin of monotony and disproportion, is that it perpetuates the position of group inferiority even in crying out against it. For it leaves and speaks under the shadow of a dominant majority whom it harangues, cajoles, threatens or supplicates." "Art," Locke argued, "in the best sense is rooted in self-expression and whether naive or sophisticated is self-contained." He insisted that "genius and talent" must "choose art and put aside propaganda." Over the issue of art versus propaganda, Du Bois was thus at odds with two of the other most important black intellectuals of the Renaissance.[29]

The responses from Du Bois's NAACP colleagues are also illuminating. They suggest differences of opinion about how art should be approached, but all the answers reflect a consensus about the usefulness of the arts to the cause of racial equality. They were not all comfortable calling for "propaganda," but in their own way they advocated this approach. Joel Spingarn wrote that a novel can be two things: "it may be considered a contribution to the *literature* of the world or as a contribution to the *culture* of a race." A "mediocre" book might be rejected from the world's literature, but "from the standpoint of Negro culture it may be important that some writers should get a hearing, even if their books are comparatively poor." Spingarn believed this was necessary because black culture was only just emerging; in time, the race too would be judged on its artistic merit. He dismissed as a "childish formula" the "art versus propaganda" debate and claimed that something did not need high artistic value to have worth. Jessie Fauset suggested that black writers must "learn to write with a humor, a pathos, a sincerity so evident and a delineation so fine and distinctive that their portraits, even of the 'best Negroes,' those presumably most like 'white folks,' will be acceptable to publisher and reader alike." She blamed white publishers for "considering only certain types of Negroes interesting," and like Du Bois, she saw the creation of a large, book-buying black audience as a partial solution. Mary White Ovington argued that publishers wanted art, not propaganda. It seems, however, that she saw "propaganda" as writing about the "sordid, foolish and criminal." In the last few years, she claimed, the "true Negro writer" had dropped this propaganda and was "painting reality." The "reality" she referred to was one that was middle class and respectable. Ovington played her own part in encouraging the Renaissance, writing a column in which she reviewed and discussed novels and that was reprinted in a number of black newspapers.[30]

Walter White responded to Du Bois's questions about the "Negro in Art" with a call for artistic freedom. He regretted that "at a time when Negro writers are beginning to be heard there should arise a division of opinion as to what or what not he should write about." White refuted the suggestion that upper-class African American life was no different from white life and therefore was of no interest. "Upper class Negroes have through that very struggle sharpened their sensitiveness to the intense drama of race life in the United States," he argued; therefore, the "lives of so-called upper class Negroes have advantages as literary material." He believed that upper- and middle-class blacks provided as much material for dramatic representation as the lower classes. This, however, was not the only topic on which African Americans should write; rather, he argued that all areas of black life were worthy and that writers should have artistic freedom. White asserted that the "Negro writer, just like any other writer, should be allowed to write of whatever interests him whether it be of lower, or middle, or upper class Negro life in America; or of white" and "should be judged not by the color of the writer's skin but solely by the story he produces."[31] White was less concerned with the content of black culture. Instead, he saw the very creation of culture as a political act. Nevertheless, in his own literature he deliberately produced images that would challenge white stereotypes of the race. His first novel, *The Fire in the Flint,* was filled with respectable, middle-class blacks who battled against the prejudice of a white world.

The NAACP's engagement with the Harlem Renaissance involved debates and theorizing, but it also took a more practical form. Association staff, particularly James Weldon Johnson and Walter White, played a personal role in mentoring the "New Negroes" of the Renaissance. Their interaction with these young artists and writers was born of a belief that this group of African Americans could help advance the race through a demonstration of their creative talent. It was also driven by a personal interest in and love of the arts and the accompanying socializing. Johnson saw his involvement with the Renaissance and his own creative work as separate from his day job as executive secretary of the NAACP. In his autobiography he remembered, "My own literary efforts and what part I played in creating the new literary Harlem were . . . mere excursions; my main activity was all the while the work of the Association."[32] This work, for Johnson and his colleagues, included investigating lynchings and race riots, defending fugitives from the South and homeowners in the North, fighting the white primary and residential segregation, pushing for legislation, and lobbying politicians. However, the NAACP's cultural strategy was intended as a complement to this other work, not an alternative. The hope was that it would challenge white attitudes toward the race, that it would make it easier for whites to accept desegregation or to see blacks as something other than violent rapists who should be lynched.

Furthermore, evidence from the NAACP Papers suggests that there was in fact a close link between both Johnson's and White's cultural activity and their roles as executive and assistant secretaries. Johnson had joined the association in 1916 as field secretary, and White arrived in 1918. Johnson and White used their positions within the NAACP and the power and influence they gave them to assist black artistic talent. Both men were widely known and respected within Harlem circles and in black communities throughout the country. They often used NAACP resources, contacts, and knowledge. The files of the NAACP Papers are full of letters relating to the Renaissance. The majority can be found in the "Personal Correspondence" file, but they were often written during work, typed by their NAACP secretaries, and sent out on the association's headed paper. White and Johnson gave NAACP mailing lists to publishers in order to send out circulars advertising their latest releases, and NAACP branch members were used as salesmen.[33]

James Weldon Johnson's biographer, Eugene Levy, writes that he "did what he could for young black writers by praising them in his [*New York*] *Age* column and by including them in both editions of *The Book of American Negro Poetry.*"[34] In fact, Johnson and Walter White did much more than this to help African American artists. There is voluminous correspondence between the two men and some of the leading lights of the Renaissance, including Countee Cullen, Claude McKay, Langston Hughes, Nella

Larsen, Rudolph Fisher, Willis Richardson, and Aaron Douglas. They contacted publishers on their behalf; introduced them to philanthropists; encouraged their endeavors; offered advice (both practical and artistic); and even raised money for, fed, and entertained these youngsters. There are many examples of White and Johnson promoting their work. For example, after the publication of *Color* (1925), Countee Cullen wrote to White to thank him for his help in publicizing the book: "I think Harper Brothers or I ought to pay you. If the book has any sale at all, much of it will surely be due to the fine spirit of cooperation you have shown in the matter."[35] The NAACP men wanted the public to read and buy the work of the New Negroes. Only in this way would the world be made aware of the talents of the race.

White often tried to mediate between writers and publishers, with varying degrees of success. This was done out of a wish to help the younger writers but also out of a desire to further his own position as an arbiter of the Renaissance. White was friends with George Oppenheimer and Harold Guinzburg, of the newly formed Viking Press, and he acted as a talent scout for them. He tried to persuade Claude McKay to publish with Viking. He urged McKay "as a friend" to "get your novel ready for publication as soon as possible." White boasted, "There are three or four first rate publishers who have asked me to keep an eye open for likely material." He had in mind "one firm in particular recently organized and known as the Viking Press. . . . If you want me to, I will put you in touch with them." White was offended when, concerned about publishing with such a new firm, McKay ignored his advice: "I think you know me well enough to know that I would not have recommended The Viking Press to you in preference to another if I were not absolutely sure that it was the best bet possible." He reassured McKay that a new firm with a smaller list would put its full weight behind every book it published. "However," he sniffed, "it is your own novel and yours is the final decision to be made." White did not like having his advice ignored. Nevertheless, alongside critic Arthur Schomburg, he continued his attempts to find a publisher for McKay's work. The saga continued for many months, until McKay resigned himself to the idea that the book would never be published.[36] This example shows that White did not always have the temperament for dealing with some of these young artists. His own considerable ego meant that he was easily offended, and at times he appeared more interested in furthering his own reputation than assisting others. He reveled in his position as elder statesman because it gave him power and prestige. Thus, while this liaising and corresponding did have a potentially political consequence, in that it helped bring the achievements of these writers to the attention of the American public and therefore might change the image of the race, it could also be driven by self-interest. At times this work became divorced from any cultural strategy and was simply a matter of ego.

Compared to White, James Weldon Johnson had an easier relationship with many of the "New Negroes." His temperament was perhaps better suited to the role of mentor. He was much friendlier with Claude McKay, despite the poet's often prickly nature. McKay clearly liked and respected the NAACP secretary; he wrote in his autobiography that Johnson was "my favorite among the NAACP officials. I liked his poise, suavity, diplomacy and gentlemanliness." Johnson encouraged and helped Sterling Brown, and the younger poet appreciated his assistance, thanking Johnson for his "inestimable help." He corresponded with Langston Hughes, Countee Cullen, and Zora Neale Hurston, who playfully called him "Lord Jim." The older man offered advice, critiques, and encouragement to these young writers, in whom he invested much hope.[37]

Johnson and White both played significant roles in the "Cultural and Artistic development of the Negro." A number of historians of the Harlem Renaissance have found the two men to be key figures. David Levering Lewis identifies them as two of six "notables" who helped to create in Harlem a significant cultural scene. Cary Wintz writes that Johnson, alongside Alain Locke and Charles Johnson, was one of the "major boosters" of the movement. Of the three, Johnson was "strategically placed to make the greatest contribution, because he, far more than any other black intellectual, was able successfully to bridge the gap between artists and critic or promoter." Kenneth Janken acknowledges that while White did not necessarily have a "sophisticated awareness of art," he did know "the connoisseurs and could harness their expertise." Such qualities were essential to building a cultural movement.[38] Johnson's and White's involvement in the Renaissance was closely linked to their "day jobs" within the NAACP. They used the influence, reputation, and resources of the association to help not just the stars of the movement but also lesser-known artists. They wanted people to hear of these artists and their achievements. Black literature and art needed an audience, both black and white.

This desire for readers and consumers brought White and Johnson into contact with the white publishers and financiers of the movement, and with this came one of the central dilemmas of the Harlem Renaissance: white control of a black movement. White and Johnson served as intermediaries between publishers and new writers. Both the NAACP men and the publishing houses appeared to gain from the situation: the publishers had people to notify them of the latest talent and work; White and Johnson had direct access to the financiers of the movement. Johnson in particular during the 1920s had a national profile, thanks to his position in the NAACP, and his name and endorsement was a powerful commodity. Publishers used his favorable reviews and comments to help sell books. Johnson, who was acknowledged as a leading black critic of the period, was highly respected, and his evaluations could decide the fate of a manuscript. Knopf, for example, often sent manuscripts for his reaction before it would publish them.

The relationship between the NAACP officers and white publishers was more than one of business; they were often friends. Indeed, interaction between the races on a social plane was a significant aspect of the Harlem Renaissance. Much of this took place in the clubs and cabarets for which Harlem was famous and in the homes of the great and good of New York. Tales abound of drinking and dancing into the night with celebrities, musicians, dancers, actors, artists, and writers. Walter White and James Weldon Johnson, along with their wives, were the hosts for many such gatherings. They provided an opportunity for whites and African Americans to discuss the issues of the day, to form friendships, and to make contacts. White, Lewis suggests, turned his apartment at 409 Edgecombe Avenue "into a stock exchange for cultural commodities, where interracial contacts and contracts were sealed over bootleg spirits." If his home was a "stock exchange," then White was a broker, earning influence and prestige from these transactions. Langston Hughes described the Whites' apartment block as "quite a party center." Walter White "was a jovial and cultured host, with a sprightly mind, and an apartment overlooking the Hudson. He had the most beautiful wife in Harlem, and they were always hospitable to hungry literati like me." From a practical standpoint, these parties were an opportunity for black artists to be introduced to white publishers, critics, and wealthy patrons. Johnson wrote that he made many of his literary contacts at such Harlem gatherings: "[I] went to a great many 'literary' parties. At such gatherings I met and came to know a large number of American literary and artistic celebrities." Men such as Johnson and White, working as they did for an interracial organization, were comfortable mixing with those from a different race.[39]

These parties may sound frivolous, but to the NAACP mindset, socializing with whites was one more step along the road to acceptance by white

America. This might not sound like a "political" activity, but given both the enforced and voluntary segregation between the races during the early decades of the century, it did provide an opportunity to break down social barriers and form alliances between black and white. After all, at the same time that its leaders were wining and dining with the great and good, the NAACP was fighting a protracted battle against residential segregation. It was a fight that was dramatized in the mid-1920s by the case of Dr. Ossian Sweet, a black physician who bought a house in a white area. Local whites took exception to this, and when a large mob gathered for a second night, Sweet's brother fired, killing one man. The NAACP organized the black men's defense, persuading renowned attorney Clarence Darrow to take the case and helping to secure a dramatic victory.[40] The association wanted to protect African Americans' right to live wherever they chose and to desegregate all areas of life. Entertaining whites was thus a step, albeit a smaller one, toward the racial integration and equality that the Sweet case represented. However, it was also a chance to have a good time, and as a political strategy it certainly left much to be desired. It may have appeared significant to Johnson and White and their small circle of acquaintances, but this type of activity had little relevance for the rest of black America.

Johnson and White acted as "tour guides" to Harlem, showing interested liberal whites the sights and sounds of black America. Mr. Raymond McKelvey wrote to Johnson telling him that their mutual friend Elisabeth Freeman, an investigator for the NAACP, had led him "to believe that you might be willing to give me some enviable glimpses of Harlem life which would ordinarily be denied to a white outsider." White led a party on a "tour" of the neighborhood. He took English novelist Rebecca West and writer Konrad Bercovici to Harlem, where they visited the Abyssinian Baptist Church and met some of the locals. White wrote, "Both of them were tremendously impressed and we made plans for other visits which I think will materialize in interesting articles or what the really worth while colored people of New York are doing and are capable of doing." A year later Konrad Bercovici wrote an article for *Survey Graphic*'s "Harlem Number" entitled "The Rhythm of Harlem." It refers to visits to Harlem where he heard black preachers and music and saw plays and dances and may well have been based on White's tour. White and others could be accused of treating Harlem as a theme park for their celebrated white friends. The place and its people were exoticized for white consumption and pleasure; it was a place where whites could enjoy the decadence and reckless abandon of the "Jazz Age" before disappearing again to their safe, comfortable lives. However, White no doubt would argue that he was trying to challenge the view of Harlem as a playground. He showed white people the "worthwhile" of Harlem, not its underbelly. It was another way of introducing white America to the best of black life. [41]

This interaction between white and black was criticized because while African Americans might host parties, whites controlled the purse strings. The Harlem Renaissance might have been a black cultural movement, but it was financed by whites.[42] The people and organizations that put their money behind the Renaissance—the Harmon Foundation, established by the wealthy real estate developer William E. Harmon, which funded black artists through prizes, sponsorship, exhibitions, and sales; individual patrons such as Charlotte Osgood Mason, who assisted Zora Neale Hurston and Langston Hughes; publishers Harold Guinzburg, George Oppenheimer, and Alfred Knopf, who published many of the key texts of the Renaissance—were all white. Du Bois, for one, believed that white financing led to white control and subsequently had a damaging effect on the work being produced by black artists. Johnson's and White's actions, however, suggest they did not share his concerns. They tried to make the best of the situation and even believed there were advantages to this arrangement. When White was having difficulty getting his first novel published, H. L. Mencken asked him if there were black publishing firms he could use. White replied that even if there were he would not publish with them because he wanted his books to be read by whites.[43] He saw white publishers as a way of reaching a white audience, which was crucial if literature was to play a part in combating prejudice. White Americans needed to be made aware of the achievements of black writers; once they had read a novel or a collection of poetry by an African American, they would surely no longer be able to deny him his civil rights. White's comment reflects the integrationist attitude of his organization: the NAACP did not want to create separate black institutions but rather to work with white ones to the race's advantage.

Johnson was particularly outspoken in his defense of white publishers; he denied that they affected the work produced by African Americans. In an article for the *Crisis* he dismissed the complaint that "the leading white publishers have set a standard which Negro writers must conform to or go unpublished" and that "this standard calls only for books depicting the Negro in a manner which tends to degrade him in the eyes of the world; that only books about the so-called lower types of Negroes and lower phases of Negro life find consideration and acceptance." Johnson listed all the novels published in recent years that depicted the "upper" levels of Negro life, a list that included novels by Jessie Fauset, Walter White, and Nella Larsen. He drew up a similar list for those showing the "lower" levels, such as *Cane* and *Home to Harlem.* The "score is eight to six" in favor of the "upper" levels. He did the same for nonfiction and found "the score is nineteen to two." He concluded, "I believe that Negro writers today who have something worth while to say and the power and skill to say it have as fair a chance of being published as any other writers."[44] Johnson, of course, had a vested interest in defending the publishers: part of his literary reputation came from being seen as someone who could influence publishers, and he played a role in the publishing process. Therefore, he was defending himself as well as the publishing houses.

Du Bois was deeply concerned about the effect that white control was having on African American art. He believed that African Americans, rather than whites, should buy and judge work by black writers. Du Bois complained that the "American Negro as a race and in accordance with his numbers does not read books, does not support periodicals, does not buy pictures." He urged African Americans to learn to read and buy books, journals and pictures, for "only in this way can we give to the world a new Negro American art." African Americans were encouraged to be consumers and judges of black culture in order to provide an alternative to white patronage and control. Otherwise black writers would think they had to distort their depiction of black life in order to get published and paid. In a letter to Amy Spingarn he argued that "if the young colored writer writes naturally, expressing his own life and his own reaction to the environment about him, it is still hard for him to get his work published." Therefore he is "tempted" to "cater to what white America thinks that it wants to hear from Negroes."[45] Du Bois seems to have forgotten that Amy Spingarn was herself a white patron who financed the literary competitions of the *Crisis* (discussed in the next chapter). Presumably white money was acceptable to Du Bois when he decided where it should go. He wanted artists to be free from what he saw as the constraints of writing for a white audience. But at the same time, he wanted to be able to instruct black artists to create work that was useful to his cause. He advocated the "truth," but it was his own truth that he wanted to see on the page; he set the rules. If black writers transgressed, then he would chastise them. This meant that he became increasingly distanced from many in the Renaissance. However, an examination of his role as *Crisis* editor, as undertaken in the next chapter, raises questions about the extent to which he tried or was able to control the work produced by black artists.

James Weldon Johnson, on the other hand, despite his many pronouncements on "Negro art," was more interested in assisting than controlling young black artists. He could see the benefits of positive depictions of African Americans, but he was more tolerant than Du Bois of those that did not conform to the standard of the Talented Tenth. He believed in the power of artists to change white perceptions but argued that this would be achieved through the very act of creating art. This was why he spent so much time and energy encouraging and promoting black artists: he wanted to show their gifts to the world. At times it seems Johnson and Walter White were seduced by the Harlem Renaissance and that their work had nothing to do with a political or cultural strategy but was an end in itself, something to be enjoyed and celebrated. They saw the benefits of this arts approach for themselves and their small circle of friends—they benefited financially and socially from engaging with the arts—and therefore they assumed that this strategy would work more broadly. They hoped that their advancement would work its way down to the rest of the race and that others could replicate it by following their model.

This shows the limitations of the NAACP's strategy and, indeed, of the Harlem Renaissance more generally. It was never able to affect the underlying economic, social, and political causes of inequality. The Depression of the 1930s put these limitations into stark relief. Art and literature seemed unimportant in the face of unemployment, homelessness, and starvation. As Langston Hughes wrote, "Ordinary Negroes hadn't heard of the Negro Renaissance. And if they had, it hadn't raised their wages any." Historians of the Renaissance have largely recognized this failure. Nathan Huggins argues that its participants were naïve to think that culture could make a difference and that this illusion was shattered by the Depression. Similarly, David Levering Lewis claims that the Harlem Renaissance was always going to fail "as a positive social force"; the Depression merely accelerated the process. Culture could not change the way whites treated blacks. A few of the "Talented Tenth" might have been able to achieve some level of assimilation, but it wasn't a path that could be followed by the masses.[46]

The Renaissance did, however, achieve other, more intangible changes. Hughes conceded that it "did a great deal to make possible a public willing to accept Negro problems and Negro art." In other words, it may have helped change white attitudes toward African Americans even if it did not immediately improve their condition (though this, of course, suggests the flaw at the very heart of the NAACP's strategy). Anne Carroll also suggests it helped to create a new identity among African Americans themselves; new ways for blacks to see and define themselves emerged. As Huggins concedes, the Renaissance contributed to "a new sense among black people that they had something of value in common." Furthermore, a gradualist approach is understandable when it is considered within the context of the racial violence of the period. NAACP officials were only too aware of the dangers inherent in the race question. In the Red Summer of 1919 both the national secretary John Shillady and Walter White had close brushes with mobs. It might seem strange that against a backdrop of such violence the NAACP should turn toward the arts as a solution. On the other hand, when black lives were so routinely threatened and taken, perhaps a more subtle, less confrontational approach to the racial question was exactly what was needed.[47]

The NAACP's engagement with the Harlem Renaissance should not be seen in isolation from the rest of its work. In 1920 NAACP representatives James Weldon Johnson, Walter White, William Pickens, and James Cobb appeared before the House Census Committee to give evidence on the disenfranchisement of African Americans. Johnson argued that the "Negro today is not the Negro who was emancipated, illiterate [and] penniless." He was, the NAACP's new secretary insisted, ready for and deserving of the vote. Although Johnson did not explicitly say it on this occasion, proof of this qualification included his artistic achievements. As he wrote later in the decade,

> Through his artistic efforts the Negro . . . is impressing upon the national mind the conviction that he is an active and important force in American life; that he is a creator as well as a creature; that he has given as well as received. . . . In this way the Negro is bringing about an entirely new national conception of himself; he has placed himself in an entirely new light before the American people. I do not think it too much to say that through artistic achievement the Negro has found a means of getting at the very core of the prejudice against him.[48]

Culture, then, had the potential to be political; the very act of artistic creation was a challenge to racism. It might not have been able to bring racial prejudice to its knees in the 1920s, but the hope that the arts could weaken prejudice was shared by many others during that decade. Furthermore, it was an idea that did not go away. As will be seen, it helped to shape many African Americans' involvement in the cultural projects of the New Deal. For its part, the NAACP started to move away from its emphasis on black people as creators of culture by the Second World War era; however, it did not give up on the notion that culture was another avenue for securing civil rights.

The Harlem Renaissance provided an exciting opportunity for the NAACP to engage with black culture, but it raised a number of troublesome issues. The most problematic was the question of white control. Johnson and White tried to take advantage of white money and use it for the benefit of themselves, other individuals, and the race as a whole. They were realistic about the position of black culture at the beginning of the century: they knew that there was neither the money nor the power within black institutions to challenge white control of the culture industries; the fight against *The Birth of a Nation* had taught them that lesson only too well. Du Bois, on the other hand, was extremely critical of white control of the Renaissance, which he was convinced distorted African American art. Du Bois, of course, had already come up with a potential solution, or at least an alternative, to white patronage and control. It was a place where black writers could contribute free from the shackles of their white paymasters, where African Americans could find discussions on the history of their culture, and where they might see pictures of their race: it was called the *Crisis,* and it was to prove one of the most important and influential black magazines in the opening decades of the century.

3

# Du Bois's *Crisis* and the Black Image on the Page

The front cover of the April 1911 issue of the *Crisis* shows a hand-colored photograph of a young African American woman in profile (figure 1). She is dressed smartly and demurely, wearing a high-necked and long-sleeved blouse, trimmed with lace. She is looking down at a hand-drawn copy of the *Crisis*. The photograph was taken by Addison Scurlock, photographer to black Washington, DC. Scurlock was known for his images of famous African American figures, society ladies, businessmen, and the great and good of the capital. A number of Scurlock's photographs appeared in the *Crisis;* they were consistent with W. E. B. Du Bois's ethos of using images that showed a side to black life that challenged racial stereotypes. This photograph is just one example of how the NAACP's cultural strategy was put into practice in the magazine. Creative work was used in numerous ways, from showing black accomplishment and challenging stereotypes to encouraging racial pride and establishing an African American identity. The black image on the page, in its many guises, was thus part of the NAACP's campaign against racial prejudice.

*The Crisis: A Record of the Darker Races,* the NAACP's monthly magazine, established by W. E. B. Du Bois in 1910, was a tool with which the association could fight racial discrimination. This battle was waged through its editorials, reports, investigations, essays, and articles on every area of black life. From the first issues it included paintings, short stories, poems, and plays by and about African Americans. The *Crisis* used the arts to combat racism in a myriad of ways. It provided a space to demonstrate the artistic talents and achievements of African Americans. This reflected the NAACP's belief that one way of demonstrating black equality was to show that the race could produce great works of art and literature. The association encouraged this artistic endeavor not only by providing an outlet for publication and an alternative to white patronage but also

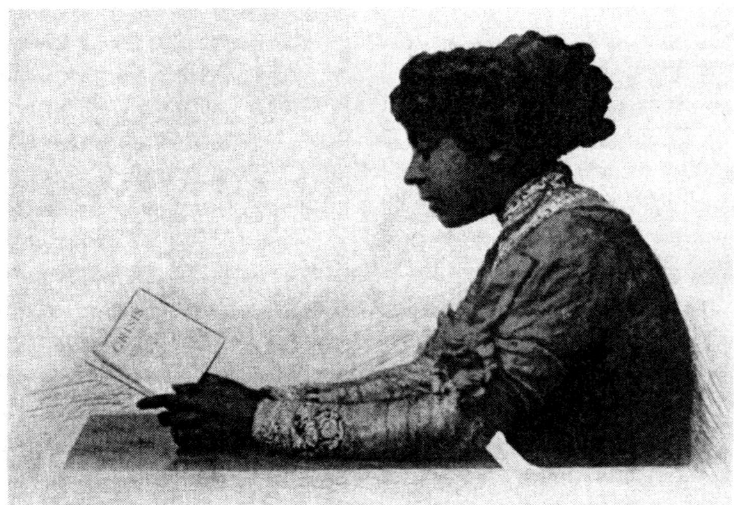


Figure 1. Photograph by Addison Scurlock, *Crisis* (April 1911): front cover. Image from the Library of Congress.

by establishing competitions that rewarded and raised the profile of black participation in the arts.

Yet there was much more to the NAACP's cultural strategy than simply proving that African Americans could create works of art and literature. The body of work in the *Crisis* helped to forge a collective black identity that was crucial to the NAACP's fight. It created a sense of racial pride, not only by demonstrating the talent of fellow race members but also by foregrounding black faces and characters and black life. The magazine became a place where African Americans could see pictures, photographs, stories, and dramas about themselves. The issue of how these black faces appeared is complicated and contentious. The NAACP has been accused of favoring lighter-skinned members of the race, reflecting its supposed assimilationist tendencies. The images of women in particular provide a fascinating insight into this debate; there are numerous examples of fair-skinned beauties on the front cover of the magazine, such as the one described above. However, notions of a shared black and African identity complicate the message about racial pride.

The representations of African Americans in the *Crisis* challenged prejudice by offering alternative images to racial stereotypes. The depiction of black women provides one example of how this was done. Another is the prevalence of representations of the black middle classes. Depicting black professionals and successful, hardworking, and decent members of the race exposed as false the claim that the race was lazy, foolish, or bestial. If the images in the *Crisis* were supposed to represent the magazine's readers, this suggests that a collective black identity was to be built around the middle class. The issue, however, is more complicated than simple arguments that the magazine reflected an interest in only this section of black society. It raises the question of the extent to which Du Bois censored material to fit his own ideas. Furthermore, it is complicated by the representations of other African Americans, such as workers, in the creative texts of the *Crisis*.

The importance of the *Crisis* in encouraging and shaping the arts has been recognized by scholars. They have discussed its role in providing a forum for black expression and in laying the groundwork for the Renaissance.[1] Most of these studies of the *Crisis* consider the general role and tone of the magazine. They tend to focus on how Du Bois used it as a forum to air his own views on the purpose of the arts (the debate about the "Negro Criteria of Art" is much discussed). Very few consider specific examples of the art and literature published within its pages. Notable exceptions to this are Amy Kirschke's *Art in Crisis* and Anne Carroll's *Word, Image, and the New Negro.* Kirschke is interested in the visual imagery that Du Bois published in his magazine and, as she puts it in her book's subtitle, his "struggle for African American identity and memory." Alongside his editorials, Du Bois used visual images to create a sense of collective identity and historical memory, which challenged white distortions. I examine this idea of collective identity when examining both the visual and the literary texts in the *Crisis.* Carroll is interested in composite texts, that is, the combination of diverse texts and images, which were used for both protest and affirmation. They were used to protest against injustice and violence but also provided a way to counteract the dehumanizing effect of such images and offered the chance to celebrate black success. Creative texts showed the "inner lives" of African Americans. Carroll examines essays and articles in black magazines, but she does not go on to demonstrate how these ideas worked in art and literature; an examination of such pieces is undertaken in this chapter. Thus, this study adds to the debate by testing Kirschke's and Carroll's theories against a greater range of creative work and by suggesting additional uses of culture in the NAACP's magazine.[2]

The first issue of the *Crisis* was published in November 1910. It cost ten cents, and all one thousand copies were sold. The NAACP was a fledgling organization, and the magazine was essential in spreading the word about its activities and principles. However, it did much more than simply inform people about the association's work. In theory the *Crisis* was the official organ of the NAACP; in reality it was, for the first twenty-four years of its publication, the magazine of its editor, W. E. B. Du Bois. He was responsible for the content of each issue, and he set the tone. Du Bois saw the *Crisis,* his "soul-child," as his most important contribution to the work of the NAACP. With his usual modesty he claimed that if it "had not been in a sense a personal organ and the expression of myself, it could not possibly have attained its popularity and effectiveness." Under his editorship the *Crisis* was more than "the dry kind of organ that so many societies support for purposes of reference and not for reading." While it did bring news of branch activities and reprint the association's annual reports, it also included his fiery editorials, articles on subjects from history to politics, and news of current and world affairs. To Du Bois, the *Crisis* was bigger than the NAACP. And for a time it was, with circulation figures almost twice those of NAACP membership. It was even, for a period, financially independent. Du Bois "crow[ed]" in a 1917 editorial that as of the previous year his magazine was "self-supporting and entirely out of debt." This financial freedom gave Du Bois a mandate for controlling the magazine the way he, and not the NAACP Board of Directors, saw fit. This, of course, often led to conflict, and as the *Crisis*'s financial situation worsened and Du Bois became increasingly dependent on the goodwill of the board, those tensions increased.[3]

The question of who *Crisis* readers were is important when determining its role as a cultural and political tool. Some scholars have argued that the magazine cut across class divides. For instance, David Levering Lewis contends that in "an era of rampant illiteracy," when there was little time for reading a "Harvard-accented editorial," the *Crisis* "found its way into kerosene-lit sharecroppers' cabins and cramped factory workers' tenements. In middle-class families it lay next to the Bible." Du Bois himself believed it was read by African Americans from all social backgrounds. He defined his readership as including "Negro workers of low income." It seems likely that the majority of its readers were middle-class blacks (a reflection of the membership of the NAACP itself at this time), who had the income, time, and inclination to read such a magazine, but that it was also known and discussed among a larger section of the African American community. Manning Marable claims that while the magazine was written "primarily for the Talented Tenth, it also spoke to a broad spectrum of Americans, from rural southern blacks to white northern liberals." The NAACP journal's readership was biracial, as was its membership. By the end of 1919 it was estimated that of the 91,203 NAACP members, nine-tenths were black and one-tenth were white. White readers, like members, were in the minority. In 1916 the white readership was estimated at only 20 percent. Thus, Charles Kellogg argues, "in determining the make-up of the magazine and its editorial policy, [Du Bois] kept in mind the fact that eighty per cent of all *Crisis* readers were Negroes." At the same time Du Bois did publish material to appeal to whites. They may have made up only a small percentage of the readership, but they were important if the NAACP's cultural strategy was to succeed. Of course, the *Crisis* was preaching to the converted: the mainly northern, liberal whites who read the magazine would already have been sympathetic to the black cause. Nevertheless, they too needed to fully accept positive representations of African Americans, and Du Bois's journal helped put such images in the public domain.[4]

Du Bois is clearly central to any discussion of the *Crisis* during this period, but so too is Jessie Redmon Fauset. As literary editor between 1919 and 1926, Fauset helped shape the cultural content of the magazine.

Carolyn Sylvander notes the many contributions Fauset made during those years: she "discovered" Langston Hughes and Countee Cullen; she corresponded with authors and smoothed relations between contributors and Du Bois; she ran the office and selected work for publication. The *Crisis* might have been Du Bois's vehicle, but Fauset clearly helped to keep it running and took a leading role in shaping the literary policy of the magazine. A discussion of the artistic content of the *Crisis* must necessarily acknowledge the influence of Jessie Fauset.[5]

The pages of the *Crisis* were filled with drawings, poems, stories, plays, and essays on the arts. In his editorials Du Bois set out his agenda for the arts in the *Crisis*. He wrote of the important contribution that African Americans could make: "We are likely to forget that the great mission of the Negro to America and the modern world is the development of Art and the appreciation of the Beautiful." The *Crisis* was to play a role in this development: "We shall stress Beauty—all Beauty, but especially the beauty of Negro life and character; its music, its dancing, its drawing and painting and the new birth of its literature." The *Crisis* "shall encourage it in everyway—by reproduction, by publication, by personal mention— keeping the while to a high standard of merit, stooping never to cheap flattery and misspent kindliness."[6]

Between 1910 and 1934 seventeen plays, 137 works of fiction (short stories), and 755 poems were published. During the 1910s the figures fluctuated, with an average of almost twenty-one pieces of literature published a year. After 1921 this number began to rise (though not consistently), with an average during the 1920s of forty-three pieces a year. The increase during this decade reflected the *Crisis*'s policy of actively encouraging and promoting the Renaissance. According to Lewis, Du Bois had withdrawn his magazine from the Renaissance by August 1927. In fact, the greatest number of pieces published during the 1920s was in 1928 (sixty-eight), and the peak during this period was in 1931, when eighty-two pieces appeared. Du Bois might have become disillusioned by the direction of the Renaissance, but he continued to find space in his magazine for work by black writers. The writers and artists published in the magazine represented some of the leading lights of African American arts. Langston Hughes was the most frequently published poet in the *Crisis,* followed by Georgia Douglas Johnson. There were short stories by Charles Chesnutt and Jessie Fauset and artwork by Aaron Douglas and Laura Wheeler. Du Bois and Fauset also published work by new and lesser-known artists.[7]

The most obvious way the *Crisis* could use the arts to fight racial prejudice was to demonstrate the creative talent of black America. The publication of short stories, drama, poems, and sketches put to the test James Weldon Johnson's assertion that "no people that has produced great literature and art has ever been looked upon by the world as distinctly inferior." A magazine with a national, biracial readership was the perfect place to showcase the artistic skills of African Americans. A contributor's race was often made explicit, by either a short biography or an accompanying photograph. The prize-winning entries published during 1926 were all printed with a photograph of the winner alongside.[8] Not everything that was published in the *Crisis* had an overt political message, but it all conformed to the NAACP's broad cultural strategy, in the sense that every piece produced by an African American was further proof of the race's merit. The paintings of sailboats and the poems about love all played a part in the NAACP's strategy to overcome racism with culture.

Du Bois believed that to establish a body of black culture, he needed to encourage and promote African American creativity and that one way to do this was to offer incentives. The first full-scale competition was introduced in 1924, with six hundred dollars in prize money donated by Amy Spingarn, wife of NAACP chairman Joel Spingarn. There were prizes for stories, plays, illustrations, essays, and poems, ranging from ten to one hundred dollars. The winners were announced the following year. The panel of judges included literary luminaries H. G. Wells, Charles Chesnutt, and Eugene O'Neill. Rudolph Fisher won first prize for his short story "High Yaller," the winning play was *The Broken Banjo* by Willis Richardson, and Countee Cullen won the poetry contest.[9]

The competition ran again the following year and received six hundred entries. Du Bois gave out the prizes at a ceremony held in New York in October 1926. Arna Bontemps read his prize-winning poem, and the winning story, "Swamp Moccasin," was read by its author, John F. Matheus. The Krigwa Players' Negro Theater, Du Bois's pet project, presented the second-prize play, *Foreign Mail* by Eulalie Spence. The Negro String Quartet played, and there was "dancing until 11.59 PM." The competition continued, in a number of guises, until 1931. The last reference is to the "Du Bois Literary Prize." The money was donated by a Mrs. E. R. Matthews, who suggested the prize be awarded in Du Bois's name as "an inspiration to the Negro youth of future generations." He accepted the honor with a "lack of modesty" because he had "hopes that this substantial prize, as the years go by, will draw the thought and genius of our young writers . . . to a more human and truthful portraiture of the American Negro in the 20th Century."[10]

According to Du Bois, "the great object of these contests is to stimulate effort, set a standard of taste and enable persons to discover in themselves capabilities."[11] He wanted to encourage blacks to pick up a pen or a paintbrush. The statement also tellingly demonstrates his desire to control the work produced by African Americans; he wanted to be the one to "set a standard of taste." These competitions, and indeed the *Crisis* more generally, allowed the NAACP to offer an alternative to white patronage and therefore white control. They also lent prestige to black artistic endeavor. By rewarding black artists with money at glitzy award ceremonies, Du Bois helped to raise the profile of their achievements. He hoped to prove to white America that blacks deserved the equal treatment that he and his organization demanded.

The NAACP was not the only organization to use literary competitions to stimulate interest in the arts; two months after the announcement of the first *Crisis* awards, the National Urban League (NUL), through its official organ, *Opportunity,* launched prizes of its own. As David Levering Lewis writes, Du Bois was not pleased that the NUL copied his idea. This incident suggests that there was competition among the different civil rights organizations when it came to championing black culture. *Opportunity,* edited by Charles Johnson, first appeared in 1923, and it included no examples of black art or literature. Indeed, it wasn't until the following year that the magazine regularly featured poems, short stories, and artwork. A number of scholars have argued that while the *Crisis* laid much of the groundwork for the interest in African American culture in magazines, by the mid-1920s *Opportunity* had taken over and become the most important black magazine it terms of the arts. Steven Watson suggests, "If *The Crisis* planted the seeds for the New Negro movement, *Opportunity* represented its flowering." On its pages appeared illustrations by artists such as Aaron Douglas; short stories by Zora Neale Hurston; and poetry by Arna Bontemps, Langston Hughes, Gwendolyn Bennett, and Countee Cullen. The last two also had regular columns in which they discussed the arts. Many of the same artists featured in the *Crisis* were also published in Johnson's magazine. There were articles and editorials on black culture, both African and American. Charles Johnson explained that his competitions were established in order "to stimulate and foster creative literary effort among Negroes [and] to stimulate and encourage interest in the serious development of a body of literature about Negro life." Johnson, like Du Bois, recognized the political role of the arts, but he also stressed artistic freedom. According to Alain Locke, *Opportunity* usurped the *Crisis* by "substituting self-expression and interpretation for rhetoric and overt propaganda."[12]

The Brotherhood of Sleeping Car Porters also published a magazine, the *Messenger,* which ran between 1917 and 1928. Its editors, A. Phillip Randolph and Chandler Owen, initially included few examples of African American art and published literature only if it served social and economic ends: "With us economics and politics take precedure [*sic*] to 'Music and Art.'" When editorial control shifted to George Schuyler and Theophilis Lewis in 1923, and during Wallace Thurman's brief tenure in 1926, greater emphasis was placed on the arts. When pictures started appearing on the cover in 1923, they were often, for a few years at least, of young, glamorous women, much like many of the *Crisis* cover girls. There was work by Wallace Thurman, George S. Schuyler, Georgia Douglas Johnson, and Robert Bagnall, as well as book reviews and articles on the arts. According to Theodore Kornweibel, the *Messenger* published more poems during the period 1923 to 1928 than either the *Crisis* or *Opportunity.* Nevertheless, of the three race journals, the *Messenger* had the least influence on artists because while it was "sympathetic to the Harlem Renaissance and the New Negro spirit [it] never committed itself to them wholeheartedly."[13]

The magazines discussed above were all linked to civil rights organizations, from which they received official, and sometimes financial, support. A more independent enterprise was set up by a group of younger artists who rejected much that these more established magazines represented. This group included Wallace Thurman, Langston Hughes, Zora Neale Hurston, and Aaron Douglas. These modernists were more experimental in the form and content of their work. They rejected the guidance and philosophies (though not necessarily the assistance) of the middle-class intellectuals, or "Niggerati," as Thurman and Hurston nicknamed them. Under the leadership of Thurman they created their own quarterly magazine, *Fire!!,* which was "Devoted to the Younger Negro Artists." Only one issue, in November 1926, was ever produced, but it provided an important statement about the group's attitude toward black culture. They rejected the philosophy of art as propaganda; they believed it was too restrictive and damaged the creative process. Ann Douglas explains that they "proudly wrote about just the things Du Bois . . . wished to downplay if not ignore: sex, color-consciousness, racism, and self-hatred" and "the Negro as . . . wild, colorful and possibly dangerous." They found the black "intelligentsia," in Anne Carroll's words, "too conservative in their representations of African Americans, too insistent on the idea of using art as a political and social tool, and too obsessed with the idea of race." These younger artists were scathing about Du Bois, particularly once he set out his propagandist stall, and about the conservatism of the NAACP.[14] Interestingly, however, many of the contributors to *Fire!!* (including Douglas, Hughes, Cullen, Bontemps, and Gwendolyn Bennett) also had work published in the *Crisis*. This indicates that their disagreements with Du Bois and his organization did not stop them from using his magazine to advance their own careers. It also suggests that Du Bois did not always censor those who opposed him.

The editor's agenda for the *Crisis,* particularly the awards and ceremonies, was directed, a least in part, toward whites. However, Du Bois also published creative work in the *Crisis* for the benefit of his black readers. He used images of African Americans, both visual and literary, to strengthen a sense of collective black identity. Kirschke argues he did this by highlighting the prejudice and difficulties African Americans faced in all aspects of their lives and demonstrating the areas, such as education, where they could make advancements.[15] I would argue that he also did it in a more simplistic way; by simply featuring black faces and black characters, he allowed his readers to recognize themselves on the pages of a national magazine. He wanted to instill pride in the race, to show African Americans that they deserved equality and that they should fight for it. Du Bois was keenly aware of the damaging effects of racial stereotyping on black self-worth. In one editorial he argued that African Americans had been made ashamed of their race because of stereotyping by whites. If the *Crisis* "puts a black face on its cover our 500,000 colored readers do not see the actual picture—they see the caricature that white folks intend when they make a black face." He received letters claiming that the images in the magazine were "*too* black." The race, Du Bois wrote, is "almost unconsciously ashamed of the caricatures done of our darker shades" because "they are cruel reminders of the crimes of Sunday 'comics' and 'Nigger minstrels.'" He urged his readers, "Let us train ourselves to see beauty in black."[16] Du Bois wanted African Americans to be proud of not only their race but also images of their race.

The *Crisis* featured many photographs of black people. As Du Bois remembers in his autobiography, this was an extremely unusual practice when he began the magazine in 1910: the "colored papers carried few or no illustrations; the white papers none."[17] In the annual "Children's" issue the pages were filled with photographs of readers' offspring; young black faces peered out between articles and editorials. The "Education" issue similarly published dozens of pictures of young college graduates, dignified in their congregation gowns. The regular "Men of the Month" column (which occasionally also featured women) celebrated the achievements of black businessmen, scholars, and other professionals, with accompanying photographs. Such pictures acted as a direct challenge to caricatures of grinning "darkies" with exaggerated lips and bulging eyes. Du Bois deliberately used visual imagery to create a more dignified picture of black life. This not only challenged the prejudice of white Americans but also inspired racial pride among the *Crisis*'s black readers. Similarly, virtually all the fiction that was published featured black characters. African Americans could identify with the protagonists of the short stories and dramas that they read on its pages. At a time when black literature was only beginning to receive a wide audience, the magazine played an important role in forging a sense of racial identity and pride.

This sense of identity and pride was similarly at play when the *Crisis* featured work inspired by Africa. Artists and writers often mixed elements of African and American or European culture, with the intention of instilling in African Americans pride in their heritage and therefore a sense of a shared past. Amy Kirschke argues that by including images of Africa, Du Bois "hoped to create and strengthen a sense of identity with contemporary Africa for his readers and to help them learn about their roots in the historically rich civilizations of Africa." Visual imagery of Egypt was common in the *Crisis,* and it was celebrated as an important example of a great black civilization. Aaron Douglas frequently used Egyptian iconography in his work. *Invincible Music: The Spirit of Africa* shows a figure in silhouette beating a drum, his head raised to the sky (figure 2). His position, the profile of his body, and his hair resemble those of Egyptian art. Douglas makes the African connection explicit to *Crisis* readers with his title. Many works of art and literature in the magazine highlight the cultural influence of Africa, particularly its musical legacy. The message to *Crisis* readers was that they should have pride in their connection with Africa and revel in its beauty and culture.[18]

The influence of Africa was also seen in some of the poetry in the *Crisis,* particularly the work of Langston Hughes. He stressed the connection between blacks in America and in Africa. In "The Negro" he writes, "I am a Negro: / Black as the night is black / Black like the depths of my Africa." The black man on both continents has been a slave, a worker, a singer, and a victim. He has suffered, but he has created great things; through his labor "the pyramids arose," and New York's Woolworth building was con-

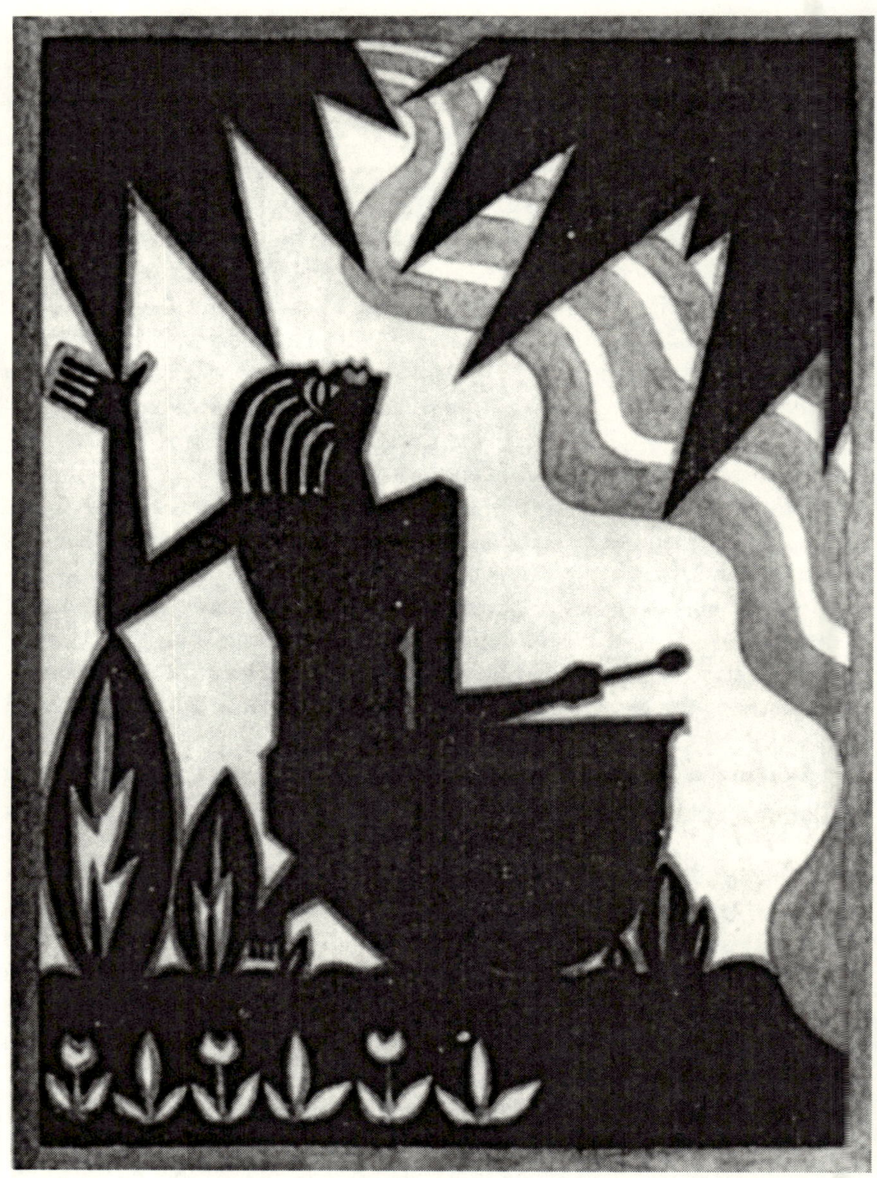

Figure 2. Aaron Douglas, *Invincible Music: The Spirit of Africa, Crisis* (February 1926): 169. Image from the Library of Congress.

structed. His music is a legacy from Africa that has created something new on American soil: "All the way from Africa to Georgia I carried my sorrow songs. / I made ragtime." Hughes highlights the shared experience of black people in Africa and America. They are linked by their history and race. At the end of the poem Hughes reasserts his pride in his racial identity when he repeats, "I am a Negro: / Black as the night is black / Black like the depths of my Africa."[19]

There are fewer references to Africa in the *Crisis*'s short stories and plays. Most were set in the contemporary period and in America. Du Bois did, however, publish some African folk parables and tales. One example of an explicit reference to Africa in fiction is "Black Fairy," a short story written by Fenton Johnson. A little black girl meets an African fairy in the garden. The fairy sings "an old African lullaby" and uses her magic to show the girl images from ancient Africa: the pyramids of Egypt, the ships, and other images of wealth and power. Then she shows the coming of slavery and blacks being shipped across the ocean. The fairy tells the girl that blacks in America, "though not entirely Ethiopian have not lost their identity." She prophesizes that in the future there will be an end to inequality and a "brotherhood of all men." The story celebrates African heritage as a source of strength to overcome prejudice and discrimination. Just as the fairy teaches the little girl about her African past, so Johnson teaches other children about Africa.[20]

In these examples the creators mix African and American culture and African and American experiences. By publishing such work Du Bois sent a message to his contributors and readers that as African Americans they were ideally placed to draw on both these influences. This is consistent with what George Hutchinson claims was the pan-Africanism promoted by the *Crisis:* in this definition, it encouraged solidarity with people of African descent, but this did not mean denying the "Americanness" of the American Negro.[21] African Americans should be proud of both their African and their American heritage. This sense of a shared past not only created pride but also forged a sense of a collective African American identity.

If black readers were to identify with the representations of their race on the pages of the *Crisis,* then this raises the question of who stared back at them when they opened the magazine. The appearance of African Americans depicted in the *Crisis* was significant. There were those within the NAACP whose light complexions opened them up to accusations of prejudice against their darker-skinned brothers. Walter White, as discussed later in this book, was attacked by those both within and outside of his organization. Many, both at the time and since, believed that the NAACP as a whole, with its biracial membership and its stance against segregation, wanted complete assimilation with the white race. If there was such a bias, then you might expect it to be reflected in the images of race found in the *Crisis*. In her article on *Crisis* cover girls of the 1940s, Megan Williams allows that there was a history of light-skinned, well-dressed, and educated African American women appearing on the pages of black journals, including the *Crisis*. In this tradition, light skin was equated with respectability. Williams contends that the *Crisis* used these images to challenge derogatory stereotypes of women but that the photographs also reflected the assimilationist tendencies of the NAACP.[22] Although she is writing about a later period, her findings are also instructive when considering women in the *Crisis* between 1910 and 1934.

There are many examples of light-skinned women on the cover of the magazine, usually at least two or three a year, particularly during the earlier period. The November 1913 cover features a young woman with skin so fair she looks white (figure 3). The photograph's label, "Octoroon," clearly identifies her mixed-race heritage. Her appearance is somewhat classical, with her dark hair tied under a band and a large pendant on her chest. Her dark eyes are in shadow, and there is the trace of a frown across her face (perhaps suggestive of the stereotypical tragic mulatta). A similarly fair-skinned girl graces the cover of the March 1922 issue (figure 4). John Henry Adams presents her in profile, her chin resting on her hands as she gazes into the distance. Her clothing is old-fashioned by the standards of the 1920s: the high collar and long sleeves demurely cover her body. She is an attractive example of respectable black womanhood. Cherene Sherrard-Johnson writes that New Negro periodicals "chose identifiably mixed-race women to represent the positive and dignified face of the New Negro woman." The images are "more sentimental than modern, more Victorian than New Negro. She is beautiful, educated, middle class." These pictures suggest that the NAACP associated light skin with respectability and that such women were the acceptable face of black America.

According to Williams's thesis, placing these women on the front cover reflects the NAACP's desire for assimilation. However, this is not completely accurate; the NAACP did not want complete assimilation with the white race. In fact, the *Crisis* often celebrated a black and African heritage. Moreover, the magazine featured numerous short stories and plays that suggested that light skin could be more of a curse than a help and that passing brought about disastrous emotional and cultural consequenc-

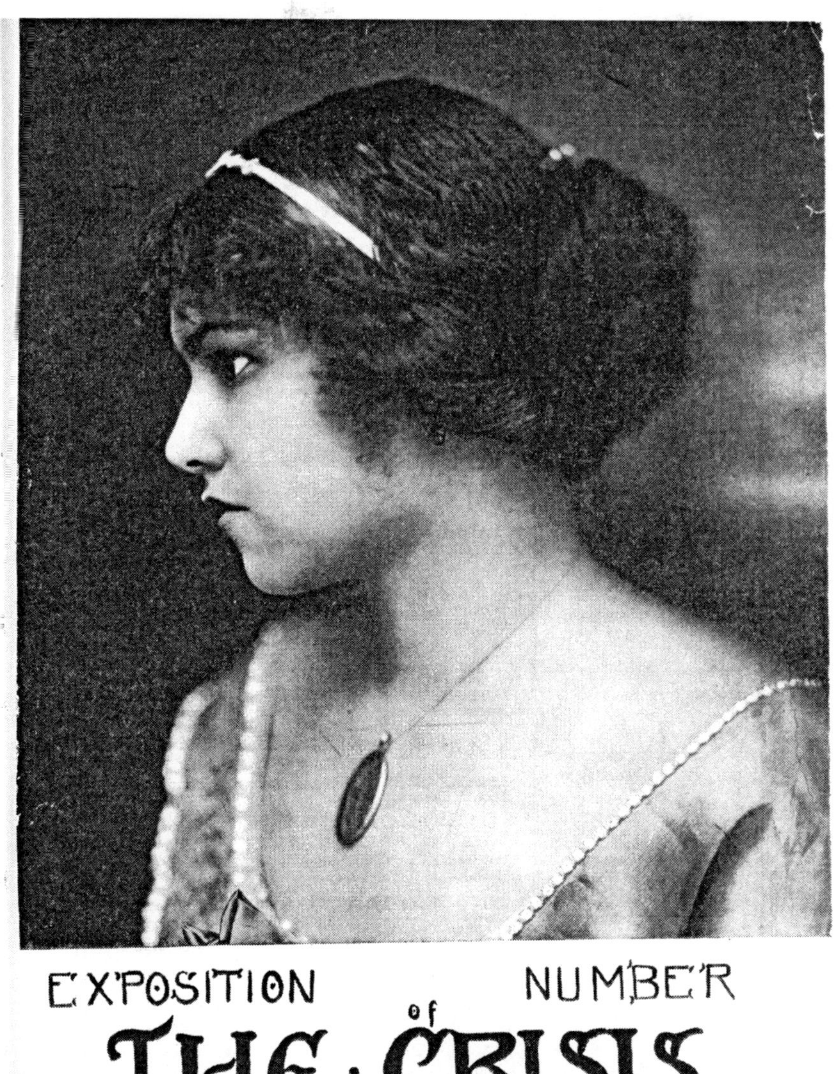


Figure 3. Anonymous, "Octoroon," *Crisis* (November 1913): front cover. Image from the Library of Congress.

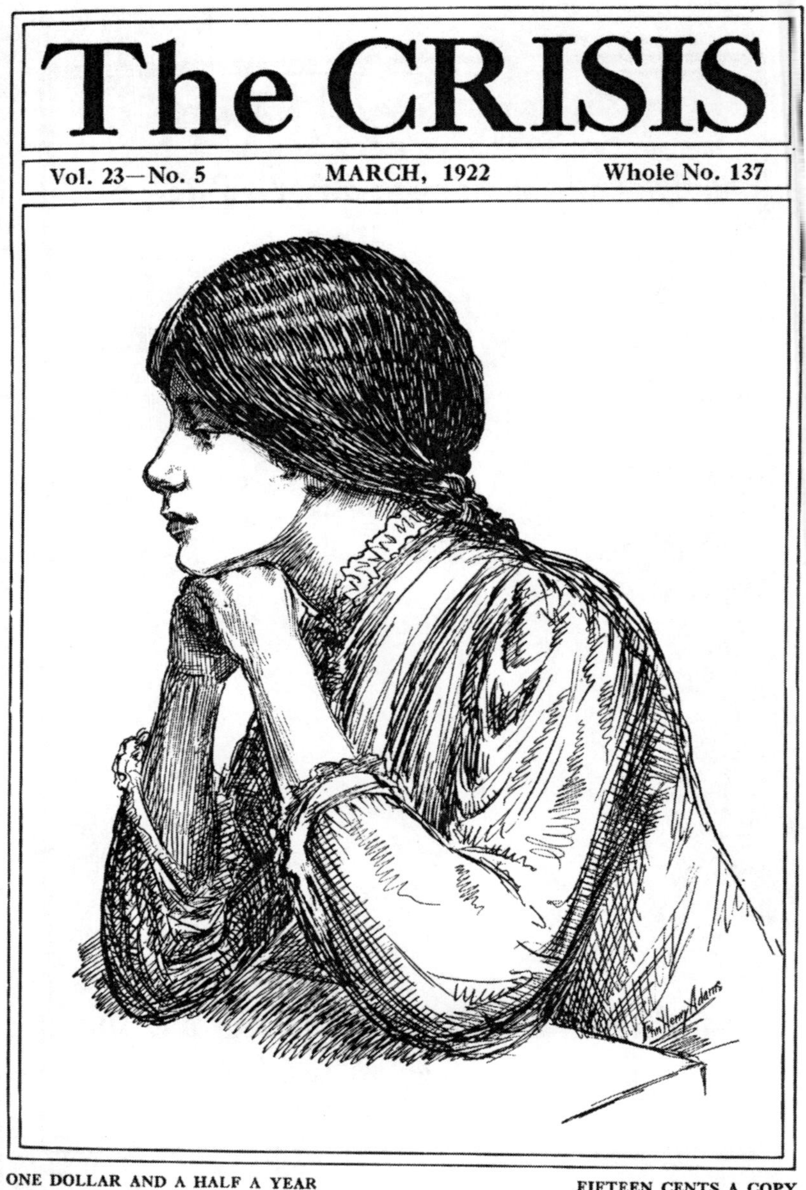


Figure 4. John Henry Adams, untitled, *Crisis* (March 1922): front cover. Image from the Library of Congress.

es. Nevertheless, the light skin of the *Crisis* cover girls was a deliberate tactic to appeal to whites. Sherrard-Johnson, for example, points out that in nineteenth-century slave narratives the mulatta was a common figure because the appearance of whiteness was used "as a strategy for gaining sympathy." A similar strategy was at play in the *Crisis;* Du Bois may have hoped that whites would be better able to identify with fairer-skinned African Americans. This suggests that there was a tension between providing positive images of black identity, which stressed racial pride and a shared black heritage irrespective of skin tone, and an appeal to whites that adopted white standards of respectability and taste.[23]

More important than their skin tone were the attire and demeanor of these women. They directly challenge white stereotypes of black women. They provide a contrast to the "Jezebel," who is overtly sexual and libidinous. The cover girl is attractive, but she is also demure. At the same time these pictures grant black women their femininity and so challenge the other dominant female image, that of the desexualized "Mammy." However, the representation of black womanhood in the *Crisis* was not limited to pictures of demure society girls. Indeed, African American women were often symbols of racial strength and dignity. Du Bois published work that challenged stereotypes of women in more interesting ways than simply showing they could be "respectable." Aaron Douglas's *The Burden of Black Womanhood* shows the figure of a black woman holding up the bottom of a sphere (figure 5). She is, like Atlas, supporting the weight of the world. In the background are skyscrapers, with a factory in between and a log cabin to the far side; Douglas was commenting on the burdens carried by women from all classes and sections of society. The woman, although she stoops a little under the weight of her burden, remains strong and poised.[24]

An even more explicit representation of the strength of black womanhood is the cartoon "Woman to the Rescue." The sketch shows a black woman using the club of the "federal constitution" to beat away the vultures of "segregation" and "Jim Crow law." She has already beaten the "grandfather clause" to the ground. In the distance is the retreating figure of a black man, calling over his shoulder, "I don't believe in agitating and fighting. My policy is to pursue the line of least resistance." Behind the woman's skirts hide two black youngsters. She is the protector of the race and its children; she fights for justice while the cowardly man deserts her. Another contrast to the delicate, feminine images of *Crisis* cover girls of the 1910s and early 1920s is seen on the front cover of the February

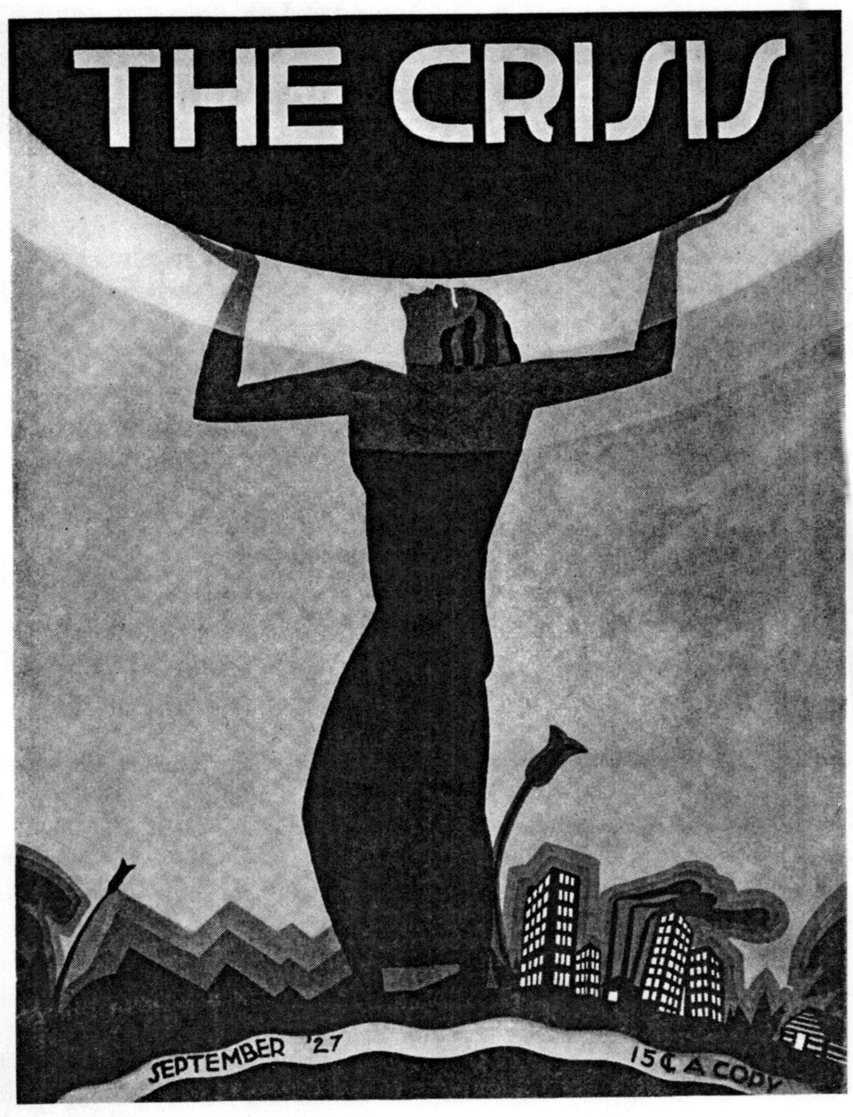


Figure 5. Aaron Douglas, *The Burden of Black Womanhood, Crisis* (September 1927): front cover. Image from the Library of Congress.

1933 issue (figure 6). The drawing shows just a woman's head. Her chin is raised, and her gaze is steady; she looks defiant and strong. The shadows on her face make it appear angular, almost masculine, but her lips are full and shiny. This image appears later than Adams's drawing and "Octoroon." Stylistically it is very different, but the woman in the picture shares the mulatta's racial ambiguity and demeanor of respectability.[25] By the 1930s there were fewer of the demure society girls on the cover of the magazine, but some of the same ideas about black womanhood remained. These cartoons and pictures show the black woman as resilient and competent, challenging white stereotypes of black women. It is also likely that Du Bois, a strong advocate of women's rights, published them to show black men that women were capable of campaigning for equality alongside them and to encourage women themselves to continue in their fight.

More unexpected, in the context of using the arts to challenge racism, are those images that show black women as alluring and overtly sexual. Given the stereotype within white culture of the black woman as promiscuous and the very real incidence of the rape of black women by whites, it is surprising that Du Bois chose to publish such pictures, sometimes on the front cover. Their presence might be explained by the fact that all these pictures use African imagery. Even in the African American mind the continent was still linked to the exotic. These images were published in the late 1920s, at the height of the Harlem Renaissance. *Dark Easter* by Richard Brown shows an attractive young woman with her dress slung low below her shoulders, showing an enticing hint of cleavage (figure 7). With her left hand she is caressing an exotic flower, and she stares at the viewer with sultry eyes. As well as the flower, her headdress and bracelets indicate her "African" status. Even more explicitly sexual is Allan Freelon's *A Jungle Nymph* (figure 8). In this cover picture a naked woman sits beside a pool. Her shoulders are stretched back, exposing her breasts. The palm trees and exotic foliage around her provide the African setting. Such images as these showcase the talents of their creators but other than that would seem to be ineffective weapons against racism. Amy Kirschke suggests that such front covers were designed to entice male readers to open the *Crisis* and that other African American magazines used similar tactics to attract new readers. Sometimes, it would seem, Du Bois was happy to simply have something beautiful on the cover of the *Crisis*.[26]

These images appeared later in Du Bois's editorship, suggesting a change in the way women were represented in the *Crisis*. The demure society girls with high-necked blouses were replaced with images of exotic

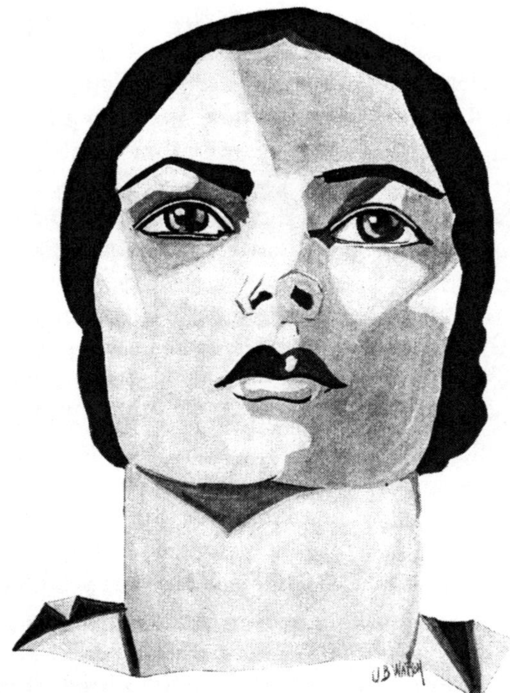


Figure 6. J. B. Watson, untitled, *Crisis* (February 1933): front cover. Image from the Library of Congress.

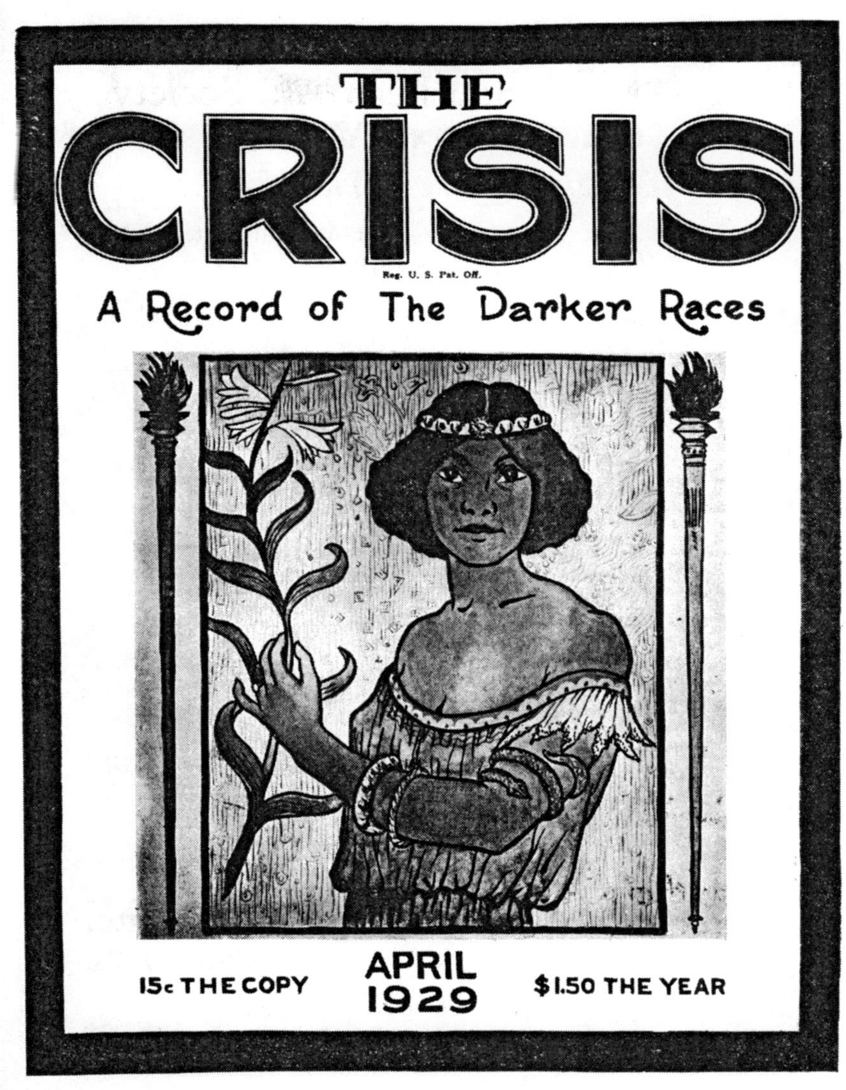



Figure 7. Richard Brown, *Dark Easter, Crisis* (April 1929): front cover. Image from the Library of Congress.

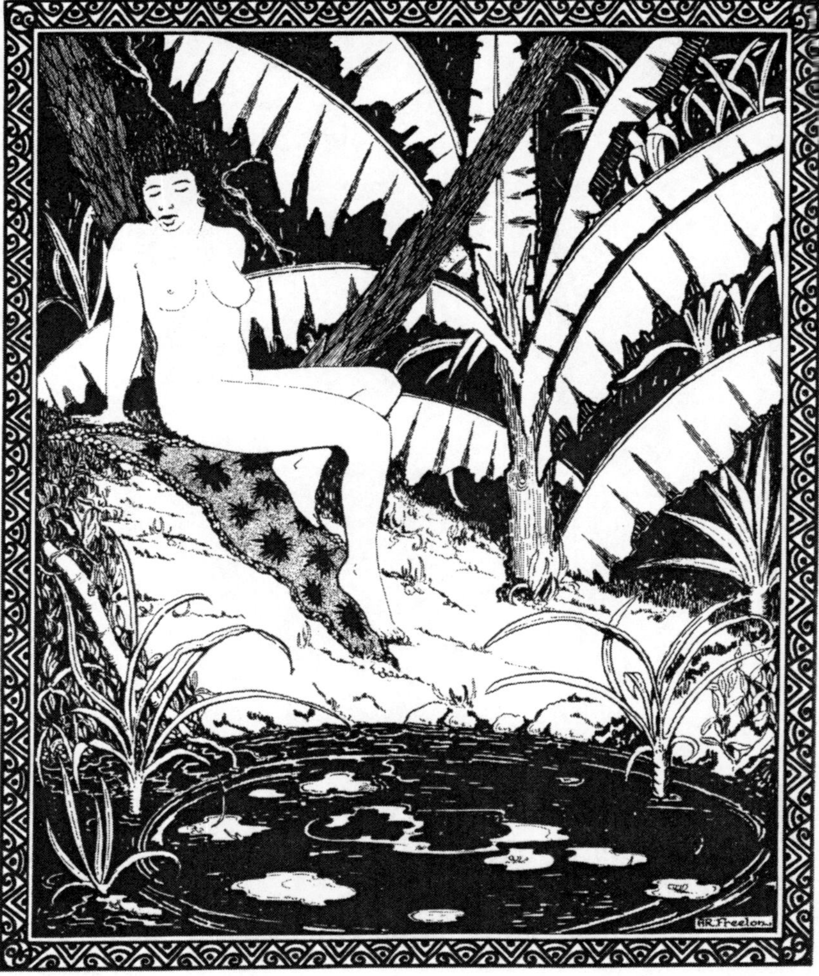


Figure 8. Allan Freelon, *A Jungle Nymph, Crisis* (June 1928): front cover. Image from the Library of Congress.

African temptresses. In part this reflected a change in artistic styles and a move toward the "modern" images of the Renaissance. It also suggests a relaxation in Du Bois's attitude toward sex in black culture. Arnold Rampersad notes that in Du Bois's novel *Dark Princess,* published in 1928, around the time these images appeared in the *Crisis,* there is nothing "conventionally prudish" about his "attitude to sex."[27] Of course, there were, for Du Bois, acceptable ways in which to deal with sex. He complained about the "lascivious sexual promiscuity" in Claude McKay's *Home to Harlem,* for example.[28] Sex should be treated tastefully, reflecting high-culture sensibilities, and preferably depicted within the context of the exotic "foreigner."

Representations, both literary and visual, of middle-class African American life abounded in the *Crisis.* This was significant in two respects. First, if images in the magazine were meant to inspire a sense of pride and identity, this suggests that the collective identity that Du Bois was striving for was that of a black middle class. Second, these representations allowed the NAACP to challenge white stereotypes of African Americans by presenting them as respectable, successful, and "American." These assertions, however, are complicated by the question of how much Du Bois actually controlled and censored the material that appeared in the *Crisis.* Furthermore, the inclusion of images of other sections of black life disrupts the dominance of black middle-class representations.

Middle-class black life certainly featured heavily in the art and literature of the magazine. The *Crisis* cover girls discussed above were not just light skinned, they were often identifiably middle class. In many of the short stories black doctors, teachers, or other professionals are the chief protagonists. The particular injustices that educated blacks had to face are examined in a story by Alice Dunbar Nelson. "Hope Deferred" is about a black man, Edwards, who has trained as a civil engineer but, despite moving to a city busy with building projects, cannot find a job because of his race. He is forced to work as a waiter, and one evening he serves one of the men who refused to employ him. He tells Edwards that he is "more fitted" to being a waiter than an engineer. This enrages Edwards, who attacks the white man and ends the story in jail.[29] Nelson exposes the discrimination that middle-class blacks faced and the humiliation of having to work in menial jobs despite their education and skills.

Du Bois filled the *Crisis* with photographs of middle-class blacks: from the annual "Education" issue with its pictures of black college graduates to the photographs of the distinguished African Americans that illustrated the "Men of the Month" columns. In February 1912 the *Crisis* featured a photograph by Addison Scurlock showing the "Social Life of Colored America" at the Mid-Winter Assembly in Baltimore. In this double-page spread men in black tie and women in evening gowns stand in a grand ballroom. They are elegant and refined, and the picture loudly, and proudly, proclaims their affluence. This is an utterly "respectable" picture of black life. So too is the photograph "Colored Los Angeles Greets *THE CRISIS* in Its Own Motor Cars." A line of half a dozen cars, with well-dressed figures sitting inside their vehicles or standing proudly alongside, stretches across two pages. The photograph is a celebration of the consumer power of a burgeoning black middle class. These images were intended to instill pride in the magazine's black readers by showing what the race could achieve. Readers were encouraged to aspire to the status of wearing expensive clothes and owning a motorcar. Furthermore, this pride was intended to reinforce a sense of black collective identity. Readers were to peruse these stories and look at these illustrations and think "that is me" (or "that could be me") and "that is my race." Such representations could also be used to fight the stereotype that blacks were lazy good-for-nothings who held only the most menial positions. They showed that blacks could be affluent. They appealed to white tastes and a white sense of social status. "See how like you we are," they seemed to be saying.[30]

Images such as these are consistent with perceptions of the NAACP as a bourgeois organization, but the creative work published in the *Crisis* did not solely reflect a preoccupation with the lives of middle-class African Americans. Other sectors of black life did receive attention. In one of the earliest issues is a drawing by John Henry Adams called *The Christmas Reckoning* (figure 9). The accompanying text reads, "At Christmastide two million Southern Negroes make their annual wage reckoning with the plantation owners and either receive the small balance due or are remanded in debt slavery." In the picture an elderly black couple face each other across the table. They are simply but neatly dressed, and the signs of strain and worry are etched across their faces. Adams presents a sympathetic portrayal of the plight of sharecroppers, a group far removed from the middle-class car owners depicted in the photograph.[31]

A number of stories are set outside the milieu of middle-class black America. These include "The Death Game," which is set in a poor black neighborhood of Chicago. The streets are "cracked and dirty," and the houses are a picture of "general disorder and hopeless resignation." The people are no better: "loud-mouthed men" sit on the step "and pick guitars

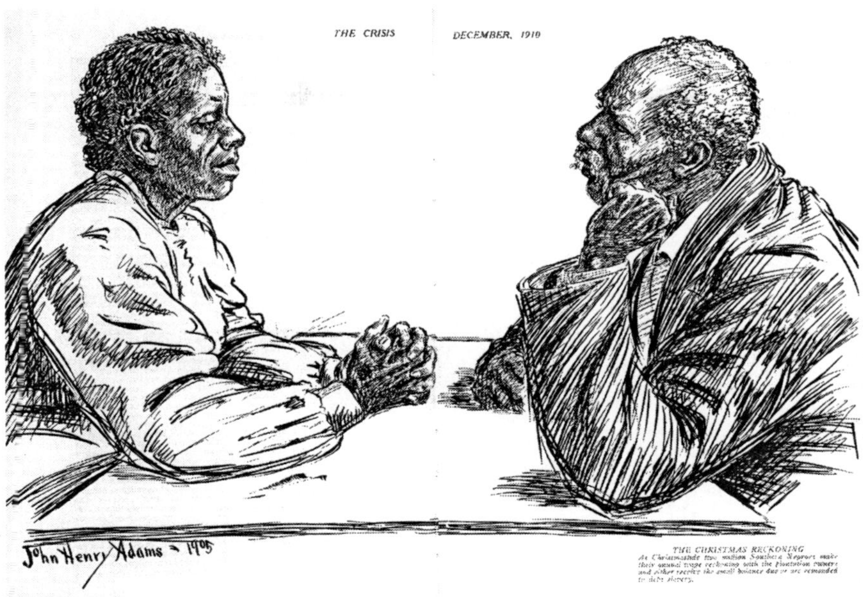


Figure 9. John Henry Adams, *The Christmas Reckoning, Crisis* (December 1910): 18–19. Image from the Library of Congress.

and dance and sing the blues," while "bold women in loose-fitting, low-necked, sleeveless gingham house dresses . . . chew tobacco and swear and let the loud-mouthed men handle them with shameless familiarity." In this area lives Nell, a white woman who works in a cabaret. Nell has a black boyfriend, Joe, but is cheating on him with another black man, Shug. When Joe finds the two lovers together he challenges Nell to choose between them. She refuses, and Shug suggests a card game to decide, the loser to be shot. But Nell tries to double-cross both men, and Joe walks away, telling her, "Nell, you ain't worth a damn." As he leaves he hears a gunshot; Shug has killed Nell. This story shows the underbelly of black life: promiscuity, gambling, drinking, and violence. It is interesting to note that the most immoral character is a white woman, living and consorting with black men, which was a particularly controversial depiction. In contrast, Joe, though a gambler, is the story's only source of morality. Sheen won second prize in the 1926 "Krigwa" competition for this entry; Du Bois and his judges obviously felt that this tale, even with its controversial content, had considerable merit. It should be noted, however, that such depictions of the seedy side of black America were extremely rare in the *Crisis.*[32]

More common, particularly in the 1930s with the Depression taking hold, were pieces of art and literature that celebrated the black worker. Du Bois increasingly saw the black proletariat as central to the struggle for civil rights. Working-class African Americans were honored in a number of examples of creative work published in the magazine during these years. In the poem "Black Man," Heba Jannath describes the work that the black man has done for his country: he has "plowed and planted cotton," "garnered in the rice fields," "laid the Southern highways," "mined for coal deposits," "blasted in the subway," "labored in the docks," and "cooked in countless kitchens." Not only that, but the black man has "fought his country's battles" and "fashioned gallant rhythms." Still, his masculinity, his humanity, is questioned by white America: "And yet, they say, he's not a man / Not equal to the rest / What, we ask, is Manhood / If this not be the test?" The poet demands that the toil and contribution of African American men be acknowledged by white America.[33]

This interest in the labor of blacks extended to visual art in the *Crisis*. On the cover of the November 1933 issue was *The Black Miner* (figure 10). This picture by J. E. Dodd shows the miner sitting in profile, his head resting on his hands, leaning on the handle of his pickax. The figure is mostly in shadow, with his torch sending a beam of light off the page. He looks exhausted; his shoulders are sagging, and his weary head is slumped. But there is something noble about his depiction; his figure is outlined, and his shadow repeats his image on the wall behind him. Furthermore, publishing such a picture on the front cover of the magazine makes the miner a figure to be celebrated and admired, just like the cover girls.[34]

The Depression hit African Americans particularly hard: they felt the effects in all areas of the country and all sections of black society. Unemployment rates for African Americans far exceeded those for whites in urban areas. In Harlem the unemployment rate was five times higher than in the rest of New York City.[35] The effects of this joblessness are portrayed in the one-act play *Job Hunter*. Set in the Public Employment Office in Harlem, it shows, in a rather impersonal manner, men coming in to look for work. Most of the characters are unnamed and are referred to by their status: "Unemployed." There are very few jobs to be had, and those that are available are unskilled and poorly paid. The play gives a sense of the dire situation these men face and shows that the few systems in place to offer help, the employment office as well as charities and churches, are

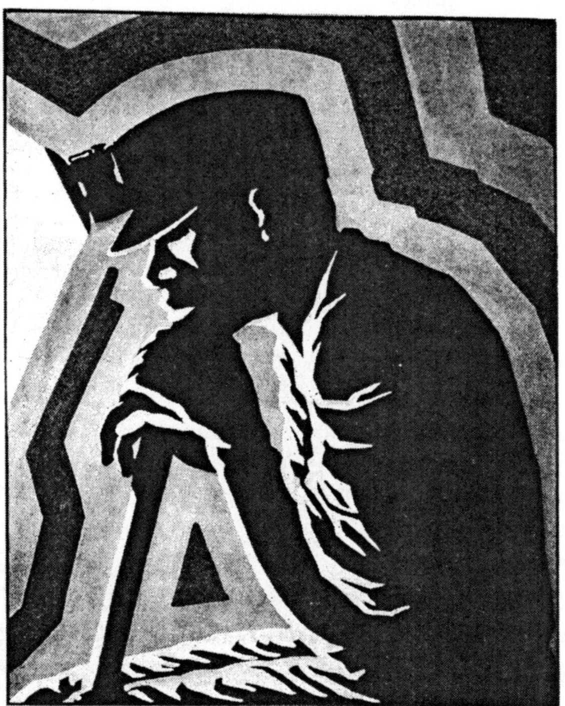


Figure 10. J. E. Dodd, *The Black Miner, Crisis* (November 1933): front cover. Image from the Library of Congress.

overwhelmed by demand. The realism of the play is emphasized. In the middle of the text is a photograph of the breadline in Harlem, and at the end it states that the play "is based on actual experience in a Harlem unemployment office."[36]

These stories and images challenge the assumption that the *Crisis* exclusively privileged middle-class life. They suggest that it was not just affluent blacks who embodied American values. The working class could also represent dignity, hard work, and respectability. In publishing such pieces the *Crisis* demanded that the labor of African Americans be celebrated by members of the race. Furthermore, it was intended that their work should be recognized by white America as grounds for equal treatment. However, it should be noted that these pieces (with the exception of Adams's sketch and "Death Game," which appeared in 1910 and 1927 respectively) were published in the 1930s. This was a period when American culture more generally was taking a more "proletarian" turn, and Du Bois was beginning to take a greater interest in the plight of black workers. Furthermore, these works of art and literature were the exception rather than the rule in the *Crisis*.

It might be expected that a study of the magazine during these years would uncover the controlling hand of its editor. After all, Du Bois had plenty to say about the type of work he thought black artists should be producing, particularly from 1926 onward, when he made his pronouncements about the "Criteria of Negro Art." However, there does not appear to be any noticeable change in the work published. One factor that might have prevented Du Bois blocking the work of newer or less conservative artists was Jessie Fauset. As literary editor from 1919 to 1926, Fauset exerted enormous influence over the arts pages of the *Crisis*. She has been disparagingly remembered as a "traditional" and "imitative" writer who avoided experimentation and radical ideas. In fact, both in her own writing and as literary editor, she displayed a considerable range of interests and a "sensibility" both "catholic and global." Fauset gave a freer hand to the young artists published in the magazine than might be imagined. It has been argued by Carmiele Wilkerson and Shamoon Zamir that after she left, Du Bois only "supported young artists whose ideals mirrored his own" and that he censored those who did not support his point of view. Those who were barred supposedly included Langston Hughes and Claude McKay. In fact, while relations with both poets were strained, he continued to publish their work in the *Crisis;* sixteen of Hughes's poems appeared between 1927 and 1933. Therefore it seems likely that it was not just the influence of Fauset but also the attitude of Du Bois himself that created space for different representations of black America in the *Crisis*.[37]

Despite some variety in the content of the work published, virtually all of the cultural forms that filled the pages of the *Crisis* could be considered examples of "high" culture: fine art and literature that were based on European and white modes of expression. This reflected the NAACP's conviction that whites would admire "high" culture and would respect those African Americans who could create it and thus would respect the race as a whole. This bias is seen in some of the African-inspired work in the *Crisis*, much of which used Egyptian imagery. According to Kirschke, Europeans had appropriated Egyptian civilization and recognized it as "high culture"; therefore it "fit into Du Bois's idea of what African American culture should strive for."[38]

A story that serves as an excellent example of this cultural elitism is "The Servant" by Fenton Johnson, published in a 1912 edition of the *Crisis*. It is a sketch about a young servant girl, Eliza, who has newly arrived in Chicago from Georgia. She feels out of place in the household of the refined and wealthy black family for whom she works. She is unsettled by her new surroundings because there are no class divisions among blacks in Georgia: "the color line obliterated every other line society should wish to draw." One evening she hears violin music and is drawn to it. Eliza goes downstairs and is allowed to sit with the group of young people. She listens as they discuss novels and plays, but, of course, "all this was Greek to the unlettered little girl." The son of the family then "started to play the sorrow songs that can never die, because they are a genuine expression of American life." The music makes Eliza recall her life in Georgia: the "little cabin," the cotton fields, her mother killed by poverty, and her father killed by whites. She feels inadequate in the face of the son's talents: he "could throw on the screen of her mind pictures of her home life by means of an instrument she could not even wield." She does not have the education or the culture to create such beauty in the same way as the children of the wealthy family: "He and his sister were versed in the lore and the music of civilization. Within her bosom was nothing save the emotions that she could feel so vividly but could not express." At the end of the story Eliza throws herself on her bed, sobbing, "Ah wants tuh luhn!"[39] The implication is that the poor, uneducated South is a source of great emotion and power in black life, but it needs educated, civilized, cultured blacks to express those emotions properly. Although the "folk" culture of the South is revered by middle-class blacks, it can only properly be expressed through high-cultural forms (such as the violin played by a trained musician). African American life can only be truly conveyed by European, in other words white, forms of expression. "High" culture triumphs over "low."

The tension between "high" and "low" is also evident in the very conspicuous neglect of jazz in the *Crisis*. During the "Jazz Age" one of the most important and popular forms of African American culture was barely mentioned. The obvious explanation for this was the NAACP's cultural elitism. Jazz was associated with working-class black life and the seedy side of Harlem. It was a form of "low" culture that did little to imbue the race with the refinement necessary for acceptance by the white world. Indeed, in the eyes of Du Bois and some of his associates, it played into stereotypes of blacks as primal and base. Ted Vincent argues that the *Crisis* "seemed to be bending over backwards to avoid mention of the jazz or blues aspects to the popular music scene." In the magazine "concern for propriety seemed to be mixed with fear of anything in Black culture that might upset or confuse the many White NAACP members."[40] In other words, Du Bois did not want to disturb the image of black life that much of the *Crisis* tried so hard to create. According to Vincent, although whites made up only a small percentage of the readership, they dictated the content of the magazine. However, this is not entirely true, as the earlier quotes from Kellogg and others suggest. Du Bois was equally if not more concerned with his black readership. Rather, the relative paucity of material on popular music reflected his personal bias and tastes.

Over the years of his editorship Du Bois frequently clashed with the rest of the NAACP leadership, many of whom felt he used the magazine for his own agenda. One example was the controversy over black involvement in the First World War. Du Bois called for the full participation of African Americans and used his position as editor to endorse his stance. As well as his controversial editorial "Close Ranks," he published a number of pictures, short stories, and poems that celebrated black patriotism and war efforts. Du Bois used work published in the *Crisis* to persuade black readers to support the war despite segregation in the armed forces, a position for which he was attacked by many, including those within the NAACP. There were a number of other battles over the years, and these disagreements were usually solved, often by the diplomacy of Mary White Ovington and Joel Spingarn. However, the issue of control of the *Crisis* continued to simmer. The financial strain of the 1930s brought matters to a head. The proportion of African Americans in the nation's cities who were unemployed was between 30 and 60 percent higher than for whites; half of those living in southern cities were unemployed by 1932. The black middle classes were also affected; in Harlem the median income for skilled workers fell by half between 1929 and 1932, and black home ownership plummeted. This, of course, had an effect on the NAACP, which saw membership fall and subscriptions to the *Crisis* dwindle. The magazine's debts increased, and in 1930 it was decided that the NAACP would pay the editor's salary. As part of this move, an editorial board was established, which included the secretary and assistant secretary.[41]

Du Bois resented having to be reliant on the association and hated the increased involvement of the then–executive secretary, Walter White. The editor was suspicious of what he saw as White's attempts to control the magazine, and there was no love lost between the two men. Du Bois, in what may have partly been an attempt to test the limits of his power, published a series of incendiary editorials on the subject of segregation, beginning in January 1934. He challenged the stance that segregation automatically meant discrimination, and he argued that there were positive sides to the separation of the races. The editor reminded his readers "that in the last quarter of a century, the advance of the colored people has been mainly in the lines where they themselves, working by and for themselves, have accomplished the greatest advance." White, and many others both within and outside of the organization, saw these pronouncements as a direct attack on the NAACP's policy. As the secretary wrote to Joel Spingarn, "If the Association's attitude is not one of opposition to segregation, then I have misinterpreted it for nearly twenty years." Du Bois's discussion took an unedifying turn when he personally attacked the secretary in his April editorial. "Walter White is white," he wrote, and he "meets no Color Line, for the simple and sufficient reason that he isn't 'colored.'" In the end the board rejected Du Bois's stance on segregation, stating that the NAACP was "opposed both to the principle and practice of enforced segregation," because "by its very existence [it] carries with it the implication of a superior and inferior group and invariably results in the imposition of a lower status on the group deemed inferior." It also voted to limit Du Bois's control over the magazine; the board affirmed that "*The Crisis* is the organ of the Association and no salaried officer of the Association shall criticize the policy, work, or officers of the Association in the pages of *The Crisis*." Du Bois, not wishing to be controlled in such a manner and finding himself in disagreement with the board over this central principle, offered his resignation. It was initially refused by the board, but when Du Bois realized that no compromise would be reached, he insisted on its acceptance. The episode is a telling reminder that not everyone within the leadership of the NAACP agreed with one another, even over key issues such as segregation. The national office was often plagued by tension, with clashing personalities and competing egos.[42]

Du Bois was replaced as editor by Roy Wilkins, who had worked as a journalist before joining the NAACP. Wilkins made clear his opinion of the *Crisis* under his predecessor: "For many years *The Crisis* has been . . . a journal definitely marked as literary and intellectual. Its style and content have been such as to appeal only to the intellectual minority." He argued that it was too "intellectual" and did not have a broad reach; in order to widen its readership and become financially self-sufficient, it must move away from a literary emphasis. In the 1930s there was a noticeable reduction in the number of works of art and literature published in the *Crisis*, and although these started to reappear with greater frequently in the 1940s and although Wilkins himself later claimed that it "continue[d] the Du Bois tradition of giving young writers a start," under its new editor the magazine never truly recovered its artistic flavor.[43]

The complex and sometimes contradictory cultural agenda of the NAACP was reflected in the *Crisis*. The NAACP's strategy was shaped by the beliefs of many of its leaders, by the practicalities of the situation, and by the tone of the era. The significance of Du Bois in steering the path of the *Crisis* cannot be underestimated, but his ideas developed and changed throughout this period, and his control was moderated by the influence of Jessie Fauset. The magazine provided a space in which to demonstrate and celebrate black artistic achievements. It could be used to prove to white America that African Americans were capable of creating beautiful works of art. The works created and published were, almost without exception, "high" culture. The NAACP believed that this was the form of culture that whites would recognize and most admire and that in this way the talent of black poets, novelists, and artists could be used to challenge white stereotypes of the race. So, too, could the images produced: the fiction, poetry, and art provided an alternative to the dominant caricatures of African Americans produced by white culture.

The NAACP wanted to use creative work to instill racial pride and to form a sense of collective identity. It gave African Americans the opportunity to read stories and poems about themselves and to look at drawings and photographs of themselves. These representations were designed to increase racial self-esteem, in order to ready the race for the larger battle for equality. George Hutchinson argues that the *Crisis* represented the cultural pluralism of the NAACP, and much of the creative work published in the magazine supports this interpretation.[44] There was a stress on race: the racial identity of its creators and its protagonists was made explicit. The particular difficulties faced by African Americans, the issue of race, and how racial prejudice affected their lives were all recurring themes in these texts. At the same time these pieces emphasized their American identity. They showed how blacks both embraced and represented "American" values; there were stories that celebrated hard work, social mobility, heroism, and patriotism. Furthermore, the artists took "American," or white, cultural forms and transformed them. They mixed them with folk or African forms, and they also used them to express the condition of the black race. No easy generalizations can be made about the "type" of African American that the NAACP celebrated. There were light-skinned cover girls and characters, but similarly, many of the pieces celebrated a shared black and African heritage. Black women in the *Crisis* were often portrayed as strong, assertive, and important champions for black rights. There were doctors and teachers but also sharecroppers and miners. Du Bois wanted art and literature that would help advance the race, and this meant work that showed African Americans in what he considered to be the best possible light. It required the portrayal of decent and upstanding citizens. After all, it was the debauchery and vice in much of the work of the Harlem Renaissance that Du Bois objected to, not the class of its protagonists. Nevertheless, while working-class blacks did appear in the *Crisis,* the predominant image was still that of middle-class black America. Despite a greater breadth to its portrayal of black life than might be assumed, the NAACP's cultural strategy was still wedded to the portrayal of the black middle class.

By displaying black cultural accomplishments, forging a shared identity, and challenging racial stereotypes, the *Crisis* reflected the NAACP's complex and sometimes contradictory cultural agenda. Of course, art was just one part of the magazine's remit. Its content covered all aspects of the organization's principles and activities. Indeed, the *Crisis* was one place where the disparate strands of the NAACP's work came together. Updates on the latest court cases, calls for the government to act on cases of racial discrimination, and investigations into lynchings sat alongside the poetry and plays. This reflected more than just their placement in a magazine; the NAACP's leaders believed that these different elements complemented and strengthened each other. African Americans were more likely to donate to its fundraising appeals or to lobby politicians if they shared a sense of group identity; it would be easier to argue court cases challenging segregation if the white public had been exposed to images and proof of black accomplishment and respectability. Thus the hope and expectation was that the arts could help clear the way for the association's challenges to segregation and discrimination. Mark Schneider argues that as the 1920s wore on, the *Crisis* became more artistic and less political: "The cover and content suggested that the NAACP's magazine had become a journal of the arts, not a political movement." However, this fails to acknowledge that for Du Bois and some of his colleagues the arts were political. Schneider may be closer to the mark when he writes that Du Bois (and, I would argue, others) "overestimated the role of literature in changing society."[5] The limitations of the Harlem Renaissance were outlined in the previous chapter, and the same critique may be applied to this expectation of the cultural agenda of the *Crisis:* the arts could not change the physical realities of black life in America.

The NAACP learned this lesson, although only to a limited extent. The *Crisis* changed; Du Bois's editorship was the last time that it devoted so much space to the arts on its pages. Never again would the association be so closely aligned with an artistic and cultural movement. However, the NAACP did not give up on the idea that creative work could be used as a tool to fight racial prejudice. It continued to believe that the arts and other forms of culture influenced attitudes toward African Americans. Furthermore, it remained convinced that the arts could have a political message. Indeed, the most comprehensive example of this was its use of culture in the fight against lynching. It had already incorporated elements of the arts into its campaign, and then in the 1930s, as its position as a champion of black culture came increasingly under threat from the Left and as American culture more generally took on a political tone, it instigated what Walter White would call a "union of art and propaganda."

4

# "A union of art and propaganda"

The NAACP believed that it could use the arts to change white perceptions of African Americans, and for much of the first three decades of the
twentieth century it also used this principle to challenge attitudes toward
lynching. The NAACP's strategy for ending mob violence was based on
its conviction that the responsibility for lynching lay with the American
public. Association president Moorfield Storey told the 1922 annual conference, "The people of the United States have the power to stop lynching and for all the lynchings that occur they are responsible, since they
can if they will prevent them. . . . Our appeal, then, is to the conscience
of America."[1] Lynchings occurred because people allowed them to occur,
through either their explicit support or their acquiescence. This argument
was an extension of the NAACP's idea that racism was formed by the attitudes of white Americans. Therefore, the solution was the same: education
and persuasion. The NAACP needed to stop white approval of and apathy
toward lynching. To do this it had to educate whites about the true nature
and extent of the practice.

Education and persuasion were to be achieved, in part, through the arts.
The association helped develop and disseminate representations of lynching in a range of media. It commissioned, staged, and published lynching dramas; Walter White helped establish the Writers' League Against
Lynching (WLAL), a pressure group of authors, poets, and journalists who
used their talents to condemn lynch law; White also put together an exhibition of paintings that dealt with lynching. He was, he said, "trying deli-
cately to effect a union of art and propaganda."[2] White and his organization
wanted to use the arts to bring about political change. The plays, paintings, and poems were used to expose the truth about lynching, to change
white attitudes toward mob violence, and to elicit support for antilynching legislation. The NAACP did not always admit that it was using art as
propaganda, particularly during the period when it laid those very charges

against Communists. In the 1930s, the Communist Party threatened not only the NAACP's position as chief protector of black rights but also its role as champion of African American culture. Ironically, although neither side wished to admit it, both the Communists and the NAACP used culture in similar ways during this decade.

Lynching—"the summary execution by a mob of an individual who had committed an alleged crime or a perceived transgression of social codes"—was an American phenomenon. Figures from the Tuskegee Institute show that 4,743 people died in the United States at the hands of lynchers from 1882 to 1968. It was also primarily a racial phenomenon. Of those victims, 3,466, or almost 73 percent, were black. Lynching was a form of control that punished any violation, or considered violation, of the racial order. It was used to keep African Americans as an underpaid and exploited workforce, particularly in the South under the sharecropping system. Mob violence could also halt economic progress by punishing those who forgot their "place" or became too successful. Lynchers themselves argued that lynching punished, and therefore deterred, the "usual crime" of black men raping white women. But in his 1929 book on the phenomenon Walter White argued, "Lynching has always been the means for protection, not of white women, but of profits." Lynchings during the first decades of the twentieth century were notable for their use of torture and mutilation and as spectacles. The victim was often burned, hanged, or shot in a public place, sometimes in front of a crowd of hundreds or thousands who had traveled to see the event. The taking of mementos—whether photographs or body parts—was common, and the body was frequently displayed for days after the attack. These practices further degraded and dehumanized the victim and, indeed, all African Americans. Lynching was thus a crime not simply against an individual but against an entire race.[3]

In the South there were some moderate whites who looked on lynching less favorably. Some southerners, while not necessarily opposed to mob violence on moral grounds, had concerns about its impact on the reputation and development of the region. The South was newly industrializing, and they feared that reports of burnings and torture would deter potential investors. Furthermore, one of the South's greatest economic assets, its labor supply, was disappearing with black migration out of the region. The NAACP wanted to encourage what Walter White called "enlightened selfishness" among moderate Southerners. It made an appeal based on expediency rather than justice. It also believed that many whites did not actively support lynching; they simply did nothing to speak out against it. Moorfield Storey claimed, "Silence, indifference, acquiescence prevail. No one approves the barbarism and injustice . . . but few indeed are the men who condemn it."[4] The NAACP hoped to shake whites out of their apathy and turn this acquiescence into condemnation. It did have some support from a southern-grown antilynching movement—most importantly the Commission on Interracial Cooperation and Jessie Ames's Association of Southern Women for the Prevention of Lynching—which combined arguments of both expediency and justice.

Lynching was such a pervasive and destructive force that the NAACP knew it could not be stopped simply by persuasion and education. As in its broader fight against racial inequality, it did not rely solely on changing attitudes. It also used the courts and legislation. Indeed, the principal focus of its antilynching campaign was its effort to lobby for federal intervention. The first real push for antilynching legislation came in 1919 when the NAACP backed the bill of Leonidas Dyer, a Republican from Missouri. The Dyer Bill, which provided the basis for all subsequent antilynching bills, defined lynching as the murder of any citizen of the United States by a mob of three or more people. It passed the House of Representatives in 1922 but was defeated in the Senate by a Democratic filibuster and because of the reluctance of Republicans to challenge the stalling tactics. A number of arguments were made against such legislation. The most common was that lynching was murder and therefore should be dealt with by the state and not the federal government. Even liberal groups such as the Commission on Interracial Cooperation opposed the NAACP's campaign for a federal law. However, the association was not dissuaded, and the second concerted effort came in the 1930s. Democratic senators Edward Costigan of Colorado and Robert Wagner of New York introduced a federal antilynching bill into Congress in 1934. Throughout 1934 and 1935 the NAACP pushed for the passage of this legislation in the Senate. It used its cultural projects, such as the art exhibition and the Writers' League, to stimulate support for legislation. However, the bill suffered a similar fate as the Dyer Bill. Indeed, the US government has never passed an antilynching bill.[5]

The retelling—by lynchers and their apologists—of the lynching story, through newspaper reports, verbal accounts, popular culture, and visual images, was an important aspect of the phenomenon. As Angelina Weld Grimké wrote, "That people could see and hear about these events far away from and long after the fact of their occurrence is part of the act of lynching itself, for representations not only function to preserve the act in perpetuity, they also allow the act to be committed again." A number of scholars have analyzed lynching narratives alongside studying the cultural aspects of and explanations for lynching. Grace Elizabeth Hale places mob violence in the context of the culture of segregation in the South. Even as incidents of lynching became less common, their increasingly ritualized and standardized nature—with the rise of spectacle lynchings—made them ever more powerful. Lynching narratives, which also took on standard forms, were central to this impact. More recently, Amy Louise Wood has also focused on the spectacle nature of lynching; she explores the relationship between mob violence and other early twentieth-century forms of spectacle. Wood argues that lynching's symbolic power was reinforced through representations and that these representations were used, in different ways, by both white supremacists and antilynching activists. Lynching narratives created a record of lynching in which the act was justified and even celebrated. Furthermore, they allowed the lynchers to reenact the event. If one of the purposes of lynching was to control African Americans through the threat of violence, then replaying the act served to reinforce its message of black vulnerability. Re-presenting the capture, torture, and killing further degraded and dehumanized the victim. The murdered African American often lost his individual identity, and the act became an assault against the whole race. Despite lynching's frequency, most Americans had not witnessed a lynching firsthand. The accounts disseminated the ideology of white supremacy that lynching enacted. Lynchings often followed ritual patterns: the location, the use of torture, the method of killing, the taking of mementos, and the displaying of the body all had symbolic significance. Lynching narratives re-created this ritual and assumed standardized forms. They emphasized both the fiendishness of the African American victim and the outrage of the community over his crime. He was always presented as guilty, often of an assault on white womanhood. The cruelty and frenzy of the mob were downplayed; the participants were either upstanding citizens carrying out their moral duty or unknown members of the lower classes.[6]

Such narratives appeared not only in white newspapers but also in novels, plays, and motion pictures. American culture repeatedly condoned and even glorified the practice of lynching. Antilynching activists, including those in the NAACP, were all too aware of the power of these representations. The association had fought *The Birth of a Nation* in part because of the film's glorification of lynching and its justification that the act punished the rape of white women by blacks. Activists realized that, unless challenged, white accounts would remain the primary record of lynching. This was particularly pertinent because of the gap in the statistics on mob violence. No official records were kept, and many incidents were unreported or misreported in both local and national newspapers. Most scholars believe that the actual number of lynchings is likely to be higher than recorded.[7] African Americans kept their own records. Figures were compiled by the Tuskegee Institute from 1882 onward, and the *Chicago Tribune* kept and published its annual record from 1885. The NAACP also kept its own annual tally of lynchings and printed it in the *Crisis*. It attempted to verify some of this information through correspondence with local people, and it was often informed of lynchings that had not been reported in the press. The NAACP also investigated numerous lynchings, sending either staff members or reporters to gather information about events. It published and widely publicized their often-shocking findings. The reports exposed the identity of the lynchers (usually as a section of society but sometimes as individuals), explained the real reasons for the killings, reported in often graphic detail the torture of the victim, and stressed the brutality of the mob. Even this approach was limited, however, because the NAACP did not have the resources to investigate and publicize every incident of lynching.

It was therefore necessary to have more than just a factual record of lynching: activists needed a further way of remembering events. The arts provided a way of fulfilling this need. Through their plays, fiction, and paintings, artists constructed narratives that challenged white representations of lynching. They exposed some of the myths surrounding lynching, restored to the black victim his identity and history, and highlighted the brutality of the mob. They could remember or reimagine events from an African American perspective. By encouraging cultural work in its fight against lynching, the NAACP helped create an alternative interpretation of the "history" of mob violence. It did not want the record of lynching to be the one left by whites; out of its campaign came a body of work that challenged white representations and created a new record of both lynching and African American resistance.

One of the earliest examples of the NAACP using the arts in its antilynching campaign was the performance of *Rachel* in 1916. For the next twenty-five years the NAACP encouraged, commissioned, published, and staged a number of lynching plays. Kathy Perkins and Judith Stephens define a lynching drama as "a play in which the threat or occurrence of a lynching, past or present, has a major impact on the dramatic action."[8]

The works discussed below were all written by black women, and they tended to focus on the domestic life of African American families. They deal either explicitly or implicitly with the theme of mob violence, and all strongly condemn the psychological, physical, and social effects of the phenomenon.

Angelina Weld Grimké's *Rachel* was first performed in 1916 under the auspices of the NAACP's Drama Committee in Washington, DC, and then again in April 1917 in New York City. An announcement in the play's program stated its intention: "This is the first attempt to use the stage for propaganda in order to enlighten the American people relative to the lamentable condition of the millions of Colored citizens in this free republic." Some scholars have suggested that the play was commissioned by the NAACP to counter *The Birth of a Nation,* but in fact, Grimké had started work on the manuscript before the film's release. Nevertheless, the NAACP's decision to stage the play may well have been in response to Griffith's film. It could not make a film that challenged the vicious propaganda of Griffith's production; the next best thing would be a stage play. Theater was one of the cultural forms to which African Americans and the NAACP had access.[9]

The play tells the story of Rachel, her mother, Mrs. Loving, and her brother, Tom, and is set in their "scrupulously neat and clean" southern home. Over the course of the three-act play, Rachel changes from being optimistic, joyous, and loving to feeling bitter and jaded by the racism she sees around her. The most extreme example of this prejudice is lynching. After keeping it secret for ten years, Mrs. Loving tells her children the story of the death of their father and brother, who were lynched when their father denounced the mob killing of another black man in his newspaper. Rachel cannot bear the inequality that she sees and experiences and that she suffers physically and emotionally. She refuses an offer of marriage because she decides it is not fair to bring a black child into such a cruel world. Rachel laments, "Everywhere, throughout the South, there are hundreds of dark mothers who live in fear, terrible, suffocating fear" about the future of their babies. "Why—it would be more merciful—to suffocate the little things at birth."[10]

When her play was published in 1920, Grimké had to answer the charge that it "preaches race suicide." She maintained that "the appeal is not primarily to the colored people, but to the whites." She said her target was white women; she wanted them to "see, feel, [and] understand" the effect of racism on the "souls of colored mothers everywhere." Grimké hoped that then "a great power to affect public opinion would be set free and the battle would be half won." There is some evidence from the reviews to suggest *Rachel* was successful in provoking sympathy. The critic for the *Buffalo Courier* found "a terrible tragic note throughout the [play], which compels one to think, and if possible to lend aid to try and remove the prejudice against the colored race." The *Catholic World* concluded, "As a protest against white prejudice it makes its mark." Grimké's explicit intention was to change white attitudes toward lynching, but not everyone on the NAACP's Drama Committee was comfortable with this approach. It was divided over whether the function of drama should be propaganda or art. A minority did not agree with the use of propaganda; they split from the committee and went on to form the Howard Players, led by Alain Locke, which promoted an "artistic" approach to theater.[11]

The *Crisis,* in a reflection of Du Bois's belief that art should have a political message, provided a publication outlet for antilynching literature. This included two lynching dramas: Alice Dunbar-Nelson's *Mine Eyes Have Seen* and Myrtle Smith Livingston's *For Unborn Children. Mine Eyes Have Seen,* published and performed in 1918, raises the question of whether African Americans should fight in a war for a democracy that had been denied them at home. Set in a "manufacturing city in the North," it features Chris, Dan—who has been injured in an industrial accident—and their sister, Lucy. Their parents are dead: their father was lynched, "shot down like a dog for daring to defend his home," and their mother died of "pneumonia and heartbreak" after they moved north. Chris has been drafted and is reluctant to join up. He asks, "Must I go and fight for a nation that let my father's murder go unpunished?" The issue is debated between the siblings and with their neighbors, and finally, Chris is persuaded to go. Although Dunbar-Nelson raises some of the contradictions of blacks serving in the American army, the overwhelming message of the play, as with most of the work Du Bois published in his magazine at this time, is one of patriotism. It ends with "The Battle Hymn of the Republic" playing in the background as Chris's siblings convince him that it is his duty as an African American to go to war.[12] Lynching is not the primary issue in *Mine Eyes Have Seen;* it is used as just one example of racial injustice. The play stresses the physical (the family was forced to move north, a move that killed their mother and led to Dan's accident) rather than the emotional effect of racism. Whereas Grimké ends her play on a note of hopelessness, Dunbar-Nelson concludes that even these hardships should be overcome for the sake of the nation and for the good of the race.

*For Unborn Children,* by Myrtle Smith Livingston, won third prize in the 1925 *Crisis* competition and was published the following summer. Leroy Carlson is a young African American lawyer who falls in love with Selma, a white girl. They want to go north to marry, but Leroy's family disapproves. His sister, Marion, condemns intermarriage for its effect on black women and asks him, "What is to become of us when our own men throw us down?" His grandmother is worried about miscegenation; she tells him to think of the "unborn children you sin against by marrying her." She confesses to Leroy that his mother was white and that "she hated you because you weren't white." At the end of the play a white mob comes to the house for Leroy. He rejects the notion of race mixing and tells Selma, "Forget me, and marry a man of your own race; you'll be happier, and I will too, up there." He goes out to meet his death willingly. The religious imagery at the end of the play—"he is transfigured; a gleam of holiness comes into his eyes"—equates black suffering with Christian martyrdom. He tells his family his death is "a sacrifice for unborn children." However, Livingston's comment on miscegenation is ambiguous. As Remi Omodele notes, it could be read as a "commentary on the consequences of the irrational and inhumane segregation laws," or Livingston could have been advocating a Garveyite nationalist ideology that condemned race mixing. The play appears to be more of a comment on racial separatism or intermarriage than a condemnation of white brutality. Nevertheless, it can be considered an antilynching drama because Leroy's actions can be read as an attempt to reassert black control: he chooses to make his death an act of martyrdom.[13]

One of the most prolific writers of lynching dramas was Georgia Douglas Johnson. She wrote a number of plays with explicit antilynching messages but found it difficult to secure their production or publication. *A Sunday Morning in the South* (1925) is set in the home of Sue Jones, who cares for her two grandsons, Tom and Bossie. A neighbor calls round with news that the whites are "trying to run down some po Nigger they say that's tacked a white woman last night." Moments later the police arrive looking for Tom. They claim he fits the description of the attacker—"Age around twenty, five feet five or six, brown skin"—and convince the white girl to positively identify him. Tom is quickly taken, and from the reports of neighbors Sue learns that he has been lynched. In Johnson's play *Safe* (1929), a black mother hears the lynching of her neighbor, Sam Hosea, while in labor and kills her newborn son to save him from future lynchers. The lynching is averted in *Blue-Eyed Black Boy* (1930) when Tom

Waters's mother calls on the governor—who is also his father, a secret she has always kept—to save him. The first two plays in particular are uncompromising in their condemnation of the psychological repercussions of lynching. It is mob violence specifically that destroys the peace of the Sunday morning and forces a young mother to kill her newborn son.[14]

It was this bleak outlook that led to the plays being rejected by the NAACP. Johnson had sent a number to its Youth Council for possible production. However, they were returned because of concerns that they "all ended in defeat" and "gave one the feeling that the situation was hopeless." By the 1930s the NAACP was optimistic—incorrectly, as it turned out—that antilynching legislation would be passed and that the practice would come to an end. While it wanted work that showed the full horror of lynching, it also wanted plays to suggest there was a solution. The NAACP did recognize Johnson's talent as a playwright, and she was asked in 1938 to write a short play about the Wagner-Van Nuys-Gavagan antilynching bill, which was making its way through Congress (and was, by the beginning of 1938, stalling in the Senate). Johnson responded by writing *And Yet They Paused* and *A Bill to Be Passed,* slightly different versions of the same play. Both recount the story of an antilynching bill's passage through the House of Representatives alongside the story of a lynching in Mississippi. The NAACP had originally intended to use the play during an antilynching demonstration, but last-minute changes meant it wasn't ready to be included. However, it kept copies on file to send out to "the numerous white and colored groups throughout the country who constantly write us for anti-lynching plays." Johnson was told, "Your play will indeed be a contribution." The staging is simple, and Johnson wrote that she deliberately made it "easy to prepare and easy to commit." It alternates between two scenes, one in a southern black church and the other outside a room in the Capitol. Most of the action—the lynching and the congressional debate—happens off stage and is overheard and retold by those on stage.[15]

The NAACP commissioned the work (though Johnson wrote it at no cost to the organization, except for typing and printing) as a piece of propaganda. On reading an early draft, Juanita Jackson, a national staff member, suggested that "there is an excellent opportunity for bringing in the arguments of those opposed to the Anti-Lynching Bill, and convincing answers to those arguments."[16] Johnson does this by having her characters repeat and comment on the speeches made in the House. However, handwritten comments on the script calling for more arguments in favor of the bill suggest the NAACP wanted the propagandist element of the play to be strengthened. The portrayal of the lynching is dramatic, and the scenes in the church, with the use of music and prayer, are more like Johnson's earlier work. However, it lacks the emotional depth of her other plays. This play was intended purely as a piece of propaganda, and it is effective in its simplicity. It is a clear example of the NAACP prioritizing propaganda over art.

These lynching dramas (with the exception of *A Bill to Be Passed*) share many characteristics. They all take place within a domestic setting and center on the black family. This allows the playwrights to create a picture of "normal" black life on which violence and racism then impinge. The family is always respectable and often relatively prosperous. For example, in *For Unborn Children* the Carlsons are described as a "refined family, evidently of the middle class." Rachel and her family are educated and well spoken. Grimké said she drew her characters "from the best type of colored people" in order to challenge the usual theatrical stereotype of "the darkey." The NAACP wanted cultural work that presented the "best" black characters in order to appeal to middle-class whites. Setting the plays in the domestic sphere also creates a focus on black motherhood, with a matriarchal figure (mother or grandmother) at the center of the piece. She is less "threatening" to a white audience than the black male and therefore more likely to elicit sympathy, particularly, as Grimké hoped, from white women. Indeed, some of the characters distinctly resemble the Mammy stereotypes with which many whites were so comfortable. Sue Jones in *A Sunday Morning* "wears a red bandana handkerchief on her grey head, a blue gingham apron tied around her waist and big wide old lady comfort shoes." The NAACP seemed to accept those stereotypes it challenged so vociferously elsewhere. This reflects the extent to which it wanted to reach whites; it was willing to compromise in order to get them on its side.[17]

The plays tend to deal with the "aftermath," to use the title of Mary Burrill's play, of mob violence.[18] This decision has practical implications, and no doubt these playwrights had issues of staging in mind because it would have been difficult to realistically show a lynching on the stage. It also allows the play to deal with the consequences and impact of racial violence on the black family and on future generations. Even in those plays that end with a lynching, such as *A Sunday Morning,* the audience is asked to imagine the effect of the act on the family left behind. Trudier Harris accuses these playwrights of disguising the horrors of lynching by ignoring the physical reality of the act. She believes plays like *Rachel* and

*Aftermath* "shy away from directly treating the issue," so much so that "we might ask if these are truly anti-lynching plays."[19]

There certainly is a distancing in the plays, in terms of both staging and language, from the physical act of lynching. Nevertheless, the plays have an undeniable emotional impact, although they do veer into melodrama and sentimentality at times. Furthermore, the women rarely shy away from criticizing white society for the evils done in its name and from linking lynching to wider social and economic injustice. In this way, they reflect the NAACP's stance on culture and antilynching. The association wanted plays that condemned whites and showed them the harmful consequences of lynching. It staged, published, and commissioned such plays because their message was in accordance with its own. The NAACP was clearly happy to use theater for the purposes of propaganda. This is one of the clearest examples from its cultural campaigns of the association using art with a specific political message. The situation was so extreme—the threat of violence so real and so deadly—that it needed a direct approach. The plays' significance is also demonstrated by their creation. At a time when racial violence was a very real physical threat to African Americans, the fact that black women were writing such uncompromising and critical works of drama was remarkable in itself.

In 1933 the NAACP faced growing pressures. The Great Depression had hit African Americans particularly hard, and this, of course, hit the NAACP, which depended on its black members for funds. To compound these difficulties, it was (as will be discussed later in the chapter) being challenged from the Left in the form of the Communist Party. As Robert Zangrando suggests, the association had to "reassert itself," and reviving its antilynching campaign was one way to try to reclaim its position as the preeminent champion of civil rights. It returned to the fray with a new antilynching bill. Around the same time that the NAACP reopened its drive for legislation in Congress, Walter White and some of his associates had the idea to use their contacts in literary and journalistic circles to increase publicity and public support for the antilynching campaign. They formed the Writers' League Against Lynching to act as a "hell-raising committee to influence the country through writing, pronouncements and the like." White explained the motivation behind the league: "Stirred by the recent increase in the number and viciousness of lynchings and the growing spirit of mob violence throughout the country, a group of us met to determine in what way we writers could best help to formulate public opinion against such lawlessness." By 1934 it had over 150 members from the literary and media worlds, including some of the brightest stars, such as Sherwood Anderson, Gertrude Atherton, E. Franklin Frazier, Sterling Brown, Erskine Caldwell, Countee Cullen, Virginius Dabney, Theodore Dreiser, Sinclair Lewis, Alain Locke, Edna St. Vincent Millay, Upton Sinclair, Jean Toomer, and Carl Van Vechten. White boasted, "I think it is safe to say that it represents the most distinguished list of writers yet organized to fight for social justice."[20]

The league operated in two ways: it encouraged its members to take up the theme of lynching in their work, and it acted as a pressure group of distinguished Americans to call for antilynching legislation. It sent a telegram to President Roosevelt, who, fearful of losing the support of southern Democrats, was reluctant to back a federal antilynching law. Members also signed an open letter to Congress supporting the Costigan-Wagner Bill. The league kept its members informed about incidents of racial violence in order to encourage them to write about lynching. Though ostensibly an independent organization, it was closely linked to the NAACP. Walter White was a founder, and numerous NAACP staff were members. It had the same postal address as the association, and funds raised by the league were put toward the NAACP's antilynching campaign. The league reflected the association's ideas about lynching: people's opinions about the phenomenon had to be changed in order to bring an end to lynching, and one of the best ways to achieve this was to educate them about its full horrors. Literature was an effective way of exposing the brutal nature and racist causes of lynching. The target audience was the white American public, but works of literature could also be used to try and influence politicians. In 1940 White told the Senate Judiciary Committee considering antilynching legislation, "If [they] are sufficiently interested and concerned about these conditions to want to find out what the atmosphere is, in a town where lynchings are possible, let me urge them a reading of [*Trouble in July*]."[21] Erskine Caldwell's 1940 novel is about a southern sheriff who fails to stop the lynching of a young black man accused of rape. White clearly felt this fictional representation could help sway these politicians in a way the facts and figures could not.

The theme of lynching and racial violence, of course, had appeared in American literature long before and would continue after the league's or the NAACP's campaign. There are numerous examples of white and black writers including it, explicitly or obliquely, in their work.[22] These antilynching texts form a record of lynching that contrasts with that created by apologists by challenging the standard lynching narrative in a number of ways. Many question the claim that the mob acts to punish the "usual crime" of rape. According to Trudier Harris, black male writers in particular were conscious of the "oppressive shadow of white women upon their lives" and returned to the theme of sexual taboo many times.[23] In a number of the texts there is an accusation of rape, but this is exposed as false to the reader and at times to the characters.[24] Some black writers directly challenged the standard lynching narrative by creating ironic representations of newspaper reports. Walter White finished his novel *The Fire in the Flint* with a mock newspaper report on the lynching of the central character, in which it is charged that he attempted to assault a white girl. In fact the black doctor was trying to treat her, and the reader knows that white resentment lies behind the attack. White is thus able to expose the hypocrisy of both the lynchers who committed the acts and the press that reported them.

Walter White knew all too well white newspapers' propensity to manipulate the facts of lynchings. He attempted through his work to correct the imbalance of reporting. Some of these accounts provided inspiration for fictional retelling. In 1918 White went to investigate a series of lynchings in Brooks and Lowndes County, Georgia. He found there had been eleven lynchings; the most horrific of those was the killing of Mary Turner. His graphic report was reprinted in the *Crisis:*

> At the time she was lynched, Mary Turner was in her eighth month of pregnancy. . . . Her ankles were tied together and she was hung to the tree, head downward. Gasoline and oil from the automobiles were thrown on her clothing and while she writhed in agony and the mob howled in glee, a match was applied and her clothes burned from her person. [A] knife was taken and the woman's abdomen was cut open, the unborn babe falling from her womb to the ground. The infant, prematurely born, gave two feeble cries and then its head was crushed by a member of the mob with his heel. Hundreds of bullets were then fired into the body of the woman, now mercifully dead, and the work was over.[25]

White's investigation, which was reprinted in a number of newspapers, was in itself a direct challenge to the standard narrative because it exposed the full brutality of the lynch mob. Turner's story inspired a number of artistic responses. In her short story "Goldie" (1920), Angelina Weld Grimké made a direct reference to the incident; she describes a man returning to the South to find his sister and her husband have been lynched: "Underneath those two terribly mutilated swinging bodies, lay a tiny unborn child, its head crushed in by a deliberate heel." This story is particularly revealing because Grimké comments on the repression of lynching stories, the tales—such as that of Mary Turner—of which no one speaks. She warns that the truth will out and that the consequences for the lynchers and those who ignore their deeds will be dire.[26]

An example of White explicitly attempting to provoke an artistic reaction with a real-life incident occurred when he sent WLAL members the NAACP report on the lynching of Claude Neal in Jackson County, Florida, in October 1934. Neal was seized from jail, held captive, and tortured for two days while news of his impending lynching was broadcast throughout the region. He was finally shot by his captors, his body mutilated by a mob of hundreds and hung from a tree in the courthouse square. The premeditated, visible, and gruesome nature of this lynching shocked many, as did the authorities' apparent inability, or unwillingness, to do anything about it. In his covering letter White wrote, "If the writers of America will on every possible occasion use their efforts to arouse public opinion against such bestiality as [this lynching] they can do much toward putting an end to it."[27]

A month after White sent the letter a selection of verses by George Schuyler, a league member, appeared in the *Crisis*. At the top of the page was a quotation from the report into the Neal lynching, which found that 75 to 80 percent of the people in the county where he was killed went to church. Schuyler had cleverly reworked passages of scripture: thus the Lord's Prayer was rewritten as "The Lyncher's Prayer"; the hymn "Onward Christian Soldiers" became "Onward Christian Lynchers"; Psalm 23 began with the line "The Coon is our victim; we shall not want"; and "Genesis" told a story of violence rather than creation. The collection of verses provided a bitter and ironic indictment of white society's claims of Christian morality. On the opposite page of the magazine was a reproduction of Reginald Marsh's drawing *This Is Her First Lynching* (discussed later in the chapter), and on the next page were letters from senators expressing support for the proposed antilynching bill and a box of text explaining that only one-sixth of lynchings were to punish an allegation of rape. These pieces were deliberately positioned in this way: the artistic responses to lynching were intended to arouse readers' emotions; they would then turn over the page and see what was being done by the NAACP to combat this evil and what they could do to help (contact their senators to demand passage of the bill). This provides a clear example of how the NAACP used cultural work to try to bring an end to lynching. [28]

It is difficult to judge the effectiveness of the Writers' League Against Lynching, as its records in the NAACP files are slight. Furthermore, it is unclear the extent to which members were prompted or inspired by the league to write about lynching. Walter White himself felt the enterprise was a success, and, as he recounted in his autobiography, "the committee kept writers supplied with carefully checked facts about lynchings and there has been ever since a continuing concern which has been reflected in articles, fiction, plays and other writings."[29] It may not have been directly responsible for the work cited above, but the establishment of the Writers' League was nevertheless a significant gesture. It demonstrated the importance of protest literature in the antilynching campaign. Writers could create alternative stories of lynching. They challenged the standard narratives of lynching apologists and alerted readers to the crimes being committed against African Americans. Through their novels, stories, and poems these writers made moral and emotional appeals for an end to lynching. Of course, not all writers deliberately created campaigning literature; they explored lynching for a variety of reasons. However, the Writers' League shows how the NAACP hoped such work would be read and understood.

From the beginning of its antilynching campaign the NAACP also used visual culture to provoke outrage about mob violence. In the *Crisis* it printed photographs of actual mob killings, and in 1935 it organized *An Art Commentary on Lynching,* an exhibition in New York with contributions from black and white artists. Du Bois (as editor of the *Crisis*) and Walter White (as the curator of the exhibition) knew visual images had the power to shock and could provoke an emotional response from the viewer. They hoped this would encourage outrage about lynching and stimulate action against the practice. The exhibition in particular was closely linked to the association's attempts to secure passage of federal legislation, which at that time was in Congress. Furthermore, visual images formed part of the lynching narrative established by white racists, and photographs, cartoons, and paintings were another way of retelling the story from an African American perspective.

Lynching photographs were usually taken by whites and intended for white audiences. They were sold as souvenirs and provided a further way of degrading African Americans by prolonging the white gaze on the (usually dead) black body. The NAACP was able to obtain such pictures, and it attempted to subvert their meaning by using them as part of its antilynching campaign. One example followed the killing of Jesse Washington, an eighteen-year-old young man who was seized by a mob from a courtroom in Waco, Texas, in 1916, taken to the town square, mutilated, and burned alive in front of a crowd of thousands. Alongside her report for the *Crisis,* the NAACP's investigator, Elisabeth Freeman, was able to provide Du Bois with photographs of Washington's burning body, the white crowd, and his charred remains. These had been taken by local photographer Fred Gildersleeve and sold for ten cents apiece. Local officials belatedly realized that the photographs would further damage the reputation of the town, and Gildersleeve wrote to Du Bois, telling him, "We have quit selling the mob photos, this step was taken because our 'City dads' objected on the grounds of 'bad publicity.'" It was exactly this "bad publicity" that the NAACP hoped to provoke with the photographs. Du Bois used a number of them in a *Crisis* supplement, "The Waco Horror," and the front page carried a picture of Washington's burned body.[30]

These photographs are shocking, and the use of such images is troubling. It could be argued that in reprinting images of black victims. the NAACP was continuing the abuse and dehumanization of the black victim. However, the association was able to alter the context in which such pictures were viewed and understood. When the photographs were originally taken and viewed, the victim was usually anonymous, identified only by his race or his alleged crime. In the *Crisis* the name of the victim, his background, and the circumstances of his death were usually recorded. Often the accusations made against the victim were shown to be false, and the white mob, the local community, and the authorities who had allowed the extralegal killing to take place were strongly condemned. In some cases the NAACP inverted the mob's message completely by drawing attention away from the black body to the white crowd. A photograph of Rubin Stacey, who was lynched in Florida, showed his body hanging from a tree, surrounded by smiling white children. The NAACP published it with the accompanying command, "Do not look at the Negro. His earthly problems are ended. Instead, look at the seven white children who gaze at this gruesome spectacle."[31] This version of the picture inverted its original message; the white community that had gloatingly stared at the black body was forced to look instead at itself.

The use of visual imagery in the antilynching campaign culminated with *An Art Commentary on Lynching,* an ambitious exhibition of artwork that dealt with mob violence. This exhibition has been discussed by a number of art historians, and the following discussion draws on the

close readings of the paintings offered by Helen Langa, Margaret Vendryes, and Marlene Park. These scholars also discuss the exhibition within
the context of the antilynching campaign of the 1930s; this is crucial for
understanding the intentions of the artists and the curator and for considering the impact of the show.[32] Walter White had the idea for an exhibition
toward the end of 1934 and in a few months had organized the show, under
the sponsorship of the College Art Association. He told a friend, "This,
of course, seems and is morbid. But even a morbid subject can be made
popular if a sufficiently distinguished list of patronesses will sponsor the
exhibit and the right kind of publicity can be secured for it." White wanted
the audience for his exhibition to be liberal, moneyed, northern whites.
He compared it to the involvement of "snooty society girls" in the anti-
Prohibition movement and understood that such people could greatly influence society's opinions on a contentious issue. By using fine art, White
hoped to attract those who would normally shy away from a subject as un-
palatable as mob violence and to provoke the many apathetic whites who
"have become hardened to the point where they accept without second
thought the inevitability of the practice." This appeal to the middle classes
was common throughout both the NAACP's cultural campaigns and its
antilynching work.[33]

White was able to secure 183 sponsors, including Sherwood Anderson,
Dorothy Parker, Carl Van Vechten, Countee Cullen, and George Gershwin.
He wanted these patrons not only to give the show a certain intellectual
status but also to create some distance between it and the association. He
wrote, it "will be an indirect approach to the subject of lynching in which
the hand of the NAACP will not be evidenced." In response to accusations
about the political nature of the exhibition, White wrote, "The exhibit is
not sponsored by organizations but by a number of distinguished individuals." He claimed that this was to "broaden the bases of the fight against
lynching and to enlist new recruits." The show was designed to attract
more than just the usual NAACP supporters. White went on, "I want also
to clear up any notion that the exhibition is for the purpose of support
of any given anti-lynching bill. Instead, the purpose is to focus attention
on lynching." It is true that one of White's aims was to arouse opposition to the practice of lynching generally. However, the exhibition *was* for
the express purpose of garnering support for antilynching legislation. The
Costigan-Wagner Bill was introduced to Congress in 1934, and the timing
of the art exhibition was not coincidental. The senators' names were on the
list of exhibition sponsors released to the press. Furthermore, in the exhibi-

tion catalog Erskine Caldwell explicitly linked the show to the legislation when he wrote, "It is the duty of the Congress of the United States to pass the necessary legislation."[34]

White wrote to artists to ask them to submit specific works or to produce something for the exhibition. *An Art Commentary on Lynching* featured over forty pieces by thirty-eight artists, including eight African Americans.[35] It opened on February 15, 1935, and ran for two weeks. The artists approached the subject of lynching in a number of different ways. *Death* (1934), a sculpture by Japanese American artist Isamu Noguchi, is a contorted, faceless metal figure, hanging from a rope. George Bellows's posthumous contribution, *The Law Is Too Slow* (1923), also depicts the act of lynching. A black figure is tied to a stake in a burning fire, his back arched as he struggles against his torture. The lynchers are present, too, men crowded around the fire. Bellows, as Dora Apel notes, has left space in the foreground that "makes way for the viewer as a potential participant." The painting reinforces the NAACP's message that all white Americans are potential mob members when they do nothing to stop lynching. Walter White believed the picture had such a powerful message he used it as the frontispiece for his study of the causes of lynching, *Rope and Faggot*. The practice of castration is portrayed most graphically by Harry Sternberg in his *Southern Holiday* (1935). An African American male is bound to a ruined pillar, with the smoking chimneys of industry in the background, a comment, Langa argues, on the conflict between America's claims for progress and civilization and its treatment of its black citizens. There is blood running from a wound between his legs and his face is contorted in pain.[36]

Both Bellows and Sternberg were white, and Apel discusses the highly problematic nature of such depictions of the black male body. Their use of nudity may be read, she argues, as signifying inferior social status, and the allusion to castration "reifies the stereotype of the virile black man" at the same time that it subverts the figure's power through his emasculation. The artworks also expose "the helpless and mortified body to the commanding gaze of the viewer who may take pleasure in the looking even while appalled."[37] However, nakedness is also suggestive of innocence, and the artists may well have been clearing the victims of assumed guilt. Furthermore, it could be argued that Sternberg and Bellows are drawing attention to the *irrationality* of the fear of the virile black man rather than reinforcing the stereotype. When read in such a way, the pictures' antilynching message is potentially more powerful. Not all white artists incorporated such graphic depictions of lynchings. Reginald Marsh removed the black body from his picture altogether and instead depicted a crowd of whites in the glow of the lynchers' pyre. The figure of a young girl being held aloft by her mother gives the piece its title, *This Is Her First Lynching* (1934). As with the NAACP's use of the photograph of Rubin Stacey, the picture is a comment on the impact of lynching on whites rather than African Americans.

When comparing the pieces contributed by black artists to those by whites, some broad themes emerge. Helen Langa points out that only two of the black artists portrayed explicit violence; the others used images of black grieving and religious metaphors as symbols of the violence. This "allowed them to downplay both the frenzied white violence and demeaning black victimization." Margaret Vendryes likewise argues that the black artists tended to focus on "victimhood" and appealed to the "morality of the viewer." For example, in *I Passed Along This Way* (1935) E. Simms Campbell drew Jesus carrying the cross with the figure of a black lynching victim behind him. Other examples include Hale Woodruff's *By Parties Unknown* (1935), in which the victim's body is left on the steps of a church, and *The Crucifixion*, by Malvin Gray Johnson. There was certainly a conscious effort by black artists to preserve the dignity of the African American victim. In Wilmer Jennings's *At the End of a Rope* (1935) the face of a black male lynching victim is peaceful, almost serene. It is placed in a jungle setting that evokes an African heritage, and the coils of rope are not immediately obvious; it is only once the viewer has noticed them that the scene is transformed. Black artists were wary of the dehumanizing effect of reproducing the lynching scene.[38]

Those African Americans who did explicitly depict acts of white violence had a different focus from white artists. The black body, or face, became the center of the frame. Allan Freelon's *Barbecue: American Style* (1934) shows, in the words of the artist, "that moment when the victim first feels the flames begin to lick at his body."[39] He focuses on the black man's pain-filled body, as he pulls against his restraints and strains upward from the fire. All that can be seen of his white torturers is a line of feet. *The Lynching* (1934), by Samuel Brown, gives a bird's-eye view of a hanged man, his agonized face dominating the picture. The white mob is reduced to barely discernible drops on the ground far below him. Both these pictures are graphic and disturbing images of black suffering. However, in focusing on the black figure the artist forces the viewers to confront that suffering and encourages them to empathize with the victim.

The exhibition received mixed reviews in the northern press. The critic for the *Brooklyn Daily Eagle* found the portrayals of actual lynchings to be the least successful, claiming that "as propaganda they are rather innocuous" and arguing that "the painters were more preoccupied with problems of space and coloring than they were with social issues." Others found them to be too hard-hitting and complained that propaganda took precedence at the expense of aesthetics. The *New York Times* critic complained that Noguchi's *Death* was realistic "to a disastrous extent" and concluded that while it might be an effective protest against lynching, as a work of art "it seems merely sensational and of extremely dubious value." There were, however, reviewers who were more comfortable with the political nature of the exhibition. One critic concluded, "No spoken or written argument against lynch law could be as hard-hitting as the work of these artists." The reviewer for the *New York World-Telegram* articulated the NAACP's hopes for the show when he predicted it "may do much to crystallize public opinion" about lynching. The writer warned that it was not an exhibition for "softies" but concluded, "if it upsets your complacency on the subject it will have been successful."[40]

According to the NAACP over two thousand people from all over the country and overseas attended the exhibition. It toured briefly, but this was cut short due to lack of funds. Walter White judged the exhibition to have been a success.[41] In terms of notoriety it seems it was, thanks in no small part to the controversy over the show's sudden cancellation, as discussed below. Taken together the exhibits offered a varied and vigorous condemnation of lynching. Many of the pieces turned the usual apologist's arguments about lynching on their head. It wasn't the African American who was savage and guilty of some brutal crime, but the white mob. Images of black figures contorted in agony while gleeful spectators, including women and children, looked on challenged notions of American civilization. The repeated use of religious imagery allowed a more dignified portrayal of black life and challenged white claims to superiority and Christian charity. Most of the exhibits did not depict specific events. This allowed the artist to comment symbolically on the general practice of lynching and to condemn the phenomenon rather than just one occasion of it.

Many representations of lynching, particularly those that are visual, are problematic. In the 1930s the NAACP faced the dilemma of needing to show black torment to elicit sympathy while at the same time replacing the notion of black victimization with a sense of collective resistance. The exhibition had to show lynching as a horrific crime and at the same time offer hope for a solution. The artists too had to decide how literally or realistically they wanted to depict black suffering. Sometimes the images of lynching were sanitized, either to make it more palatable to a white audience or to spare the black viewer. Some, such as Brown's and Freelon's pictures, were intended to make the audience uncomfortable and to challenge them to act on this feeling. Such images were the most effective, when judged against the NAACP's standards. After all, the NAACP's primary aim was not to curate a show of fine art but to create a piece of propaganda. In this respect, it was the exhibition itself, as an event that drew crowds and attracted publicity, that was more important than the work it showed. As with much of the NAACP's cultural work, propaganda took precedence over aesthetics. Whatever the merits of individual paintings, it could be argued that the decision to exhibit a collection of images of naked male bodies, castration, torture, bloodthirsty whites, and black Christ figures was the boldest choice of all.

Another antilynching art exhibition took place in New York at the beginning of 1935. This "opposition show," as Walter White sneeringly called it, was not only a rival to *An Art Commentary;* its Communist-affiliated organizers directly and deliberately challenged the NAACP event. The Jacques Seligmann Galleries, where the NAACP show was due to be held, pulled out at the last minute, allegedly due to pressure from the Communist Party. According to an NAACP press release, "The Seligmann Galleries authorized the statement that 'political, economic and social pressure had been brought to bear' to induce them to cancel their donation of space for the exhibit." Fortunately for his venture, Walter White was able to secure space at the Arthur U. Newton Galleries, and publicity about the cancellation only increased the media's and the public's interest. The Communists objected to the association's proposed antilynching legislation and threatened to boycott the show. They believed that the Costigan-Wagner Bill was too conservative and that the NAACP was too cautious in its approach to mob violence. It proposed its own legislation, the Bill for Negro Rights, which demanded the death penalty for lynchers. This clash over the art exhibitions reveals the increasing tensions between the NAACP and the Communist Party (CP), which was beginning to challenge the NAACP as both the champion of black rights and sponsor of black culture. [42]

The Communist exhibition, *Struggle for Negro Rights,* opened at the ACA Gallery on March 3 and ran for two weeks. It was organized by the John Reed Club in conjunction with the League of Struggle for Negro Rights (LSNR), the International Labor Defense (ILD), the Artists' Union, the Artists' Committee of Action (ACA), and the Vanguard. The exhibition catalog set the tone. It was written by Angelo Herndon, a black Communist who had been sentenced to twenty years on a chain gang for organizing workers, and was titled *Pictures Can Fight!* He criticized the NAACP's support of the Costigan-Wagner Bill and argued that "we can only stop lynching by STRUGGLE—by mass organization of white and Negro workers, by mass defense, by mass pressure for a real fighting anti-lynching bill like the Bill for Negro Rights and the Suppression of Lynching."[43] The show included fifty-six works by forty-five artists, including four that also appeared in the NAACP's show. None of the exhibitors was known to be black.[44]

The pieces in *Struggle for Negro Rights* dealt with issues such as Scottsboro, racial solidarity among workers, and the threat of fascism. These themes were as prevalent in the pictures as lynching itself. This reflected the Communist belief that lynching must be linked to a wider class struggle that could only be overcome by interracial cooperation between workers. Stephen Alexander's review in *New Masses* compared the two exhibitions. Alexander argued it was not enough "merely to arouse indignation or sympathy or horror. . . . We must attack the social forces responsible for lynching." This is what the Communist exhibition did more successfully than the NAACP show. The exhibits in the Arthur Newton Galleries focused on the physical, emotional, and spiritual *impact* of lynching, whereas the ACA show raised questions about the *causes* of racial violence and suggested class struggle as a primary reason. The Communist exhibition attempted to explore economic factors and to suggest a solution to lynching that was not simply legislative. This, Langa argues, was a deliberate critique of what the Communists saw as the NAACP's elitist and gradualist approach to lynching. It could also be argued that because the Communist Party was a predominantly white organization, it was more detached from the threat of violence against blacks. This allowed it to analyze the broader causes in its exhibition, whereas the NAACP show emphasized the emotion of black vulnerability.[45]

The CP and the NAACP had come to blows before the exhibitions of 1935. Since the end of the 1920s, Communists had taken an explicit interest in the race question. Initially, they believed the enemies of black self-determination and revolutionary change were not just white oppressors but also the black middle class. Therefore the Communist Party worked to undermine organizations such as the NAACP and set up rival organiza-

:ions; the competing art exhibitions provide one example of Communists acting in direct competition to the association. This approach was reversed in 1935 with the introduction of Popular Front policies. Communists were urged to form alliances with the black middle classes, and attempts were made to work alongside liberals and the black intelligentsia. They even put their support behind the NAACP's antilynching legislation. The most famous example of the tensions between the two sides began in Alabama in 1931 with the arrest of the nine "Scottsboro boys," who were charged with raping two white girls. The NAACP and the ILD tussled over who should represent the defendants, with the latter eventually seizing control of the case. The NAACP did reenter the case in 1933 (when it agreed to help the ILD with expenses), and it was one of five groups that formed the Scottsboro Defense Committee in 1935 (when, in line with wider Communist policy, the ILD sought to form alliances with black organizations). Nevertheless, the incident, which dragged on throughout the 1930s, provides an example of the differing approaches and tactics of the CP and the NAACP toward the question of race. The tension was exacerbated because the NAACP felt threatened by the Communist Party, not least because there were calls from within the association to rethink its direction and focus more directly on the economic turmoil and the hardships of black workers. (In the end, it largely ignored these calls, as it was brought further into national politics and continued to build its legal program.)[46]

Despite their many differences, Communists actually used the arts in ways similar to the association, to spread their message and to recruit African Americans to their cause. There has been some debate among scholars as to the consequences of the Communist influence on black culture. During the Cold War many scholars were highly critical of this relationship and argued that it stifled black creativity and that the Communists used black culture for their own political purposes.[47] In the last twenty-five years there has been something of a reassessment by scholars. They have uncovered a less exploitative and a more nuanced relationship, which allowed for a two-way process of influence and creativity.[48]

Studies such as these suggest the NAACP faced competition in its attempts to shape and encourage African American culture. Groups such as the John Reed Club and the Vanguard provided opportunities for black and white artists to meet and exposed many African Americans to Communist ideas. *New Masses* was a radical magazine with an artistic and literary tone that published work by African Americans and articles on racial issues. Significantly, many of those the CP attracted through its cultural work were from the black middle class, the NAACP's core constituency. According to Mark Naison, the CP's "cultural policies were far more attuned" to middle- rather than working-class "artistic tastes" or "more to the point *aspirations*." This approach is very similar to that of the NAACP: it promoted artists producing "high" cultural forms and then attempted to persuade African Americans to become consumers of this art. By targeting the same sections of the black community as the NAACP, Communists posed a direct challenge to the association's role as cultural sponsor.[49]

The similarities between the cultural work of the two sides are telling. They targeted the same groups, they used the same artistic forms, and, perhaps most important, they used that work for the same purpose: propaganda. Both *An Art Commentary on Lynching* and *Struggle for Negro Rights* were designed to influence public feeling. *Struggle* dealt with a broader range of issues than simply mob violence, and it promoted a Communist doctrine. For example, it included paintings that showed class struggle and interracial cooperation between workers. The NAACP exhibition focused instead on the single issue of lynching, and it was held to increase support for the passage of the antilynching legislation. Nevertheless, both shows were united in calling for political and racial change. Walter White and company would no doubt object to the comparison between the two groups. The NAACP was scathing about the CP's use of propaganda because it was either directed against it or a challenge to its own work. White tried to distance the NAACP from accusations of propaganda; he claimed the art exhibition was not political. But in this he was being disingenuous. The show was held with the explicit intention of rallying support for antilynching legislation and was, therefore, a political act. Furthermore, an examination of the NAACP's use of the arts across its campaign against lynching demonstrates how readily and frequently the association used art as propaganda in the 1930s.

The creation and use of African American culture during this decade needs to be understood in the context of the New Deal. Lauren Sklaroff has studied the development and significance of black cultural production through a wide range of federal agencies. Many African Americans believed that culture could have political implications. Sklaroff argues that "African American political leaders and program participants considered New Deal cultural projects as tantamount to organized challenges against economic and social inequality." This, of course, was much like the NAACP's own approach to culture, not just during the 1930s but throughout the first half of the century. Harold Ickes, director of the Public Works

Administration, commented after seeing the Federal Theater's all-black *Swing Mikado,* "No people . . . can consistently be suppressed on the basis of race, color or creed, when they persist in making cultural contributions of real importance and benefit." His comments echo James Weldon Johnson's assertion during the Harlem Renaissance that "no people that has produced great literature and art has ever been looked upon by the world as distinctly inferior." Indeed, much of the emphasis on the production and potential of culture during the New Deal was reminiscent of the hopes of many African Americans a decade earlier. [50]

The association closely monitored all aspects of New Deal provision, challenging examples of segregation and discrimination. It also tried, not always successfully, to exploit the more liberal atmosphere to push for civil rights. Its engagement with the federal government extended to its involvement with cultural production during the 1930s. The NAACP forged close links with a number of New Deal agencies, including the cultural wings of the Works Progress Administration (WPA). It protested against examples of racial discrimination and cuts to funding from programs such as the Federal Writers Project and the Federal Theater Project (FTP). In a reprisal of his role during the Renaissance, Walter White, who was on the advisory board of the WPA's Five Arts Project, sought out "good plays dealing with Negro life" from writers such as Sherwood Anderson and Sidney Howard. The association monitored the work being produced by different projects, including protesting against what it saw as unsuitable material. For example, Roy Wilkins complained to Emmet Lavery, director of the National Service Bureau, about plans for the Newark Negro Unit to stage Octavus Roy Cohen's play *Come Seven.* Wilkins's colleagues referred to it as an "Uncle Tom" play, and the assistant secretary warned Lavery that the "vast majority of colored people" objected to Cohen's "caricatures of the race." He went on to criticize the FTP, claiming "inaccurate and ofttime vicious interpretations of Negroes have been passed by uninformed play readers and consultants." White people, he explained, could not accurately judge material about African Americans. (This seems somewhat ironic, given that Walter White had been busy asking white writers like Anderson and Howard whether they had any material to contribute.) While Wilkins did tone down his criticism when Lavery defended the FTP and assured him that the play had been withdrawn, the exchange demonstrates the NAACP's concern about the ways in which African Americans were represented by these federal projects. The association saw there was an opportunity to help shape images of the race. Furthermore, the climate of the decade validated the NAACP's approach. Skarloff writes that, although they faced resistance, African Americans during the New Deal "conceptualized culture and politics as inherently intertwined."[51] The NAACP—with its antilynching plays, art exhibition, and writers' pressure group—was not alone in linking culture and civil rights.

The NAACP's aim in using cultural forms in its antilynching campaign was twofold. Primarily, it hoped to change white attitudes toward lynching in order to bring an end to the practice. It also understood that the production of written and visual texts would create an alternative record of lynching, a history that challenged that produced by lynchers and their apologists. It is difficult to measure the extent to which the NAACP was successful in changing white opinion about lynching. The number of lynchings began to fall in the second half of the 1930s. In 1933 there had been twenty-eight reported incidents, but the total number for the last four years of the decade was lower, and there were only three lynchings in 1939, the lowest number since records started being kept. While the decline in lynchings could have been due to a number of factors, there are suggestions that opinions were beginning to alter. When a 1937 Gallup Poll asked, "Should Congress pass a law which would make lynching a federal crime?" over 60 percent of respondents answered, "Yes."[52] Although such legislation was never passed, the response indicates that there was growing support for federal intervention.

Of course, although there was a gradual shift in public opinion, this was not necessarily due to the efforts of the NAACP and antilynching activists. It has been argued that southern support for lynching, in its contemporary form, began to wane for reasons of self and economic interest.[53] However, antilynching activists can be credited with applying pressure on whites, not just in the South but throughout the nation. They opened many eyes to the brutal nature, the extreme scale, and the consequences of the lynching problem in the United States. Whether their reaction was based on moral or selfish impulses, Americans began to turn against lynching as it was understood in the 1930s. Certainly the NAACP felt its approach was successful. Walter White wrote that "through magazine articles, books, lectures, and personal contacts," the NAACP "kept the issue of mobbism constantly before the public and thus helped to change apathy and hostility to interest and support of the campaign against Judge Lynch." Similarly, journalist Philip Dray argues that "most indispensable" to lynching's demise was "the steady pressure from the reformers and writers who never quit insisting that we were too good to be a nation of lynchers."[54]

The artistic work created in response to lynching and as part of the campaign against it forms an alternative history of lynching. There is a gap in the "official" historical record of lynching: the statistics are incomplete, and we can never know exactly how many people were lynched. Anne P. Rice argues that writers are able to help to fill in this gap. The text "carries the burden of remembering and working through the past."[55] For the NAACP the value of this cultural work was limited when taken in isolation; it had to exist alongside its investigations and its publication of statistics. Nevertheless, these alternative narratives serve an important function. They re-create the elements missing in standard narratives: the victim's identity, his family and community, the identity (as a collective group) of the lynchers. The dominant white representation of lynching was thus challenged and an alternative story of lynching created. This body of work exists today as a reminder of a shameful period in America's history and as a form of resistance against white brutality.

Artists, poets, playwrights, and novelists were responsible for rewriting, and thus righting, the lynching narrative. They took the standard motifs of lynching and subverted them or replaced them completely. In these works the psychological and emotional impact on blacks and whites is emphasized. So too is the destructive legacy on the black family and the African American community at large. In many works the physical reality of lynching, the brutality of it, is explicit. In others, religious imagery is used to find spiritual solace in suffering and the Christian strength to overcome. Many of the works challenge the stereotypes and myths that surrounded white perceptions of mob violence. In the antilynching narratives the victim is often given back his identity: he is named and given a family and a community. Perhaps contradictorily, the universal nature of lynching is also shown. Lynching is presented as a crime against both an individual and his race. This accords with the NAACP's arguments for federal intervention. In order to show that lynching was not only murder but a crime that came under the jurisdiction of the states, activists had to show that the lynchers were "acting under the pretext of service to justice, race, or tradition."[56] Again, the NAACP used cultural works that reflected its own views toward lynching and how to end it. The lynching record that was created by activists and artists was thus a key weapon in the fight against lynching. Using cultural forms allowed the NAACP to reach those who chose to ignore or had become immune to the brutal facts of racial violence.

The NAACP was operating during a difficult period. Although it seemed that the liberalism of the New Deal, combined with the Democrats' growing base among African Americans, would offer opportunities to push for civil rights, there was reluctance in the Roosevelt administration to align itself too closely with measures that would alienate the white South. When it came to antilynching legislation, as Zangrando explains, "the black community lacked allies willing to sacrifice and perhaps suffer a little politically on its behalf." In this context it is perhaps unsurprising that the NAACP, alongside its lobbying efforts, tried alternative methods, ones that were less dependent on a political capital that it did not have. Sklaroff suggests that government officials saw arts projects as substituting for "'real' racial politics," as a way of stymieing other demands. It could be argued, then, that culture was a distraction; it avoided the heart (that is, the structure) of an issue. However, just as African Americans involved in the New Deal saw culture as an opportunity to secure actual political change, so the NAACP believed the arts could make a real difference. Thus the cultural elements of the antilynching campaign were designed to work both in and of themselves and as a way of furthering the association's political and legal ends.[57]

The arts provided the NAACP with a powerful way of making a moral appeal to Americans. The positive reviews of *Rachel* and the art exhibition, for example, indicate that the arts could successfully provoke sympathy for the antilynching cause. Furthermore, the NAACP believed that most whites were simply apathetic about lynching rather than staunch supporters. If this was the case, then emotive and powerful artistic representations of mob violence may have been enough to shake them out of this apathy. The association probably reached only a small minority of liberal, northern whites with its use of "high" cultural forms. This, of course, was part of its strategy. It thought it had the best chance of persuading middle- and upper-class whites of the desirability and necessity of an end to lynching. The NAACP hoped these whites would then use their influence—in politics, in business, and as public-opinion formers—to persuade others and to press for political changes. This reflects its broader approach to racial inequality (that it was caused by ignorance and could be combated with education and persuasion), and it also mirrors the NAACP's cultural strategy. It often used "high" culture to reach and impress the upper sections of white society.

However, the focus on "high" cultural forms at the expense of all others highlights a weakness in the NAACP's strategy. It might have been able to reach an even broader audience if it had embraced other "popular" forms of culture. Probably the best-known example of a cultural response

:o lynching was a song, "Strange Fruit," made famous by Billie Holliday. *Time* magazine described it as "a prime piece of musical propaganda for the NAACP."[58] In fact, it is unclear what the NAACP's reaction to the song was or whether it was associated with it in any way. Perhaps its long-standing wariness of jazz or the left-wing politics of the song's composer, Abel Meeropol, made the NAACP reluctant to incorporate the song into its antilynching campaign. An important reason why the NAACP's antilynching campaign focused on "high" culture at the expense of other forms was that these were the ones that the organization was most able to influence. It did not have the resources or contacts to make an antilynching film, for example. It did, however, have a history of reacting to those films that dealt with racial violence. After all, one of its chief complaints about *The Birth of a Nation* was that it condoned and actively encouraged lynching. When MGM released *Fury* (1936), in which a man narrowly avoids being lynched, the NAACP called it "one of the strongest educational features against lynching that has ever been placed before the public." In fact, all references to race were removed from the final movie; the lynch mob's intended victim is played by the white actor Spencer Tracy.[59] The NAACP's overenthusiastic reaction to a film that ignored the racial history of lynching suggests the poor state of racial depictions in Hollywood movies at the time. Very few films dealt with issues of race in a sympathetic manner. Nevertheless, after *Birth* a film such as *Fury* was a step in the right direction. There was, however, still much work to be done. Walter White hoped that a painting hanging in a gallery could influence a person's attitude toward lynching; he was convinced that motion pictures held an even greater power over public opinion. So, as the 1930s drew to a close, the NAACP secretary took the tactics of lobbying and persuasion he had honed in his battle for an antilynching law and the principle that cultural representations of African Americans could influence attitudes, and he headed to Hollywood.

5

# White in Hollywood

Walter White had a somewhat utilitarian attitude toward the arts and popular culture: he tended to see them in terms of how they could assist the African American struggle for equality. He promoted the artists of the Harlem Renaissance because he admired their talent but also because they were shining examples of black culture and achievement. He formed the Writers' League Against Lynching and organized his art exhibition in order to drum up support for antilynching legislation. Similarly, when he watched a motion picture, he assessed whether it would reinforce or challenge racial prejudices. He was concerned that films were having a damaging impact on race relations by reinforcing white stereotypes about African Americans. So he resolved to go to Hollywood and bring about a change in how African Americans were depicted on the screen. White used some of the tactics he had developed in earlier campaigns: he targeted the rich and powerful and white; he conducted business over luncheons and drinks parties; he lobbied and cajoled; he appealed to people's consciences; and he made the most of every opportunity to press his organization's arguments. White's cultural campaign during the Second World War reflected a new strategy toward motion pictures: rather than protest a film once it had been made and call for it to be censored, the association attempted to intervene before and during production. White went to Hollywood, the heart of American filmmaking, to tackle the problem at its source.

During the late 1920s and the 1930s the NAACP was largely silent on the matter of motion pictures. There was the odd skirmish against *The Birth of a Nation,* but the association devoted little time to the question of black images in films. Its resources were depleted by the Depression, and it was distracted by other issues, such as the fight against the nomination of Judge John Parker to the Supreme Court and the battle for an antilynching law. Nevertheless, it continued to keep an eye on what was coming out of Hollywood and was hopeful for any sign of improvement.

For example, in 1929, with the Harlem Renaissance still in full flow, two musicals with black casts were released, *Hearts in Dixie* and *Hallelujah.* The NAACP called the former a "fine film" and had particular praise for the second, which it said was a "great drama." However, as Donald Bogle has shown, the same old stereotypes prevailed, with the servant figure particularly common as a figure of reassurance in a time of upheaval and difficulty. Despite this, black actors were often able to give their characters dignity and humanity. For example, Louise Beavers was applauded in the *Crisis* for her part as a black cook in *Imitation of Life* (1934). The NAACP did not seem overly concerned about either the stereotypes or the signs of improvement. While there were occasional references to films in NAACP correspondence or reviews in the *Crisis,* the association devoted little attention to the business of motion pictures until the decade drew to a close. This is particularly surprising, as the movies held an increasingly important place in American lives during the 1930s. The lack of a systematic campaign reflected the fact that the NAACP had not yet discovered a way into the closed world of the white film industry and that the broader national climate had not yet provided it with the opportunity for action.[1]

When the NAACP turned its attention once more to the motion picture industry, it did so with a new approach. Its strategy was shaped by a number of factors, including the leadership of Walter White and, most significantly, the changing national and international climate brought about by the rise of fascism in Europe and the outbreak of the Second World War. White became the NAACP's permanent executive secretary in 1931 and was a dominant figure after the resignation of Du Bois in 1934. The NAACP's growing involvement in the motion picture industry was driven by White's own interests and concerns. By 1942 he considered "the matter of the treatment of the Negro in the motion pictures of such importance that it takes rank over some other phases of our work."[2] It was White who spearheaded the NAACP's campaign in Hollywood, and it was he who spent his time on the West Coast and in correspondence with movie men and women. He was a man who enjoyed the chance to mingle with celebrities and powerful people, as had been seen in the previous decade during the Harlem Renaissance. There is no denying that the focus on Hollywood during the early 1940s reflected, in part, White's enjoyment of the work. While this chapter focuses on the work and attitudes of White, he was not the only one within the organization who was interested in the film industry. He was supported in his venture by Roy Wilkins, who was his assistant secretary, and Julia Baxter, who worked for the NAACP's Division of Information and whose role involved watching movies and reporting back to White and the board on their content. However, as would be seen in later years, not all of White's priorities and plans would be supported by his colleagues and NAACP members.

Nevertheless, Walter White's work in Hollywood corresponded with the NAACP's approach to the depiction of African Americans in the arts and popular culture. The association believed that negative representations of the race exacerbated racial tension and prevented African Americans from progressing by reinforcing the prejudices that held them in place as second-class citizens. The motion picture was a particularly pernicious medium. Walter White argued that the movie was "the most widely circulated medium yet devised to reach the minds and emotions of people all over America and the world" and that it "was perpetuating and spreading dangerous and harmful stereotypes of the Negro." These stereotypes were doing incalculable damage to white perceptions of the race and therefore to the race itself. As Walter White told a meeting of Hollywood producers: "Restriction of Negroes to roles with rolling eyes, chattering teeth, always scared of ghosts, or to portrayals of none-too-bright servants perpetuates a stereotype which is doing the Negro infinite harm. And showing him always as a mentally inferior creature, lacking in ambition, is one of the reasons for the denial to the Negro of opportunities and for low morale . . . as it constantly holds the Negro up to ridicule and disparagement." The depiction of blacks in motion pictures reinforced white prejudice. Furthermore, White believed it damaged the psyche of African Americans themselves and contributed to a lack of racial pride among some sections of the black community.[3]

Walter White and his colleagues were not the only ones to be interested in and concerned about the effect of motion pictures. By the 1930s, there was a growing argument within academia that movies had a psychological and educational effect. The Educational Research Committee of the Payne Fund, in conjunction with the Motion Picture Research Council, conducted a four-year study into the effects of films on children. They analyzed children's viewing habits, the content of movies, and their emotional, physiological, and behavioral effects and concluded that they could have a considerable and often damaging impact on young people. As part of the study, they found "a town where almost no child had even seen a Negro. They tested the school children and found them practically without race prejudice." They arranged a viewing of *The Birth of a Nation* and afterward found that "race prejudice had grown like a weed." The October

1937 issue of the *Crisis* included a speech by psychologist Edgar Dale, who was part of the Payne Study, entitled "The Movies and Race Relations." Dale argued that for many white Americans their lack of contact with other races meant their "mental portrait" was based on "second-hand or indirect contact" through literature, radio, and motion pictures. This last form of media was particularly important; it "not only entertains," Dale explained, but "also educates." He quoted a number of studies that had found that motion pictures shaped attitudes and that this had damaging implications for relations between races. The NAACP's long-standing belief that the way blacks were culturally represented affected the way they were perceived was now supported by a powerful consensus of opinion. The black press also monitored Hollywood, and black film critics frequently attacked the film industry's stereotypical portrayals of African Americans. According to Daniel Widener, black activists and artists in Los Angeles during the Second World War critiqued black images on screen and sought entry into the motion picture industry. Many others, it seemed, shared the NAACP's belief that white Hollywood's representation of the race could be damaging.[4]

The NAACP's solution was to replace negative depictions with more positive images of the race, ones that would show African Americans in a new light and prove to white America, and to blacks themselves, that they were deserving and capable of full equality. This meant lobbying for professional, middle-class black characters to appear on screen. It did not necessarily mean that these should be the only images. Walter White claimed, "I strongly believe that Negroes, like every other group, should guard against hypersensitiveness. There are Negro sharecroppers and there is no reason why in moving pictures, fiction or elsewhere their existence should not be acknowledged." However, and this was the crux of the NAACP's argument, "there are also Negro artists, doctors, lawyers, scientists, teachers, business men and others who have made and are making very material contributions to their own and the country's advancement. We contend that these others should be shown in the films as well as the sharecroppers, the comedians and the menials."[5] The NAACP did not protest every time a black servant appeared on screen, but it objected to those films that featured blacks only in these stereotypical roles. It wanted the race to be more "fairly" represented. In other words, it wanted middle-class, respectable characters on the screen. This reflects the NAACP's bias toward the "Talented Tenth," the people who made up the leadership and the majority of its membership. These were the people that the NAACP believed reflected the "best" of the race. Furthermore, the association's cultural campaigns were designed to appeal to the white middle classes; it hoped to show these whites that African Americans were just the same as them.

Walter White wanted these characters to appear in mainstream, white films. He was opposed to the idea of the all-black cast, in which African Americans and black communities were shown as separate from the white majority. He told a friend that when he and his ally Wendell Willkie went to Hollywood, they made it clear "that neither of us favored the all-Negro picture," their reasoning being that "90 percent of movie goers in the United States are white and they will just not go to see an all Negro picture unless it has some unusual merit."[6] White was a pragmatist, and he recognized filmmaking as a business. He knew that the studios were motivated primarily by profit, and he worried that poor box office returns could jeopardize his efforts. His attitude also reflects the integrationist philosophy of the NAACP: motion pictures should reflect the integrated society for which the association strived. In this society African Americans would be accepted as equals and would live and work alongside whites.

Much of the philosophy behind the NAACP's cultural campaigns remained the same, but its strategy for tackling motion pictures was beginning to change from the days of *The Birth of a Nation*. As Walter White told a friend, "The problem of the Negro in the cinema is not now so much that of deletion as it is of getting the moving pictures to present the Negro as a normal human being and an integral part of human life and activity."[7] By and large, it moved away from a strategy of censorship toward one of persuasion. White decided that he and his organization stood a better chance of success if they could intervene before and during the production of films, rather than waiting until they were made and having to resort to calls for suppression and cuts.

The most useful studies of Walter White's forays into Hollywood include those by Thomas Cripps, Lauren Sklaroff, and Kenneth Janken. They all explore White's work in the context of the Second World War, explaining that he used this opportunity to call for an improvement in how African Americans were portrayed in the movies. Cripps argues that White saw his film industry work as linked to the wider civil rights struggle. Janken, given his biographical focus on White, goes further in analyzing the NAACP secretary's motivations. White, he argues, was driven in part by his personal ambition; he wanted to be part of the glamour of Hollywood. But he was also fully aware of the power of the movies. However, Janken does not examine the nature of this power. Sklaroff does; she writes that

"White's desire that Hollywood present African Americans more accurately was connected to his larger hopes for the improvement of America's racial psyche." Racially stereotyped depictions affected both white attitudes and black "opportunity." However, as it is not their focus, these scholars do not explore in detail how the secretary and his organization believed movie depictions could help their wider objectives. The aim of this chapter, then, is to put Walter White's campaign in Hollywood into the wider context of the NAACP's philosophy and changing cultural strategy.[8]

The first film that really captured the attention of the NAACP after its fight against *Birth* was *Gone with the Wind* (1939). Walter White was just beginning to turn his attention to the film industry, and, although it was a somewhat halfhearted campaign, it provides examples of the arguments and tactics he would use in subsequent years. When the association heard that Margaret Mitchell's 1936 novel of the same name was to be made into a film, it was apprehensive. Many people had criticized the novel for its sentimental portrayal of the antebellum South and its depiction of freed blacks during Reconstruction. Writing in the *Crisis,* George Schuyler argued that it might be a Pulitzer Prize winner, "but it is just another Rebel propaganda tract to the colored citizen who knows our national history and knows the South." For Schuyler it was "an effective argument against according the Negro his citizenship rights and privileges and sings Hallelujah for white supremacy."[9]

Mitchell challenged some of the romanticism of the Old South (for example, the O'Haras are middle class, not aristocrats in a white-columned house on the plantation, as they would become in Selznick's movie), but nevertheless she left many of the conventions in place, particularly when it came to the issue of race. All the named black characters are loyal black slaves, and they include the usual "Mammy" figure. Mammy is devoted to "her" white family, particularly to the novel's heroine, the wayward and stubborn Miss Scarlett. She is joined by the often hysterical and comically useless Prissy, the stoic Pork, and Big Sam, who at one point in the story saves Scarlett from an attack. These are the faithful blacks who choose the security of the past over the opportunity of freedom after the war. They are the African American characters who "prove" that slavery was a benign institution, who free the North of any responsibility for contemporary race relations, and who show that white southerners know better how the deal with "their Negroes" than northerners. During the Reconstruction section of the novel, there are the usual freed blacks on the rampage, examples of black violence against whites, and attacks on white women, complete with references to the subsequent reprisals of the Ku Klux Klan and lynchings.

The film's makers were well aware that aspects of the novel were offensive to African Americans. David O. Selznick, whose Selznick International produced the film, was worried about potential controversy or black pressure on his picture. No doubt he had seen the reaction of African Americans to *The Birth of a Nation,* some twenty years earlier. In 1937, as he began work on the film, he opened a clerical file labeled "The Negro Problem." Selznick and his screenwriter, Sidney Howard, were particularly concerned about the references to lynchings and the Ku Klux Klan in the novel, albeit relatively minor ones compared to *Birth.* In what may have been a reflection of the NAACP's success in highlighting the issue in the 1930s, Howard wrote that due to "the lynching problems we have on our hands these days, I hate to indulge in anything which makes the lynching of a Negro in any sense sympathetic." Similarly, Selznick feared the KKK's presence in his film might be an "unintentional advertisement for intolerant societies in these fascist-ridden times." These aspects of the story were thus purged from the film.[10] This can be read as a belated success in the NAACP's campaign against *Birth.* Selznick and Howard must have been conscious of the storm stirred up by the association over Griffith's glorification of the Klan and lynching. The NAACP, even if it had not rid Hollywood of them completely, had succeeded in making such images controversial.

With production well under way by the summer of 1938, the NAACP kept a close eye on proceedings. It had been perturbed by the book, but it was extremely worried about the film. For the NAACP the change in medium signaled a change in potential damage. Walter White explained that the "motion picture, appealing as it does to both the visual and auditory senses, reaches so many Americans, particularly of the middle classes, that infinite harm could be done in a critical period like this one when racial hatred and prejudices are so alive."[11] This comment reaffirms the NAACP's concerns over the link between films and racial prejudice. The harmful representations became more "real" and therefore more powerful when they appeared on the screen compared to the book. They were brought to life by light and sound. Moreover, by the end of the 1930s motion pictures reached larger audiences than even the most popular books, so the potential to influence people's attitudes was increased still further. Most telling is White's comment that motion pictures reach the middle classes. There is some debate about which social class dominated cinema audiences during this period, but what can be said is that during the golden era of the motion picture more people than ever before were watching films and that this included people from all classes.[12] Middle-class whites certainly attended the cinema in large numbers during the 1930s and 1940s. This was the group that the NAACP was most concerned about; these were the opinion makers, the influential people who could help either deny or grant equality to African Americans.

The leaders of the NAACP feared that the film version of *Gone with the Wind* would be a "second 'Birth of a Nation,'" the film that remained the touchstone for its attitude toward racist movies. White contacted Selznick to express his concerns. He said that he and his staff had "found among both white and colored Americans a very definite apprehension as to the effect this picture will have" and that this was an apprehension that he shared. White recommended that Selznick "employ in an advisory capacity a person, preferably a Negro, who is qualified to check on possible errors of fact or interpretation" and suggested that his scriptwriter read Du Bois's *Black Reconstruction*. Selznick was quick to distance himself from any potential accusations of racism and "hasten[ed] to assure" the NAACP leader "that as a member of a race that is suffering very keenly from persecution these days, I am most sensitive to the feelings of minority people." (Like many in Hollywood Selznick was Jewish, and White was aware that international events could strengthen his appeal to the Jewish conscience in that climate.) He reassured White that the scriptwriter, Sidney Howard, was "also a very good friend of the colored race" and promised they would heed White's suggestions to read Du Bois's book and hire a black advisor.[13]

White replied to Selznick that his and Howard's connection to the film was "most heartening." Nevertheless, the book was "so essentially superficial and false in its emphases that it will require almost incredible effort to make a film from the novel which would not be both a hurtful and inaccurate picture of the Reconstruction era." The NAACP was not suffering from "racial chauvinism or hypersensitiveness" but rather was interested in "accuracy according to the most rigid standards of historical truth."[14] As with *The Birth of a Nation,* the NAACP worried about the "southern" depiction of historical events. It knew that the distortion of the portrayal of the antebellum period, the Civil War, and Reconstruction was detrimental to the black fight for equality.

It wasn't only the NAACP that was concerned about the movie during production; the filmmakers faced criticism from all quarters of the black community, with the black press particularly vehement. Members of the public, too, were increasingly perturbed by the rumors they heard coming out of Hollywood. By February 1939 the studio had received hundreds of letters demanding that the producer shelve the project. The pressure from the black community, or at least a fear of controversy, did lead to Selznick removing some of the most offensive elements from the movie. Thomas Cripps suggests that the film version of *Gone with the Wind* "had been stirred by [the] winds of racial change." The increased visibility of African Americans in public life, the atmosphere of reform created by Roosevelt's New Deal, and events in Europe had a liberalizing effect on Selznick and his production. However, just as these "winds" were little more than gentle breezes, so the film was racially liberal only to a degree.[15]

The debate between Joseph Breen of the Production Code Administration (PCA) and the studio over the use of the epithet "nigger" is a case in point. The PCA, established in 1934, was the means through which the Motion Pictures Producers Association (MPPA), also known as the Hays Office (after its first head, Will H. Hays, who took office in 1922), implemented its Production Code. As in earlier decades, the movie industry was still practicing self-censorship as a way to ward off governmental interference, but it was now more organized and effective. (However, as demonstrated below, filmmakers often tried to ignore the code's guidelines or pushed the limits of what would be accepted.) Breen had advised Selznick to remove "nigger" from the script as early as 1937. He wrote to "urge and recommend that you have none of the white characters refer to the darkies as 'niggers.'" Initially Breen thought it would be acceptable if black characters used the term, but he later changed his mind and decided the term should be removed altogether. The letter ably demonstrates the limits of white liberal attitudes toward race in the film industry: while balking at "niggers," Breen clearly thought the term "darkies" was acceptable. Selznick argued for the epithet to remain, suggesting it provided "historical accuracy" and arguing that it would not be offensive if it was used by "the better Negroes" in the film. When they started filming it was still in the script. It was only after uproar in the black press and when Selznick's story editor, whom he had instructed to consult with local African American leaders, had informed him "they resent it as they resent no other word" that he agreed for it to be cut from the script.[16] Selznick was motivated by commercial considerations; he did not want any controversy to damage the potential profit of his movie. The NAACP might have preferred filmmakers to be motivated by a sense of moral duty or racial justice, but in reality it was satisfied if any considerations led to improvements in depictions of the race.

When the film was released at the end of 1939, it received mixed reviews in the black press. While there was some praise for Hattie Mc-Daniel's Oscar-winning performance—the *California Eagle* praised her "brilliant work"—many were critical of the film as a whole. Melvin Tolson of the *Washington Tribune* said it was "more dangerous than 'The Birth of a Nation'" because *Birth* was "such a barefaced lie that a moron could see through it . . . [but] 'Gone With the Wind' is such a subtle lie that it will be swallowed as truth by millions of whites and blacks alike." Du Bois, meanwhile, waved it aside, arguing that while the 1915 film had been "a cruel libel," *Gone with the Wind* was only "conventional provincialism about which Negroes need not get excited." A review in the *Chicago Defender* was more damning, criticizing its historical distortions. It claimed the film "has lied about the Civil War period shamelessly" and "has glorified slavery."[17]

In contrast to this condemnation, the NAACP's reaction to the finished film was strangely muted. Roy Wilkins's review appeared in the January 1940 edition of the *Crisis*. According to the editor, anyone who read the novel "had reason to be apprehensive over the making of a moving picture from it. The novel contained much objectionable material on Negroes and sought to show that the colored people would have been better off as slaves and were totally unfit to be citizens." Wilkins reassured his readers that "happily" the film "eliminates practically all the offensive scenes and dialogue so that there is little material, directly affecting Negroes as a race, to which objection can be entered." He warns that there "are two or three uses of the word 'darky' which may make some spectators wince," as well as "a fleeting scene of carpetbaggers and Negroes." Furthermore, "there is the emphasis upon the devotion and faithfulness (to white folks) of the 'Uncle Tom' servant type." But "the inflammable dialogue in the novel has been omitted."[18] He told the secretary of the NAACP's Brooklyn branch there was "very little direct anti-Negro material" in the film, compared to the book. He conceded that "the whole theme glorifying the South's civilization under slavery and the South's point of view in the Civil War is one with which Negroes cannot agree" but concluded that "there is no good reason why we should advise colored people not to go to see the picture."[19]

Wilkins's review seemed to miss the point about what made a film offensive; it was not a question of racial epithets but rather of the message it sent out and the characters it included that could damage opinions about the race. His comments demonstrate that he was aware of the racist ideology that underpinned *Gone with the Wind*—he complains about its racist "theme"—but he appears to have been appeased by Selznick's small improvements. The producer had launched a public relations campaign, wooing black leaders and journalists, and it seems to have worked on the NAACP. Perhaps the association felt that because some concessions had been made, it was not able to continue complaining.

Walter White could not remain entirely silent on the matter of Selznick's film. A few months after its release he wrote to the producer, informing him that the success of his film had led to a revival of *The Birth of a Nation* and that "out of this revival and other situations has come an alarming recrudescence of the Ku Klux Klan." He repeated reports that some white southern women who had previously been supporters of federal antilynching legislation had turned against it and embraced "the Confederate and anti-Yankee spirit" after seeing *Gone with the Wind.* In reply Selznick expressed his horror at such reports and again pledged his support for the black cause, offering to join the NAACP and make an annual donation.[20]

Other than this exchange, however, the association did little to challenge the film upon its release. For an organization that had been and would continue to be so sensitive about racial representations in movies, the halfhearted response to *Gone with the Wind* was surprising. Leonard Leff suggests that its indifference "probably derived from a combination of White's general apathy toward American film and his organization's inability to incorporate Hollywood into its agenda of legal-judicial reform." The NAACP was "ill-suited to affect movies at their source and weary from two decades of pursuing its bête noire, *The Birth of a Nation.*"[21] There are elements of truth in this; certainly it had learned a hard lesson from the relatively ineffective campaign against Griffith's film, and it realized that once a motion picture had been released, it was very difficult to do much about it. However, the NAACP *was* able to incorporate a concern with popular culture into its "agenda of legal-judicial reform." Admittedly, when it came to Hollywood it was still finding its feet. It had not yet found a strategy for tackling films at their source, but the ever-resourceful and determined White (who was not apathetic about film, but rather deeply concerned and interested) was beginning to sense the time was right for action.

Indeed, White was, in 1939, on the cusp of launching a concerted effort to lobby Hollywood and persuade it to improve its depiction of Af-

rican Americans. He was both prompted and assisted by world events
The outbreak of the Second World War and America's subsequent involvement opened up opportunities for change in race relations. The country
was fighting a war for what Roosevelt called the "Four Freedoms," yet
the fact that some of its own citizens were denied such freedoms had become embarrassingly obvious to both America and its enemies. African
Americans were quick to realize that the changing climate might offer an
opportunity to press for improvements in the treatment of the race. Many
got behind the *Pittsburgh Courier*'s "Double Victory" campaign, which
called for freedom at home as well as abroad. A. Phillip Randolph established the March on Washington Movement and with other black leaders
was able to pressure Roosevelt into issuing Executive Order 8802, which
established the Fair Employment Practices Commission and called for an
end to discrimination in the defense industries. Although in many ways
this turned out to be a disappointing compromise, the successful forcing of
the president's hand demonstrated the level of governmental concern over
the potential disruption of racial conflict.

The government knew it needed to keep all sections of American society behind the war effort, and it established a number of agencies whose
job was to improve morale and to "sell" the war to the public. The Office of War Information (OWI) was the leader in this propaganda effort.
The OWI had a somewhat confusing bureaucratic history. It had its beginnings in the Office of Government Reports, which was formed in 1939 and
headed by Lowell Mellett. A number of other government propaganda and
information agencies existed at this time, and to simplify the situation the
Office of Facts and Figures (OFF) was established in 1941, with Archibald
MacLeish in charge. Mellett became coordinator of government films, and
in April 1942 he set up a Hollywood office, headed by Nelson Poynter, to
liaise with the film industry on the West Coast. When the Office of War
Information was created in June 1942, with radio presenter Elmer Davis
at its head, Mellett's film liaison office became the Bureau of Motion Pictures (BMP). The BMP's responsibilities included releasing government
shorts, and Poynter's office continued to be the main point of contact with
Hollywood.

As the creation of Mellett's bureau indicates, considerable emphasis
was placed on the role films could play in the process of selling the war to
the American people. President Roosevelt called the motion picture "one
of our most effective media in informing and entertaining our citizens"
and declared that it could make a "very useful contribution" to the war ef-

fort. The BMP attempted to persuade the film industry to use its movies to help secure an Allied victory. The OWI-produced handbook "Government Information Manual for the Motion Picture Industry" asked filmmakers to consider this central question: "Will this picture help win the war?" The OWI acted in an advisory role, with most studios passing their scripts to Poynter's office before they went into production. Poynter could then ask the studios to change aspects of a film he and his staff found unsuitable, or he could offer suggestions for how it could help "win the war." The government shared the NAACP's utilitarian approach toward motion pictures. It was a case of persuasion rather than coercion, as there was no federal censorship of the movies, and the OWI had no powers to force Hollywood to comply. Hollywood resented outside interference and was wary of being accused of making propaganda films. However, the OWI's links to the state censors and overseas distribution agencies gave it some leverage. This, combined with a degree of patriotic and ideological belief in the war among studio executives and screenwriters, allowed the OWI some influence over the films of the period.[22]

The government was particularly conscious of the need to "sell" the war to African Americans. A poll taken by a government agency produced "formidable evidence of the degree to which racial grievances have kept Negroes from an all-out participation in the war effort." The government feared the potentially damaging effects of such resentment, so the Office of War Information became increasingly concerned with the portrayal of African Americans in films. A study by the Bureau of Motion Pictures in 1943 of the depiction of blacks in wartime movies concluded that, "in general, Negroes are presented as basically different from other people, as taking no relevant part in the life of the nation, as offering nothing, contributing nothing, expecting nothing." African Americans appeared in 23 percent of the films released in 1942 and early 1943 and were shown as "clearly inferior" in 82 percent of them. The government realized that the negative images of blacks in movies were damaging to morale and therefore potentially damaging to the war effort. Through these agencies, it put pressure on Hollywood to make films that would at the very least refrain from antagonizing blacks and, if possible, to go some way toward improving morale.[23]

The NAACP hoped to use the establishment of these agencies to its advantage. Roy Wilkins attended a conference held by the OFF in 1942, in which the participants discussed how to "build up the morale" of African Americans "to full and enthusiastic support of the war effort." Wilkins explained that it was white attitudes, rather than black, that needed changing; white Americans needed to see and treat their black compatriots in a more equal manner. He argued that "the primary job in improving the condition of the Negro as a citizen is the changing of the dominant white public opinion. Much of this opinion is not hostile, but is uninformed, or has been influenced by stereotyped treatment of the Negro." He "made several suggestions as to how the OFF might attack the problem of influencing white public opinion through the use of the radio, the films, newspapers and magazines, and speeches by government officials." Wilkins was optimistic that there were allies within the OFF and that "a goodly percentage of men" are "'straight' on the chief aspects of the Negro minority problem." He suggested that "the NAACP be as helpful as possible to the OFF in working out a procedure that will be mutually helpful to the country and to our race." Certainly during his dealings with Hollywood, Walter White consistently tried to use the influence of these government agencies to press his own program. He was in regular contact with Lowell Mellett and Nelson Poynter and their colleagues. White was aware of the unique opportunity that the war presented for the NAACP's campaign to change representations of the race. President Roosevelt had overseen the expansion of government during the New Deal and the war, and there existed legislative channels—of the kind favored by the NAACP—into areas of life previously outside the remit of the government. The association tried to exploit these channels to advance the black cause.[24]

White had been concerned about the portrayal of African Americans in motion pictures and frustrated with the NAACP's lack of action for some time. He had been to the West Coast on NAACP duty many times, and during some of these trips, including a speaking tour in support of the Gavagan antilynching bill in 1937, he had visited the studio lots.[25] During a four-week tour of the West Coast in 1940, he was invited to a lunch hosted by film producer Walter Wanger, where he discussed his concerns about the film industry with studio executives. But these were little more than brief distractions. This hiatus suggests that while the NAACP was consistently interested in culture, its priorities and focus changed over time. By 1941 White was convinced that the NAACP needed to take decisive action on what he saw as an important issue. He was frustrated because the "terrific pressure of issues that had to be handled immediately more than monopolized the time and energy of the staff," and therefore the campaign against the portrayal of blacks had been fought "more or less spasmodically." The time, he decided, had come for a "relentless campaign."[26]

In order to launch such a campaign, White needed some way to infiltrate the film industry; he needed someone who shared his concerns and could reach powerful industry leaders. His ally came in the form of the former presidential candidate and chairman of the board of Twentieth-Century Fox, Wendell Willkie. In 1941 Willkie represented the "big eight" studios during the Senate investigation into propaganda in the motion picture industry. He was a man with considerable influence in both political and industry circles, and he was sympathetic to White's concerns. During a lunch between the two men toward the end of that year, Willkie admitted to White that he "ought to have a tiny bit of influence right now . . . with the motion picture people" and suggested that they "go out to Hollywood and talk with the more intelligent people in the industry and see what can be done."[27] White did not need to be asked twice.

In February 1942 the NAACP's executive secretary headed to the West Coast, armed with a letter of introduction from the First Lady. His "mission," according to Eleanor Roosevelt, was "to see producers and others, in the effort to have broadened the roles in which Negroes are presented in the moving pictures." The trip was a rush of meetings and dinners, most of which were spent establishing initial contacts and planning the arrangements for a subsequent visit. To begin with he spent most of his time lunching with actors, including "Jimmy" Cagney, who held a lunch for him at MGM, Melvyn Douglas, and Jean Muir. He recognized, however, that the actors had little power, and as he admitted to Roy Wilkins, it was the "producers we've got to crack." "The movie job moves but so slowly," he complained. "The movie moguls are just beginning to become dimly aware that war, anti-Semitism and world collapse affect Hollywood too." White knew that he had to seize the opportunity provided by the war and convince the studios that change was necessary for the greater good.[28]

The breakthrough came on his last "feverish" day, when, as he recounted to his friend Sara Boynoff of the *Los Angeles Daily News,* he was summoned by Willkie to the Biltmore hotel to meet with Walter Wanger, producer Darryl Zanuck, and "several others whose names I did not get in the excitement." Willkie told the group White "had a legitimate complaint against the movies which had to be met." An initial proposal by White's former correspondent David Selznick was for the NAACP to pay for someone to work with the Hays Office to read all the scripts that included black characters. However, White said, "this didn't strike them, or me, as being too effective."[29] White's doubts reflected the change in the NAACP strategy toward motion pictures; it wanted inclusion rather than censorship. From the filmmakers' point of view, their objection reflected a distrust of the Hays Office and its attempts at censorship.

White felt his initial visit had at least succeeded in raising awareness of the problem. He boasted that during the meeting Zanuck "marched up and down puffing a cigar and stopped to declaim, 'I make one-sixth of the pictures made in Hollywood and I never thought of this until you presented the facts.'" White reported back to the NAACP Board of Directors that he had "conferred in Hollywood with a number of leading producers, directors, actors and actresses regarding the harmful effects of limitation of the Negro to comic or menial roles in moving pictures." In reality, very little had been achieved aside from a few lunches and some cautious comments of support by a few executives. But this was how White operated: he hoped to charm and cajole the industry into implementing changes, and he believed he had used these initial meetings to lay the groundwork for subsequent lobbying. This, of course, highlights the weakness in White's strategy. He could do little more than try to *persuade* the white film industry to change.[30]

White returned to Hollywood in July, and again his itinerary primarily consisted of a series of lunches, dinners, and parties, including the Academy Awards dinner as Willkie's guest. The high point was a lunch on July 18 given in White's and Willkie's honor by Darryl Zanuck and Walter Wanger at the Café de Paris restaurant on the Twentieth-Century Fox studio lot. Among the seventy-plus guests were William Goetz of Twentieth-Century Fox; David Selznick; Will H. Hays, head of the MPPA; E. J. Mannix, head of MGM; scriptwriter Marc Connelly; Frank Capra; and representatives from Paramount, Universal, Warner Brothers, and the Screen Actors Guild. White told his audience he "did not expect Negroes to be treated always as heroes" and reassured them that "Negroes wanted no propaganda films, because propaganda is self-defeating," and that "they did not ask motion picture companies to lose money to satisfy a minority because to remain in business the companies had to make pictures that will sell." White's pronouncement might signal a change in attitude from the 1930s, when White used art as propaganda in his antilynching campaign, and the 1920s, when he wrote his own propaganda novels. Certainly by 1942, propaganda, already a loaded issue, had been discredited by its association with the totalitarian regimes in Europe. However, it was not entirely true that White wanted no propaganda in motion pictures. Ideally, he wanted films to show blacks in the best possible light. Nevertheless, he would settle for films that at least stopped portraying African Americans in a derogatory manner. Moreover, White knew that he had to get these businessmen on his side by remaining reasonable. He did not want to be accused of oversensitivity, nor did he wish to make unrealistic demands of the industry. He did, however, tell them, in no uncertain terms, that the stereotypical images of African Americans in their films were harmful, that they damaged black morale and made the race the object of ridicule and abuse. The allusion to morale was not coincidental: White deliberately echoed wartime rhetoric to strengthen his argument. He believed his message had hit home and returned to the East Coast confidently declaring, "Negroes will hereafter no longer be restricted to comic or menial roles in motion pictures."[31]

The NAACP celebrated what it saw as the positive response of industry leaders, who gave "assurances that Negroes will be given roles more in keeping with their normal place in American life." Its press release quoted Fred Beeston, vice president of the Motion Picture Producers Association, who felt "every producer who was at the meeting was greatly impressed and will undoubtedly find ways and means of helping to put into effect some of the suggestions offered," and Al Lichtman of MGM, who promised he was "thoroughly in accord with the efforts being made for the Negroes" and would "do my utmost in whatever way I can in helping this cause. I think the program is a very intelligent one."[32] However, these comments amounted to little more than vague support for the principles of fairer representation, rather than concrete plans for radical change.

A letter from Eddie Mannix at MGM typified the view of many executives, who were happy to support vague notions of improvements but were suspicious of any interference. He recognized that what White was "actually asking for is that Negroes be used in motion pictures in the same manner in which they occupy positions in life" and promised he had "committed [himself] to this program." However, in a later meeting with White he claimed to have extracted a promise that the NAACP would not push for a black member of the Production Code Administration or for anything else that "might be misunderstood as pertaining to censorship, which might retard rather than advance this desirable program." White apparently said, "It would be much better to leave the whole matter to the responsibility of the individual studios."[33] White had learned from the fight against *Birth* that censorship was a tricky issue, and he wanted to keep the studios on his side.

Mannix was not the only one who tried to discourage White from interfering too deeply. Joseph Breen wrote to tell him about a letter Zanuck had written "to a number of the important people in the studios hereabouts, as a kind of follow-up to your visit." Zanuck "expressed himself in pretty plain language," and Breen was "certain that his letter made a profound impression on all who received it." Therefore, argued the PCA head, "I think it would be best to let the situation stand as it is now. I do not think it is necessary for you to press the matter further."[34] The movie producers were happy to listen to White's ideas over a long lunch and to make noises of encouragement, but they did not want to commit themselves to any radical changes in their industry. Nor did they want this outsider to meddle too deeply with their work. They were already feeling the pressure from the government's wartime agencies; they did not need pressure from elsewhere.

White himself recognized that he faced a difficult task. He knew there were not going to be any overnight conversions to his cause among studio executives. He was "certain that the stereotypes about the Negro are so indelibly fixed in their minds, as well as a lot of other American white people, that it is going to take a very long time to eradicate them." White was all too aware how pervasive and powerful stereotypes of the race were, and he recognized that he would have to change the film industry's attitude toward African Americans before he could expect any improvements. Nevertheless, he was able to build up relationships with executives such as Walter Wanger, Daryl Zanuck, and David Selznick and studios like Twentieth-Century Fox and MGM, who were sympathetic to his arguments. A number of White's allies in Hollywood were Jewish. There is a long and complex history of the relationship between blacks and Jews, but the historical position of Jews as outsiders in America and, even more pertinently, the contemporary persecution of their people by America's enemies made many sympathetic to black causes. White appealed to the common bond between the two oppressed groups and was able to get a number of studio heads and executives on his side.[35]

The first test of White's strategy came within weeks of his July 1942 visit, in the shape of the controversy over *Tennessee Johnson* (1942). Originally to be called *The Man on America's Conscience,* the film was a biopic of President Andrew Johnson. It was an attempt to restore Johnson's damaged reputation, and, even more controversially from an African American point of view, it depicted the man whom many saw as a champion of the race, Congressman Thaddeus Stevens, as a "heavy." It was David Platt in the Communist *Daily Worker* who first started the campaign against the film. Walter White was sent a clipping from the newspaper, and, given his recent pronouncements about his work in Hollywood, he was forced to act. The film actually included very few black characters, which was problematic in itself, given the historical context of the story. Therefore it was the portrayal of Stevens, and the glorifying of Johnson, that became contentious. On hearing of the film, the NAACP leadership must have had flashbacks of *The Birth of a Nation.* Yet again, white Hollywood was intent on besmirching the achievements of Reconstruction.[36]

White wrote to Louis Mayer, head of MGM, enclosing the newspaper reports and asking to see the script in order that he might judge for himself whether there was any cause for concern. Mayer replied, all patronizing flattery, that White's request to see the script before issuing a statement shows the "fine man and character that I believed you to be." He claimed he could not be "anti-negro" and invited White out to Hollywood to view the footage himself. In the meantime it seemed White had already got hold of the script, possibly from Nelson Poynter at the Hollywood office of the BMP. In an example of the many occasions in which White liaised with the government agency, he wrote to Mellett, head of the bureau, expressing his concern: "I regret to say that I strongly believe that the making of this picture at this time would do enormous injury to morale." "The treatment," he complained, "is historically biased to the point of gross inaccuracy," and Thaddeus Stevens is made to look "like a vulture." White suggested that "MGM could find infinitely more pertinent and valuable films to make, especially during the war period, to which it might devote its great machinery and talent." White was always careful when appealing to the BMP to place his organization's concerns within the wider discourse of the war.[37]

On the surface Mayer and his colleagues appeared to tolerate White's interference. Howard Dietz, MGM's head publicist, invited White to view the film so he could see for himself that his "apprehensions were needless." However, correspondence from Poynter indicated a less patient stance within the studio. Poynter reported that the "management of MGM is completely upset because it feels the agitation of the negroes over the picture is directly a result of the communists." MGM had asked his office, "Shall a minority in the country dictate what shall or shall not be on the screen through the Mellet Office?" The studio knew it would have an easier job dismissing complaints if it could link them to Communist agitation. Walter White no doubt could have done without what he considered the "interference" of David Platt and his comrades. As the NAACP would see even more clearly later in the decade, the issue of Communism and race in Hollywood would prove a tricky course to navigate.[38]

Despite Mayer's complaints, pressure on the studio resulted in some changes to the motion picture. Critics of the film had objected to the portrayal of Stevens, in particular scenes in which he was shown to be a gambler, a conspirator in Lincoln's murder, and the cause of Johnson's drunkenness. These scenes were cut, and the character of Stevens was "softened." The Bureau of Motion Pictures was evidently satisfied with the final product. Mellett was quoted as calling it "a forceful, dramatic exposition of the development of democratic government in this country. I believe that so far as it has any effect on popular thinking it will cause a better understanding of what it is that makes American democracy work." White, however, was not so convinced. He was "still puzzled" by the revised version. "The motion picture industry," he told Dietz, "has unwittingly become so conditioned in the treatment of the Civil War and the Reconstruction Period that it appears impossible for it to make a picture except from the Southern point of view."[39]

The NAACP had been battling Hollywood's "Southern point of view" for almost thirty years. This fight had usually taken the form of protests against finished films, but in 1942 Walter White believed there might be a chance to offer an alternative on the big screen. He wrote to author Philip Van Doren Stern about his "amicable controversy" with MGM over *Tennessee Johnson*. He told Stern about a conversation he'd had with Howard Dietz, in which he told the MGM man that "the South had completely won the Civil War, so far as Hollywood is concerned." According to White, "No Hollywood producer had the guts to make a film showing the northern side of the war," and "the Gone with the Winds completely dominated cinematic treatment of the Civil War and the Reconstruction period." Stern had been trying to find backing for a movie of his novel about the abolitionist movement and the ensuing Civil War, *The Drums of Morning* (published in 1942). The book was hailed by reviewers as a "reply" to *Gone with the Wind*. Stern's sympathetic, even celebratory, portrayal of the emancipation of African Americans and the important role of historical figures such as Frederick Douglass offered an antidote to American culture's vilifying of African American freedom and northern motivation during Reconstruction. As White explained to Stern's publisher, what was really needed was an "affirmative treatment which would show that there were people in the north who fought against slavery because they were morally convinced of the evil of the system."[40]

White mentioned the book to Dietz, who asked him to read it and send him a memorandum recommending it be made into a film if appropriate.

White boasted to Stern that Dietz told him "because of the trip Mr Willkie and I made to Hollywood in July, any recommendation that I made right now might have some effect." However, despite White's usual optimism, nothing came of his proposal. Projects such as these, while humored, were unlikely to be taken seriously by Hollywood. A motion picture of *Drums of Morning* might be noble, but if it wouldn't turn a profit, then Hollywood wasn't interested. Although White's plans for an alternative film were never realized, the NAACP remained positive about the *Tennessee Johnson* incident. It claimed MGM "had to remake a great part of the picture" and change the title because of White's protests. Thomas Cripps argues that, while the changes might have been slight, the film marked the "first victory" of the alliance of "government, liberals, and a racial minority." White was able to use the BMP and wartime rhetoric to put pressure on the studio. He cleverly couched his arguments in the language of the war effort. He knew how worried government officials were about racial antagonism and that they would transfer this concern to Hollywood. Furthermore, there were liberals in Hollywood who were sympathetic to the broader arguments about the war and were willing to translate some of them into motion pictures. The changes may have been small, but for the NAACP they were significant: Walter White's strategy, it seemed, was working.[41]

There were a number of films during the war that gave White cause for satisfaction and that he, at least, felt proved that his intervention was having an effect. These included three war films, all released in 1943, that featured African Americans in uniform: *Crash Dive* (Twentieth-Century Fox), *Bataan* (MGM), and *Sahara* (Columbia Pictures). The film that pleased White most was *Crash Dive*. It featured black actor Ben Carter as Oliver Cromwell Jones, a submarine crew member. Jones is one of the volunteers in a dangerous mission to land on a Nazi-controlled island. He fights bravely and is one of the last to return to the submarine. When the vessel returns to the port and the cheering crowds, Jones is standing up top alongside the film's two white stars. It is easy to see why White got excited about such a movie: the black character is treated in a nonpatronizing way and is shown making a brave contribution to the fighting. There is virtually no mention made of race, apart from a comic aside when the landing party are "blacking-up" their faces as camouflage, and Jones jokes that he is "the only torn commando here." White believed that the film was a result of his and Willkie's lobbying of the film industry, writing "that if nothing else comes out of our two trips to Hollywood the time and money were well spent. . . . I believe the film is going to do a lot of good."[42] *Crash Dive* was produced by Daryl Zanuck, who was the Hollywood insider most sympathetic to White's arguments. White believed that the film was an indication that Zanuck and his colleagues had responded once he highlighted to them the issue of racial representation in the movies.

White might have taken credit for the racial liberalism of *Crash Dive,* but there is little to suggest he had any direct influence over the film. With *Bataan,* however, it seems he was able to intervene. There were reports that the studio heeded his demands that a black character remain in the picture, after rumors reached him that the role was to be dropped. The film tells the story of a small patrol bravely holding up the Japanese advancement in the Philippines. The patrol includes a black soldier, Wesley Epps, played by Kenneth Spencer. Epps dies as heroic a death as any of his white comrades. It was certainly a breakthrough role: a black man dying for his country. However, some of the old stereotypes remain. Epps is training to be a preacher, and it is he who is called upon to pray over the bodies of the fallen soldiers. In many of his scenes he is in a state of semi-undress, with his upper torso exposed. Admittedly it is hot in the Pacific but Epps is the only character who is half naked, and there are echoes of savage-in-the-jungle imagery. These factors, combined with a relative lack of dialogue, subtly serve to make the character less developed and less dignified than his white counterparts. The NAACP, however, either did not see or chose to ignore these deficiencies. It endorsed the film, and White provided a blurb to be used in the production's publicity. He said that the movie "shows how superfluous racial and religious prejudice are when common danger is faced" and implored, "May we learn, too, how dangerous and divisive prejudices are before we lose here the liberty fighting men died for on Bataan." In this statement White brought out the message of unity, especially racial unity, within the film and used it to highlight the contradiction between America's war efforts and the situation at home. This was something at which White and his colleagues were highly skilled; they never missed an opportunity to hammer home their message.[43]

In the final film, *Sahara,* the black actor Rex Ingram plays a British Sudanese sergeant who joins Humphrey Bogart's ragtag patrol laying siege to the Germans in the desert. The only racism Sergeant Tambul faces is from the Nazi prisoner, thus equating racism exclusively with Nazism. He is a valuable member of the crew because he can direct them to a waterhole and is respected by the rest of the men. His death is one of the most dramatic and heroic in the film: he chases and kills the escaping German prisoner before being shot himself. Such an image of black heroism was unusual for films of the period. However, it is worth noting that Tambul was an African British, not an African American, character. Therefore *Sahara* was saluting Africa's role in the war, rather than making a comment on African American sacrifices. Again, the NAACP chose to see the film within its campaign for better black characters. It commended Columbia Pictures for Ingram's role, declaring it an "outstanding contribution" toward the objective of improving roles for blacks.[44]

It is not difficult to see why the NAACP praised these three films. They all depict a heroic black character, and this in itself represented a significant break from the stereotypes that so angered the organization. The black man was not a servant or a fool but rather a uniformed member of the armed services making a great sacrifice, sometimes the ultimate sacrifice, for the Allied cause. Looking back, there were discordant notes in these productions. In these films men of all races fight and die alongside one another when in reality segregation meant that the armed services were divided along racial lines. Hollywood was not about to make all-black war films; after all, Hollywood did not believe there was an audience for such a thing, and anyway, they might have argued, were they not making a greater contribution to morale by showing racial harmony? If there were to be any black faces in war films, they would have to appear in historically inaccurate interracial groups. Equally unrealistic was the fact that these groups were pictures of racial harmony. There were no examples of the overt racism that existed in the army. It would not be until 1949's *Home of the Brave* that the impact of racial discrimination on black soldiers would be openly discussed by Hollywood. Furthermore, none of the black characters in these films demanded anything from their country in return for their sacrifices. There was no mention of a "Double Victory," no calls for fairer treatment of troops or equality back home. They were seemingly content to fight and even die for a country that denied them equality. The NAACP, however, while it lobbied for changes to the treatment of black servicemen and servicewomen, was not concerned about these failings in the films. It wanted the fair representation of African Americans and was pleased that at least these movies showed blacks as citizens who participated in the war effort and proved their equality, even if they did not demand it. Nevertheless, it did subtly try to use the productions to reinforce its larger message about the double standards of the war. The statement from White above, in response to *Bataan,* is one example of the NAACP linking the films to the principles of racial equality. He and his colleagues constantly reinforced the message that African Americans were essential to the war effort and that in return for their considerable contribution they must be granted full citizenship.

These films indicate that Hollywood was a least making an effort to include black characters in its depiction of the war effort. Not all its attempts, however, met with the NAACP's approval. Canada Lee's role as Joe Spencer in *Lifeboat* (1944) was a disappointment to the association. Spencer was a steward—a historically accurate portrayal, as this was the only position blacks were allowed to fill in the navy in the first years of the war—among a group of survivors drifting on a lifeboat after their ship has been sunk by the Nazis. The character is sulky and remains distant from the rest of the group. The "role was a sop, a weak gesture. Absolutely the best that can be said is that it represents some slight departure from the harsher techniques of the conventional stereotypes," an NAACP staff member complained. "[Spencer] spoke generally only when spoken to, behaving generally after the manner of a steerage passenger rather than an equally beset participant in a grim struggle for survival." Roy Wilkins, in place of White, who was in Europe investigating the experience of black soldiers, wrote to the vice president of Fox to express the NAACP's "disappointment" in the production. Although it did not seem to take much to please the organization, it could not always be appeased by the mere presence of a black face. The executives at Fox were clearly disgruntled by the NAACP's criticism. Jason Joy replied that he was "very much surprised" at Wilkins's "expressed disappointment of the manner in which Negroes have been used in pictures by our company." He contended that "if Mr Walter White were here, he would substantiate our feeling that we have made a commendable effort to use Negroes in a normal manner, without attempting to exaggerate or minimize their presence." He went on to assert that since White's visit in 1942 Fox had used "approximately fifty Negroes in pictures." This exchange indicated the difference in expectations between the studios and the NAACP: Hollywood thought that any black face was an improvement, whereas the association hoped for characters that showed the best elements of the black war effort.[45]

*Lifeboat* represented Hollywood's liberal intentions, even if they were sometimes misplaced when it came to the issue of race. The same could not be said for Warner Brothers' cartoon short *Coal Black and de Sebben Dwarfs* (1943). It retold the story of Snow White using black characters, complete with jive-talking dialogue and bluesy song and dance numbers. The leading lady is a buxom, sexy diva; Prince Chawmin' a zoot-suit-wearing playboy; and, perhaps most offensively of all, the seven dwarves are black soldiers in uniform. White wrote to Harry Warner, quoting a report by NAACP staff member Julia Baxter, who complained that the cartoon "is a decided caricature of Negro life and an insult to the race." She asserted that the "segregation and indignities to which colored soldiers are subjected is in itself damaging to national unity. That they should also be held up for derision by theater-goers is inexcusable." The NAACP issued a press release calling for its withdrawal but did not take the protests any further. It was, probably wisely, unwilling to get into a battle over a short cartoon.[46]

From the NAACP's perspective the picture coming out of Hollywood was mixed: there were promising signs but still plenty of the old stereotypes. In fact, it was a government-made film that really got the NAACP excited about the depiction of African Americans in uniform. As well as monitoring Hollywood, the Office of War Information also commissioned and oversaw the production of films. It commissioned Frank Capra's *Why We Fight* series, which was shown to all American soldiers with the intention of explaining American involvement in the war. One film in this series was *The Negro Soldier* (1944), a documentary about the black contribution to American wars. Using a mixture of newsreel footage, reconstructions, and staged scenes, the film provided a unique picture of blacks in American conflicts, from the Revolution through the Civil War and the First World War up to the present conflict. It was the first time that black men and women in uniform had appeared on the screen in such numbers. They were shown in training, on the battlefield, with airplanes, and on ships. Originally produced as a training film to improve racial harmony within the services, after pressure from black organizations it was distributed in public theaters. Langston Hughes called it "the most remarkable Negro film ever flashed on an American screen." *The Negro Soldier* unquestionably provided the most positive depictions of African Americans during the war. Its positive message was embraced by most of the servicemen who watched its preview. The majority of the preview audience (which was composed of 439 black and 510 white soldiers) praised the film. Only 3 percent of blacks felt it was untrue, and only 4 percent of whites agreed.[47]

The NAACP was proactive in its support for the film. White called it "an extraordinary documentary picture which will do much to stimulate the morale of American Negroes and to educate white Americans regarding Negroes." The association supported the War Department in a legal case brought against the film. The production company Negro Marches On Inc. complained that the War Department's release of *The Negro Soldier* to commercial cinemas was an act of direct competition to private enter-prise. Jack Goldberg, the president of Negro Marches On, was worried that it would take away the potential audience for his film, *We've Come a Long, Long Way,* which dealt with similar material. The NAACP criticized his production as an "insult" to the race and filed *amicus curiae* for the War Department. "The effect of motion pictures on social attitudes is well-recognized," the NAACP brief explained, and the "substantial participation in the war program of Negro Americans has been minimized in the press and in the news reels." Therefore "a valid documentary picture such as 'The Negro Soldier,' made and sponsored by the government and offered to motion picture theaters without charge, should be given the widest circulation in the public interest." The result of the case was a settlement that allowed Goldberg's film a few days to run before *The Negro Soldier* was released.[48]

The NAACP was clearly thrilled with the film. It hoped the production would teach white America about the historical contribution of blacks to America and prove that they continued to play a role in the country's war effort. To the NAACP the production presented irrefutable proof that African Americans deserved their civil rights. However, while the NAACP might have hoped that the film would be interpreted as a call for racial advancement, in fact the overriding message was one of maintaining the status quo. *The Negro Soldier* presented a picture of the armed services based on the doctrine of separate but equal, in which African Americans were given the same level of training and opportunities as their white contemporaries. The reality, however, was a collection of marginalized black units that faced prejudice from army officials, were given inadequate training and restricted opportunities for promotion, and for the most part were limited, at least until 1944, to service or labor duties. The NAACP was all too aware of this state of affairs. It had investigated conditions in training camps in the South and instances of violence against black soldiers. In 1944 Walter White traveled to the European, North African, and, the following year, Pacific theaters of war to see for himself the experience of African Americans in the armed services. In his 1945 book, *A Rising Wind,* he reported on black troops' resentment at the separate and unequal facilities and the discriminatory treatment. Those black soldiers at a preview screening of *Negro Soldier* who felt the film was untrue thought that it "over-glamorized the treatment they received in the Army and their role in it." The filmmakers' intention when making the film was to improve black morale and to ensure blacks supported the war. Therefore they stressed harmony rather than acknowledging potentially divisive racial grievances.

The government's agenda was to further the war effort, not to promote racial advancement.[49]

Those same limitations can be seen when studying race and radio. Barbara Savage explains that the War Department and the OWI "wanted to build up black morale by integrating a more visible 'Negro' into the public sphere of patriotic rhetoric, but they did not want to endorse the racial reforms blacks sought for fear of offending whites." Nevertheless, as Savage has shown, the war offered opportunities for educational and social programming, and African Americans, fully aware of the power of the medium, took advantage of the chance to push for more positive portrayals of African Americans on the radio. One example of the openings provided by the wartime fight for democracy was the series *Freedom's People,* put together by Ambrose Caliver, a black employee of the Office of Education, and broadcast on NBC in 1941. Advisors on the programs included W. E. B. Du Bois, Alain Locke, Sterling Brown, Charles Johnson, and Roy Wilkins. The "recurring political theme of *Freedom's People* was that blacks had contributed significantly to American culture and history and had earned the right to be free and fully accepted as Americans." The series emphasized black cultural achievements in music, art, and literature and made the "subtle and sophisticated claim that their contributions were at the very foundation of what was to be called American culture." Savage explains that this argument about black history and culture was common among black leaders of the time, but it is also notable that many of the advisors were key figures in the Harlem Renaissance and that the radio programs continued the belief from that era that the arts could have a political and communal impact. Not everyone, it seems, had abandoned the philosophy of the Renaissance.[50]

The NAACP had a limited relationship to radio, particularly during the 1930s and the war years. The association monitored radio output, sending messages of complaint or support, with the former usually focusing on the use of racial epithets or derogatory comments broadcast over the air. It called for the greater inclusion of and opportunities for African Americans in radio programing. It also attempted to use the radio to highlight its work and "advertise" the organization. Brian Ward charts the NAACP's involvement with radio in the postwar years. The association, he writes, "worked harder than ever to exploit the full potential of radio—a potential that the organization was adamant existed, but that it still struggled to define and harness." Rather than simply having its representatives appear as guests or advisors, the NAACP looked to buy or, using pressure born of the growing federal disquiet with segregation, request airtime from stations.

Between 1952 and 1955, Walter White had his own weekly radio program. Produced by WLIB in New York, *The Walter White Show* was eventually syndicated to stations across the North and West. White used the show to update his audience on his organization's work, particularly its legal campaigns. In the late 1950s and early 1960s, the NAACP continued to use radio to implement and expose its work, and as the civil rights movement progressed, even its presence in the South improved.[51]

Broadly speaking, then, the NAACP, like others, saw that radio had the potential to highlight the injustices of racial intolerance and discrimination and to change attitudes toward the race, particularly in the context of first the wartime rhetoric of democracy and then the burgeoning civil rights movement. However, its involvement in radio was, compared to film, relatively limited. This was partly, as Barbara Savage and Brian Ward have explained, a question of access; commercial radio was largely closed to African Americans, the federal government only wanted to go so far in broadcasting about race, and southern radio stations in particular were either hostile toward or wary of the association and its status as a "militant" organization. It might also be explained by the fact that the emphasis of the NAACP's cultural strategy had changed. During the Harlem Renaissance and with the production of the *Crisis,* the NAACP had followed the "contributionist" approach outlined by Savage above. The association used art and literature to celebrate black achievements and strengthen black identity and pride. By the late 1930s, however, Walter White, at least, was more concerned with the inclusion and visibility of African Americans, on an equal basis, in American culture. This, it seemed, could be best achieved through the motion picture, which, for the NAACP, was the most powerful medium for influencing racial perceptions. The movies made representations more "real" and, literally, more "visible." *The Birth of a Nation* concerned the association more than any other cultural production because it was a film. Similarly, as will be discussed in the next chapter, it was not until it transferred from radio to television that the organization took issue with *Amos 'n' Andy.* The NAACP saw that radio could also change attitudes, but it treated the medium more as a forum for factual information, in the same way as newspapers. Walter White's radio appearances were similar in content, tone, and ambition to his syndicated newspaper columns.

Walter White could have a narrow attitude toward culture, and this limited the effectiveness of his campaign in Hollywood. He had a very particular idea of the type of film and the type of black character he wanted to see produced. He was critical of films that featured exclusively black casts. In 1943 he complained that he was "getting more and more disturbed about the Hollywood situation. Mr Willkie and I made it very clear when we were there that neither of us favored the all-Negro picture." He expressed his fear that "when one of these all-Negro pictures fails to make money, Hollywood will drop or greatly diminish its efforts to keep its promises to Willkie and myself." His comments were most likely in response to news of the production of two all-black musicals, *Cabin in the Sky* (MGM) and *Stormy Weather* (Twentieth-Century Fox), which were released that year. White's concern was that such productions were racial separation writ large. As Donald Bogle says of *Cabin in the Sky,* "Negroes were removed from the daily routine of real American life and placed in a remote idealized world." White and his organization were campaigning for an integrated society, in which African Americans played an equal role. His disquiet was echoed by the OWI, which, as Sklaroff writes, "critiqued these films for invoking a type of separatism incompatible with the larger war aims."[52]

White was closed to the notion that such films in fact provided opportunities for black actors and that they could showcase the talents of the race. These films were often censored in the South, as in the case of *Cabin* in Memphis, when an ordinance banned all-black films or those with "negro actors performing in roles not depicting the ordinary roles played by negro citizens" from being screened for white or mixed audiences. If, as Whitney Strub argues, white censors saw them as troubling signs of black assertiveness (and banned them for fear of provoking white anger), then it is surprising that the NAACP did not see them as positive examples of the very same. White's reaction to such films was also perplexing because at times he was not far from advocating a "head count" mentality; in other words, the more African Americans in movies, the better. In an article on White's visit to Hollywood, *Variety* reported, "Just as Hollywood now puts one out of each 15 persons in a crowd scene in uniform . . . so White desires that one out of 10 persons be a Negro in normal pursuits." *Variety* quoted White as citing as an improvement a scene in *Saboteur* (1942) "in which the crowd viewing the Statue of Liberty included a Negro." Similarly, he did not seem overly concerned by unrealistic or conservative black images in war films (such as those in *Bataan* or *The Negro Soldier*). White did not expect African Americans to have starring roles or to be pictured as heroes; he wanted white America to become used to seeing black faces on the screen. What he did object to was what he saw as the continuation of demeaning stereotypes.[53]

There were some signs of progress in the depiction of African Americans in motion pictures. Films such as *Crash Dive, Sahara,* and *Bataan* included black characters who fought and died alongside their white compatriots, almost as equals. There were other films made during the war that suggested a relaxing of the racial codes that had governed Hollywood's use of black characters. Dooley Wilson had a significant supporting role in 1943's *Casablanca* (never mind that he is stuck at a piano), and *The Ox Bow Incident* of the same year included a black man among the group who try to stop a lynching (never mind that the film was an indictment of Nazi mobbism, rather than American, and that thus the lynch victims are white rather than black). These pictures gave White and his colleagues cause to hope that Hollywood's attitude toward the race was beginning to change. The NAACP's campaign was helped enormously by the Second World War and America's involvement in the conflict. Throughout the country there was an increase in black consciousness and activism, as African Americans sensed the opportunity to press for advancement. A second wave of mass migration saw almost 1.6 million southern blacks move to the industrial centers of the North and West between 1940 and 1950. The direct participation of African Americans in the war effort, whether working in the defense industries or fighting with the services, increased black militancy, as the race began to demand the same freedoms at home that they fought for abroad. The association benefited directly from these changes. By the end of the war its membership had risen over eightfold, to at least four hundred thousand.[54]

The government was well aware of the stirrings among the black community, and it was worried that racial conflict and even the appearance of racial disharmony would derail the war effort. The Office of War Information and related departments were thus alert to potentially inflammatory portrayals of African Americans in motion pictures. Walter White was able to use these fears to further his own agenda. He used his position as an influential civil rights leader to gain the ear of government officials and thus piggybacked on their influence over the studios. He also had direct access to film industry leaders, thanks to Wendell Willkie. The NAACP leader was thus able to form an alliance between his organization, men like Mellett and Poynter at the BMP, and liberals within the studio system. Together they established a more racially tolerant tone, which would continue throughout the decade.

There were, however, limits to how much this alliance could achieve. For one thing, the different parties were motivated by different aims. The NAACP, of course, wanted significant and lasting improvements for the condition of African Americans. It saw cultural representations as one way in which this could be achieved, by changing white perceptions of the race. In contrast, Hollywood was motivated by profit. It was happy to produce films with nominal references to Allied war aims if this eased distribution and to include images of heroic (white or black) Americans if they were popular with audiences. While some in Hollywood might have supported the NAACP's aims, they worked within a business driven by audience figures and profit margins, not ideology. The government, on the other hand, wanted black morale to be bolstered in order to strengthen the war effort. Although there were many liberals in the ranks of the OWI who sympathized with the black cause, its head, Elmer Davis, tempered their "hopeful visions of the war" with the "more utilitarian notions of the policy makers." Their work was driven by the practical needs of the government and not by their political beliefs or sympathies. The OWI adopted what Deputy Director George Barnes described as "a direct and powerful Negro propaganda effort as distinct from a crusade for Negro rights." It wanted to improve morale, to get African Americans behind the war effort. It was not engaged in a fight for racial equality.[55]

Hollywood and the government agencies tried to play down the issue of race. They created films that showed the racially harmonious armed services and ignored the tensions and inequality. Or they removed African Americans from white society altogether and placed them in dreamlike settings or back on the stage as entertainers. However, they found that the best way to minimize the impact of race in the movies was to ignore it altogether. As Koppes and Black have shown, the easiest way to do this was "writing-out," in other words, removing a black character that might cause offense. It was better to have no black faces at all than to have ones that could stir up animosity and therefore damage morale. As a result, membership in the black actors' union fell by 50 percent during the war, suggesting that there was little work available.[56]

Within those roles that remained, many of the old stereotypes prevailed. A Columbia University study conducted in 1945 found that of one hundred black appearances in wartime films, seventy-five perpetuated old stereotypes, thirteen were neutral, and only twelve were positive.[57] Hattie McDaniel was still playing a maid, albeit one infused with more dignity in Selznick's liberal-minded film about the home front, *Since You Went Away* (1944). If the black characters were not in the kitchen, then they were likely to appear on the stage: black "entertainers" starred in *This Is the Army* and *Thank Your Lucky Stars* (both 1943). Despite some promising signs, by 1945 little had substantially changed in the motion picture industry when it came to race.

Walter White can be criticized for flaws in his strategy for changing racial stereotyping in film. He frequently gave the impression of being dazzled by the bright lights of Hollywood. He was too interested in fine dining and drinks parties and was easily impressed by celebrity. Much of the attraction of this aspect of his job must have been the opportunity to mingle with the stars. For this is what his campaign in Hollywood boiled down to: luncheons and parties and chatting with important people, backed up with frequent press releases and letters. Kenneth Janken criticizes White for his reliance on the "goodwill" of the studio heads. White, he argues, "mistook his access to powerful people for access to power itself." He might have been granted an audience at court, but White had no control over how these men wielded their power. Furthermore, he seemed wary of pressing too hard for his demands. Jill Watts argues that "he spent considerable energy cozying up to and even defending Hollywood." There is some merit in these evaluations, but, on the other hand, White knew that he had little leverage, and he believed that there was little to gain from antagonizing Hollywood with radical demands. He was an experienced lobbyist; he had honed his skills on Capitol Hill, and he knew how to deal with large egos. His options were incredibly limited, as they were for all African Americans. He knew that the black community could exert virtually no commercial pressure on the film industry, so he was in a weak bargaining position. He made the most of the opportunities that presented themselves. He cleverly tied his demands into the broader discourse about the war and its aims. One of the NAACP's strengths was its ability to highlight an issue and put it before the nation's conscience, as it had with lynching. This is what White was able to do in Hollywood: he alerted the industry to the problem and tried to convince it to change.[58]

Perhaps the greatest weakness of White's campaign was one for which he could be held accountable. He virtually ignored black Hollywood during his trips to the West Coast. He was so transfixed with the power and glamour of white Hollywood that he ignored African American actors, screenwriters, and filmmakers. Black actors, in particular, were infuriated by the fact that White overlooked them during his visits. They were worried about what his campaign meant for their livelihoods, and they resented his interference. In the aftermath of the Second World War, White's plans to keep up the pressure on Hollywood would bring these tensions to a head.

6

# Blacks, Reds, White

The decade or so after the end of the Second World War was a time of flux in race relations in the United States. On the one hand, there was a lingering liberalism from the New Deal and the war; there was a growing international context to understanding race; and the federal government, at least to begin with, displayed some willingness to engage with racial issues. On the other, attacks on that liberalism began to increase, and the anti-Communist fear of threats to the status quo shaped much of the period. The NAACP had to respond to a number of challenges and opportunities during these years. This was also the case in relation to culture. The organization found it difficult to chart a consistent path through this period: it wanted to be proactive but too often found itself reacting to events, and it was not always successful in judging the mood of its constituents or its potential allies. Nevertheless, during Walter White's often antagonistic dealings with black actors, the association's reaction to accusations of Communism in Hollywood, and its engagement with "message movies," battles over censorship, and protests about television, it continued to adhere to the basic premise of its cultural strategy. In resolutions condemning the television programs *Amos 'n' Andy* and *Beulah,* discussed later in this chapter, NAACP convention delegates in 1951 argued that stereotypical and derogatory depictions "strengthen the conclusion among un-informed or prejudiced peoples that Negroes and other minorities are inferior, dumb and dishonest" and that they "seriously hamper and retard the development of the work of this Association and other interested groups and associations to promote intelligent appraisal of all human beings as individuals."[1] The NAACP may have been reacting to the new medium of television, but it still believed that images of the race could shape attitudes and that, among all the other demands on its time and attention, culture remained crucial to the work of the association.

When Walter White went to Hollywood in February 1942, there had been a glaring omission from his agenda: black Hollywood. He snubbed black actors, local black newspapers, and even the local branch of the NAACP. While he could not ignore local African Americans on his return visit in July, because it coincided with the NAACP's national conference in Los Angeles, he did little to include them in his movie campaign. His omission was not simply an oversight; it reflected his priorities and prejudices. White gave little indication of being interested in the development of a black film industry. He preferred to work with the mainstream, well-funded white film industry. White might have argued this was because the objective of his work was primarily to shape the opinions of white Americans, who would not go to see black films. Certainly he was a pragmatist who knew that the money and power lay with white studio executives, not with black actors. But this distancing from black Hollywood also reflects the NAACP's attitude toward the motion picture as a form of culture. In the association's mindset, creating films, in other words, producing, directing, and acting in them, was not proof of a group's "civilization" or greatness. The motion picture was a form of "popular" culture and therefore inferior to the "high" culture of art and literature. It was a powerful medium, with the potential to influence public opinion and therefore race relations, but it did not carry any cultural cachet. During the Harlem Renaissance the NAACP held up black artists as examples of racial achievement and argued their talent was irrefutable proof that the race deserved equality. This was not the case when it came to the movies. It did celebrate some of the achievements of black actors; for example, Hattie McDaniel appeared on the front cover of the *Crisis* when she won her Oscar for *Gone with the Wind*. However, as White's behavior in Hollywood demonstrates, the NAACP did little to encourage, promote, or support the majority of black actors. White did not seek out their opinions or advice and at times belittled their work. He had a strained relationship with black movie stars, with the exception of a select few, such as Lena Horne, whose fair skin, good looks, and East Coast background only strengthened the arguments of those who claimed his personal prejudices shaped his work.[2]

Black actors resented what they saw as White's interference with their livelihoods. Thomas Cripps asserts that they "hated everything about him: his Eastern roots, his liberal friends, his access to hotels and movielots, his neglect of their stake, even his pinkish pallor and straight hair." His strategy in Hollywood was based on eliminating the parts that they had made a living from playing. In an editorial for the *Chicago Defender*, he wrote that there needed to be "a complete break with the tradition of showing Negroes as menials," because such characters were "cretinish, grinning, Uncle Tom[s]." Not content with attacking the roles, White went even further and blamed black actors for increasing their offensiveness: "One of the most important elements in that progress will be the behavior of Negro actors themselves in playing their roles with sincerity and dignity instead of mugging and playing the clown before the camera." He accused blacks of playing up (or acting down) to the stereotype and producing caricatured performances. There were examples of "mugging" blacks in Hollywood films, but African American actors often brought great dignity and humanity to their roles, even if they were cast as servants or comics. White, however, was incapable of seeing beyond the part itself.[3]

White's snubbing of the black acting fraternity in the spring and summer of 1942 incensed those in its ranks. One of the most scathing attacks came from Clarence Muse. He complained that Walter White, "as a committee of one," had been "wined and dined in the usual Hollywood fashion" but had "never seen it fit to address the Screen Actors Guild" (the actors' union, of which he was a member). Muse summarized what he saw as White's solution to the problem: "There should be only a few black-skinned Negroes, more browns and even more Mulattoes," and "all pictures should have a Negro Lawyer, Doctor and Architect." Most important, "don't have them too black." Muse accused the NAACP secretary of wanting the film business to be "white-washed." It was unfair for Muse, as others would do, to accuse the NAACP leader of intraracial prejudice. He did not call for lighter-skinned actors, and his demand for more black faces hardly reflected a desire for a "white-wash." Muse was closer to the mark with his comment about the inclusion of a black professional in every scene. The actor defended his profession and concluded that the "actor must play the part as written" and asserted that "his talent is unlimited when the opportunity presents itself. Negro actors of experience love their business and they want to protect it against selfish ambitions." Furthermore, he asserted, "Negro actors have progressed and parts are better every year." Muse was a former head of the NAACP's Los Angeles branch, and his vitriol suggests a more personal vendetta against White and the association. Nevertheless, he expressed some very real grievances shared by a number of his fellow actors who were anxious about what White's actions would mean for their careers.[4]

Indeed, Muse was not the only black actor to have noticed Walter White's forays into Hollywood. Some of the fiercest and most personal attacks on the NAACP leader and his plans were made by Hattie McDaniel. An actress who had made a successful career out of playing maids and "Mammies," she was almost paranoid in her conviction that White was specifically targeting her. She believed that he was turning black troops against her during his visits to the front lines in 1945. White was shown a rambling letter she had sent to the War Department, and although she does not explicitly name the NAACP secretary, it is clear her accusations are about him. McDaniel complained that after she had won her Oscar, she "found one of my own racial leaders launching a bitter attack against me only for accepting nurse and maid roles" and that she had "continued to be the only person named or aimed at." In a theme she would return to again, McDaniel pointed out that the "instigator of this campaign happens to be one of lighter skin than myself." She stressed her own appearance in contrast and suggested that in the eyes of someone like White, she was undeserving of success: "I, even though dark of skin and stout, must have a right to gain my economic security also." To an even greater extent than Muse, McDaniel's letter suggests that her analysis of the situation was clouded by personal dislike of White. Again, however, her comments are proof that black actors felt threatened by what appeared to be White's growing power.[5]

Walter White's plans for the NAACP in Hollywood at the end of the war only antagonized blacks further. He wanted to open a Hollywood Bureau, from which he and his organization could continue to monitor the film industry and apply pressure to the studios. In the two years since his 1942 visits White had grown increasingly disappointed with Hollywood. He was frustrated that "so little has been done to implement the promises which were made" to himself and Willkie. He praised the "few good spots," such as *Sahara, Crash Dive,* and "perhaps" *Casablanca,* but, he complained, "the same old stereotypes remain." The year 1945 and the end of the war saw the studios released from any pressure they had been under from the government and the Office of War Information. Perhaps even more significantly for the NAACP, Wendell Willkie had died, and as a result White lost much of his influence with the studios. As he acknowledged, "with the tragedy of Willkie's death in 1944 most of those responsible in Hollywood for changing the pattern appeared to feel that the pressure upon them had been removed."[6]

White believed that if his groundwork was to come to fruition, then he needed to renew his assault on Hollywood. He decided that he needed to keep a closer eye on the studios and create an agency to maintain pressure on them. His solution, supposedly suggested to him by "some of the more enlightened producers," was to establish an "information bureau in Hollywood to which producers, directors, writers and others could turn for guidance." He rejected the suggestion that such producers help finance it, lest "those who paid the bill would influence policy," and made plans to raise money to fund it. In August 1945 the NAACP head office sent a letter out to 137 members asking for their reaction to a proposed Hollywood Bureau and seeing whether they would be willing to make an annual donation. They received fifty-one replies, with forty-eight approvals and three disapprovals. There were forty-one pledges of financial support, totaling $717 annually, plus a donation of $1,000. This rather meager amount was a long way from the $15,000 annual running costs that White predicted. The pallid response indicates a lack of interest in or mistrust of the suggestion. The NAACP membership obviously felt the association had more important issues on which to spend its money in 1945, such as building a legal case against housing segregation, black teachers' salaries equalization cases, and campaigning to secure a permanent Fair Employment Practices Committee (FEPC). This mixture of political lobbying and legal strategy took priority over White's plans.[7]

White had to reassure the American Civil Liberties Union, which had been critical of the fight against *The Birth of a Nation* and was concerned that the NAACP might resort to its old tactics, "that the proposed Hollywood Bureau will in no way be a censorship bureau." Its functions, according to White, would be to "supply, upon request, exact information regarding the Negro to moving picture companies"; to "offer suggestions for more intelligent and frequent use of Negroes as normal human beings in motion pictures instead of limiting them to comic or menial roles"; and to "supply information by means of the NAACP Bulletin, 'The Crisis' and press service on the content of films dealing directly or indirectly with Negroes." In other words, it would provide the mechanism for the continuation of the work White himself had been carrying out in recent years. The bureau would allow a more cohesive, formal approach and give the NAACP a stronger representative in the heart of Hollywood. White conveniently ignored the fact that a Los Angeles branch already existed. According to Jill Watts, members of the black film community had a close relationship with the branch; this may explain why White hoped to bypass it. It was also another example of the broader tensions between the head office and the local branches. Furthermore, White wanted direct control of the Hollywood Bureau, which he could not have with the branch. He would not head the new office, but his intention must have been to play a key role in its running.[8]

Needless to say, White's plans were not well received by the black actors he once again seemed determined to overlook. White, probably unwisely, decided to announce his plans to open a Hollywood Bureau at a meeting of "all the Negro movie folks," organized by the NAACP's Los Angeles branch in January 1946. He reported on the evening's events to Roy Wilkins: "Virtually all of them came—with hatchets. . . . I presented briefly the plan for the Hollywood Bureau and invited comments. And did they come! Clarence Muse, Louise Beavers, and three or four others gave me the works. Fortunately I was in a non-belligerent mood and laughed at their cracks, some of which were to say the least slightly less than good taste. But they overplayed their hand and revealed to everybody that they were interested only in jobs for themselves and to Hell with everything else."[9] The meeting could have been seen as a genuine attempt by White to bridge the gap between himself and the disgruntled actors. However his offhand dismissal of their "cracks" suggests he was not interested in appeasing or even listening to them. He made no effort to allay their fears and did not seem to recognize their legitimate concerns about how his interference might affect their careers. If White wanted black Hollywood's help in establishing his bureau, he did not try very hard to secure it.

The gathering in January was missing a notable critic of White: Hattie McDaniel. She had written to Tom Griffith, head of the Los Angeles branch, to decline her invitation, citing the "tactics" White had used against her in the past. She accused White of speaking to her "with the tone of voice and manner that a Southern Colonel would use to his favorite slave" and repeated the accusation he was "prejudiced to those Negroes of my complexion." Her comment that "there [are] none of us that would not welcome better parts, but usually groups are portrayed the way they are in actual life and we predominate in the servant bracket," reflected exactly the sort of attitude White insisted he was fighting against. However, some of her concerns should have struck a chord with the civil rights leader. She claimed that since White had begun "meddling in the affairs of the motion picture industry," work for African Americans had "decreased some seventy to seventy-five percent." She went on to explain that because black people had no financial stake in the industry, no one was "obligated to give consideration to increased employment." As a consequence, "white stars are now playing our roles and loving it." McDaniel was right to highlight the lack of economic power that made black actors vulnerable. Other than the Screen Actors Guild, which had shown itself to be more than a little reluctant to become involved with the contentious issue of race, there was no one to speak up for them in Hollywood. During the war, opportunities for black actors had been limited, and the immediate aftermath held few signs of improvement. Film industry leaders obviously felt that removing black parts altogether was preferable to facing complaints from censors, government agencies (during the war), and civil rights organizations.[10]

White, betraying the arrogance for which he was widely known, dismissed the concerns of black actors out of hand. He wrote to Sterling Brown, whom he had in mind to head the bureau, about "the racket raised on the West Coast by a few of the brethren and sisters who don't want any interference with Uncle Tom and Aunt Jemima. This really isn't terribly important however much some of them may squawk now." White pressed ahead with his plans, determined to raise the support and funds needed. He drafted a statement explaining that the need for such a bureau "should be readily apparent to any open-minded person" because since the first motion pictures "the Negro has been pictured, with but few exceptions, as either a selfishly subservient menial or as a comic figure." He claimed the NAACP had never "taken the position that Negroes should never be shown as servants or comedians"; rather, it was its contention "that Negroes should not be limited to these two stereotypes but instead should be pictured as normal human beings playing an integral and important role in the life of America and of the World." White went on to criticize "a few Negro actors and actresses [who] object to any efforts to improve the Negroes picturization in moving pictures. Their fear seems to be based upon a belief that they will not be given work in the films. Such a fear is utterly without foundation." And anyway, he asked, "What is more important—jobs for a handful of Negroes playing so called 'Uncle Tom' roles or the welfare of Negroes as a whole? If a choice has to be made, the NAACP will fight for the welfare of all Negroes instead of a few." The statement betrayed White's true feelings on the matter: black actors should be willing to sacrifice their careers for what he saw as the good of the race. Their individual contributions meant nothing, and any personal success they might achieve was outweighed by the harm their performances did to race relationse.[11]

White's attempts to establish a Hollywood Bureau continued until the beginning of the 1950s, when they eventually petered away. It would not be until over half a century later, in 2003, that the association would eventually open such an agency on the West Coast. The idea seemed doomed to failure from the beginning. There was very little support among the NAACP membership for such a plan, and therefore the necessary funds were not forthcoming. Hollywood itself was wary of anything that smacked of censorship, and anyway, it had its own battles to fight; having been freed of one form of governmental control with the disbanding of the OWI, it would soon face another, more powerful threat, in the shape of anti-Communism. Thomas Cripps argues that the plan failed because the NAACP failed to consult with black actors, whose support was crucial.[12] Even with their backing, however, it is unlikely that a bureau would have succeeded. By the early 1950s the association was preoccupied with other, more pressing demands on its resources, such as the legal battle against segregated education. The bureau was important to White but not to other members of his organization. This division of priorities suggests a limitation of the NAACP's cultural strategy: it would never be able to replace the core tasks of the association, and when a choice (implicit though it may have been) was to be made between cultural work and legal work, the NAACP chose the latter.

The furor over the proposed Hollywood Bureau highlighted the fault lines between White and Hollywood's black community. Both sides harbored deep suspicions and accused one another of undermining their work. The situation was exacerbated by White's arrogance and the fragile egos of some of the actors. White was extremely critical of anyone taking what he saw as a stereotypical role. He did not recognize that even when playing maids or slaves African Americans could bring dignity and even subversion to the part. He was insensitive to the fact that their livelihoods and the careers they had spent years developing were potentially being jeopardized by his actions. White should have acknowledged that economic opportunities for blacks were seriously limited and that the film industry provided a shot at wealth for a lucky few. As Hattie McDaniel put it, "Why should I complain about making seven thousand dollars a week playing a maid. If I didn't, I'd be making seven dollars a week actually being one!"[13] White was not interested in celebrating the achievements of actors like McDaniel. Unlike the artists of the Harlem Renaissance, he did not see them as proof of black talent. Quite the opposite, in fact: most of the parts they took simply reinforced white prejudices about the race. This may have reflected cultural elitism on the part of the NAACP; it could only recognize the artistic value of forms of "high" culture such as fine art and literature.

For the actors' part, many of their attitudes were shaped by their own prejudices and insecurities. They saw White as an interloper from the East Coast who had come to take away their hard-earned status. The actors claimed they too wanted change in Hollywood, but at the same time they knew they could not rock the boat. Their position was extremely precarious, and although some of them were big stars, they were dependent on the goodwill of white producers and studio heads. McDaniel, Beavers, Muse, and the rest were not about to call for an end to the roles from which they made a living. The NAACP secretary's outsider status gave him an advantage they lacked. It is unfortunate that he decided not to use this advantage in a coordinated effort to improve the opportunities for black actors at the same time that he lobbied for the greater good of the race.

It is not surprising that Walter White pressed for the establishment of a Hollywood Bureau in the years after the war. He was disappointed when those tumultuous years that had promised some improvements gave way to a retreat to the status quo. It must have been all the more galling when the state of American race relations more generally gave some cause for optimism. The war had seen significant increases in black employment, union membership, and voting registration. An increasing number of blacks held senior positions and were serving in state legislatures. The NAACP had secured an important victory in *Smith v. Allwright* (April 1944), when the Supreme Court ruled that all-white primaries were unconstitutional. Its own membership had grown enormously, and it was becoming an increasingly important organization in national and even international affairs. In 1944 Gunnar Myrdal had published his groundbreaking work *The American Dilemma: The Negro Problem and Modern Democracy,* in which he predicted that America's democratic tradition would win out over its racism and called for greater federal intervention to improve the status of America's blacks. Race and racism had become national and international concerns.

These slight gains, however, were not immediately reflected in the film industry. Thomas Cripps identifies the period in Hollywood between 1945 and 1949 as one of "thermidor": "the cooling of ardour that has followed every era of disquiet" when "order seems to matter more than liberty, sameness more than novelty." There was no clearer example of this retreat to the familiar than Walt Disney's 1946 part-animated, part-live-action musical *Song of the South.* The film displayed remarkable technical wizardry, but its subject matter had more in common with the 1880s than the 1940s. Watching the contented slaves happily singing on the plantation, one might never know a world war in which African Americans had fought and died for freedom (let alone a Civil War that released them from bondage) had taken place. In a memorandum to Walter White, Hope Spingarn, niece of NAACP president Arthur Spingarn, condemned the film as a "glorification of pre-bellum plantation life" and complained of the "Negrofying" of the cartoon animals, whose body movement and dialect were caricatures of black stereotypes. An NAACP press report recognized the "remarkable artistic merit" of the film but regretted that "in an effort not to offend the South, the production helps to perpetuate a dangerously glorified picture of slavery" through its "impression of an idyllic master-slave relationship which is a distortion of the facts." White and his colleagues must have been disheartened to have to yet again take Hollywood to task for its "southern" retelling of American history.[14]

Equally disappointing was a film produced by someone White might have considered an old ally, David Selznick. In his Western *Duel in the Sun* (1946), he cast Butterfly McQueen as a maid, Vashti, once again. According to the NAACP reviewer, the character "is the embodiment of the stupid undependable servant stereotype." There were two other female roles—a Native American and a "half-breed"—which, taken together, served "to substantiate the contention that colored races are morally and intellectually inferior." The film "is a telling blow at any program attempting to better race relations through the medium of the motion picture."[15] African Americans were back in their proscribed places: the kitchen or the plantation.

It was not all bad news, however; the situation in Hollywood did show some signs of promise. A number of films in 1947—*New Orleans, The Foxes of Harrow,* and *The Boy with the Green Hair*—represented what Cripps dubs the genre of "Faint of Heart." Each film "compromised its race angle on the way to the screen, but together they took steps that stoked the liberal audience's hope for a political cinema." Even more promising was *Body and Soul* (1947, United Artists), a film about a white boxer who becomes corrupted by greed and the mob, with a much-praised performance by Canada Lee as a black boxer. When asked by *Ebony* to vote for the film of 1947 that "does most to improve interracial understanding," White replied that he had not seen *Foxes of Harrow* and voted for *Body and Soul.* This poll reflected the fact that there was a broader debate about the social effects of movies and that the black press, as in earlier decades, shared some of the NAACP's concerns and hopes about the impact of cultural representations on race relations.[16]

While these films were in production, a potential obstacle to the liberal mood in Hollywood began to loom large. Anti-Communism, an ever-constant force in American life, had gained momentum since the end of the Second World War, and it had started to turn its attention to Hollywood. The NAACP was caught in two minds about how to deal with this development. It could see that anti-Communism was being used as a stick with which to beat demands for civil rights. In relation to the film industry more specifically, it was worried that anything that challenged the status quo, including the racial status quo, would be accused of being Communist. This new mood could threaten the gains made during the war years and curtail the reemerging liberalism of Hollywood. At the same time, the association was afraid of being labeled Communist itself.

Historians have debated the NAACP's attitude toward anti-Communism during this period. Manning Marable is extremely critical of the NAACP, and Walter White in particular, for what he sees as their acceptance of anti-Communism and for siding with Cold War liberals such as President Harry Truman. He argues that, in so doing, White, along with A. Phillip Randolph and other black leaders, "retarded the black movement for a decade or more." Gerald Horne is similarly critical of what he calls the NAACP's move, again led by White, to "virulent anticommunism." Carol Anderson claims that the NAACP carried out an internal "witch hunt" and "purged" the association of "*suspected* Communists." In contrast, Manfred Berg argues that such critics of the NAACP "grossly exaggerate the extent to which the association actually joined the anticommunist crusade." More specifically he denies that the NAACP carried out the alleged purge of Communists within its ranks. Berg admits that the organization was guilty of "opportunism" and that it stayed silent during the violations of the civil rights of Communists. However, it did not "deliberately fan the anti-Communist hysteria." The tension between seeing the dangers inherent in anticommunism and the desire to protect itself from attack was clearly demonstrated in its reaction to the Hollywood blacklist.[17]

In September 1947 the House Committee on Un-American Activities (HUAC) subpoenaed forty-three people working in the film industry to answer questions about alleged links to Communism. Of these, nineteen so-called unfriendly witnesses refused to give evidence. The NAACP was worried about these developments and what they would mean for its work in Hollywood. It was afraid that the crusade would target those who were sympathetic to black causes and who were involved in changing the depiction of the race in motion pictures. Thurgood Marshall found that the NAACP's fears were being realized. The producers were "scared to death" and were determined to delete from current and future scripts any material that could be interpreted as "Communist propaganda." The interpretation of Communist propaganda was "anything in opposition to the status quo of the country as demonstrated by the well-known stereotypes," and therefore, Marshall believed, the studios would revert back to the stereotypes against which the NAACP had campaigned.[18]

The NAACP's leaders contacted J. Parnell Thomas, the chairman of HUAC, to outline their concerns. They urged him to "guard most carefully against penalizing any producer, writer, director and actor or actress who has worked to change the dangerous stereotype treatment of minorities in film particularly of the Negro." They explained the harm done by such stereotypes and praised the "thoughtful, patriotic Americans in Hollywood" who had tried to remove them. "Some of these [people] have been charged with being 'Communist' because they have tried to live up to the ideal of treating all human beings fairly." The telegram assured Parnell that "this Association is opposed to Communism, Fascism or any other kind of propaganda of any medium of public communication." "But," it explained, "we believe it equally important that responsible public officials should not fall into the equally dangerous error of labeling 'subversive' [the] honest American doctrine of freedom, justice and equality." This telegram, which was released to the press by the NAACP, suggests that the association was not prepared to stand by and let HUAC's crusade in Hollywood go unchallenged. White criticized the "unconscionable treatment and attempted pillorying of the motion picture industry" in the HUAC hearings. He claimed that it "amounted almost to a legislative lynching" and alleged that "the 'Communist' issue is used as a means of expressing vicious anti-Semitism."[19]

Leslie Perry, of the NAACP's Washington bureau, went to the hearings and reported back to White. He found the committee had not the "slightest interest in fair characterization of Negroes." His letter to White went on, "You, of course, know the record of many of those cited far better than I do: [Albert] Maltz who wrote 'A House to Live In.' John Howard Lawson 'Sahara.' And Robert Rossen who is directing 'Body and Soul' in which Canada Lee has a part." He told White he thought it was "important that we do everything possible to head off and defeat contempt citations not only because most of the writers involved have been conscious of their responsibility to handle Negro subjects with honesty and decency, but also because of the serious threat involved to freedom of speech, thought, expression and political beliefs." The lawyers for the nineteen men hoped that the NAACP and its branches would send a message to congressmen stating that it opposed the citations of contempt.[20]

White, however, was getting anxious. He told Arthur Spingarn that while his "sympathy is distinctly with the 19," several people had told him "that there is no doubt that some of the men who have been cited are unquestionably members of the Communist Party." He realized that "it is not, as yet, a crime to be a Communist in the United States," but he was clearly worried about the implications of siding with known Communists. He thought "the contempt proceedings contemptible," but he "question[ed] whether this is properly a matter for the Association to take action on." After discussing it with Spingarn and Marshall, he decided the "kind of action" suggested by Perry was "somewhat outside [the] scope of [the] Association's program." The NAACP did not side with the anti-Communists, but it was reluctant to ally itself with Communists or even those strongly suspected of being Communist. No matter the principles at stake, it was not willing to threaten the viability of the association. The NAACP's reaction to the blacklist suggests that Berg's analysis of the association and anti-Communism is closest to the mark: the NAACP was sympathetic to those under suspicion, but it did what it needed to survive.[21]

As it turned out, in the short term at least, the NAACP's fears of a devastating backlash in Hollywood were unfounded. A cycle of "message movies" appeared in 1949 and 1950 that dealt with such contentious issues as racial discrimination, passing, and race riots. It included *Home of the Brave, Lost Boundaries, Intruder in the Dust, Pinky* (all 1949), and *No Way Out* (1950). These films reflected a reemergence of the liberal consensus that had been seen during the Second World War. The NAACP was once again frequently involved in either the production or the promotion of these films. Outside Hollywood there were indications that improvements in the racial situation were possible. President Truman wanted to court the black vote in the 1948 election; he adopted a pro–civil rights plank and desegregated the armed services. The previous year his Committee on Civil Rights had issued its report, *To Secure These Rights,* in which it condemned segregation and proposed ways in which it could be eradicated, including federal intervention on issues ranging from lynching to voting rights. Human rights had become an international hot topic, and the discourse of the American civil rights movement was increasingly being heard on the world stage. It was a period of tension between Cold War conformity and increasing activism; in some parts of Hollywood the latter won out.

These films were prompted, in part, by the racial liberalism discussed above. The issue of civil rights was pushing its way onto the national agenda, and Hollywood responded. Furthermore, the growing economic importance and visibility of African Americans as a group within American society meant that they were increasingly seen as a potential audience for the film industry. Hollywood began to appeal to black audiences and also to liberal whites who were sympathetic to their plight. Some of those liberals were to be found among the ranks of the movie studios themselves, as they had been during the war. There were some familiar names involved in making the "message movies," including Daryl Zanuck and Twentieth-Century Fox and MGM. Walter White and his organization continued to play a role in the liberalizing of motion pictures. White kept up his pressure on the studios by the usual means of persuasion, consultation, and complaint. As before, he and the industry leaders did not always see eye to eye over how racial issues should be treated. But the old wartime alliance (now minus the government agencies) produced some significant cinematic representations of race.

The first of the "message movies" was *Home of the Brave* (United Artists), a groundbreaking examination of the psychological effect of racial prejudice on African Americans. It used the war setting familiar from the earlier half of the decade to examine these issues and explored the experiences of a black army private in a white patrol. Walter White praised the film for being honest and dramatic and for telling its story without preaching.[22] Although it owes much to the war films made during the conflict, *Home of the Brave* does not share the earlier films' rose-tinted view of  racially harmonious armed services. Rather, it shows that the army was one place among many where African Americans faced persecution and discrimination. The final message of the film, however, is hopeful and promises racial cooperation and integration. After all, the American armed services had been racially integrated only the year before, surely a sign, to Hollywood's optimistic liberals, that change was on its way.

A similarly hopeful ending is offered by *Lost Boundaries* (RD-DR Corp). It was based on a true story, about a "Negro" doctor and his wife who move to a small northern town and "pass," gaining the respect and friendship of the white community. White was asked by the producer to read a number of versions of the script, and he predicted that the film would "set a new and greatly to be desired yard stick in films to be made in the United States dealing with the Negro." After seeing a rough cut of the film, he was perturbed by the scenes in Harlem; he complained that the neighborhood was portrayed as a "place of filth, frustration, crime and abject poverty." This complaint was reminiscent of the debates during the Renaissance, when the NAACP objected to the depiction of Harlem as a working-class ghetto. Nevertheless, he was won over by the central character: an African American doctor who is hardworking, successful, and patriotic (he signs up with the navy during the war). White wrote that the film should make viewers proud "that democracy is still strong enough to rise occasionally above ignorance and fear" and that "the motion picture industry at long last is daring to picture the Negro and Negro-white relations as they are and not to shiver in terror at the one-man censorship boards [that threaten] fire and brimstone unless Negroes are restricted to roles as menials or comics." The comment about southern censors was prescient: the following month the film was banned in Atlanta, Georgia.[23]

Another film in the "message" cycle was MGM's *Intruder in the Dust*. Again, the NAACP was sent copies of the script. Walter White might not have been able to open his Hollywood Bureau, but he had not allowed himself to be forgotten by the studios. Based on William Faulkner's novel, the film tells the story of Lucas Beauchamp (Juano Hernandez), a black landowner, who is wrongfully arrested for shooting a white man and is saved from a lynch mob and jail by a young white boy and elderly white woman. The most impressive aspect of the film is the character of Lucas and the performance of Hernandez: here is a black man who will be cowed by no one and who refuses to play the "nigger." He is assertive, proud, and, for 1940s Hollywood, unique. White, demonstrating once again his belief that films could change attitudes, predicted that "no man who sees it, no matter how prejudiced he may be, will leave 'Intruder in the Dust' without a profound conviction that something must be done about race hatred."[24]

At the same time that Walter White was expressing his hope that the movies could shape opinions, his organization was continuing its legal battle against racial segregation. Between 1948 and 1950 the NAACP secured a number of important Supreme Court victories. These legal cases represented a clear priority for the association in terms of time, money, and effort, as compared to White's correspondence with film studios or plans for a Hollywood Bureau. Yet there are links between the two strategies. This can be seen, for example, in *Shelley v. Kraemer*, which brought together restrictive covenant cases in which whites had sued African Americans under private agreements that forbade the sale of houses to black people. The court's unanimous decision in May 1948 struck down judicial enforcement of restrictive covenants based on race. This decision marked a change in the justices' opinion, which, Michael Klarman argues, was due to changing public opinion about race as a result of a number of factors, including the democratic ideals of the Second World War, the increasing political power of African Americans, and Cold War pressures.[25] Thus some of the same social changes that helped shape a more sympathetic portrayal of African Americans in Hollywood also influenced the outcomes of these cases. Furthermore, the NAACP hoped that positive depictions would actually help further improve the racial climate, making its legal challenges to segregation and discrimination more likely of success.

In 1946 Heman Sweatt attempted to enroll at the University of Texas Law School and was rejected. The case (*Sweatt v. Painter*) was heard before the Supreme Court in April 1950; two months later unanimous decisions in this and two other cases (*McLaurin v. Oklahoma* and *Henderson v. United States*) were handed down that struck down segregation in railroad dining cars and in two higher-educational institutions (the University of Texas Law School and the University of Oklahoma's Graduate School of Education), though the justices stopped short of ruling on the constitutionality of segregation. In a particularly significant aspect of the ruling, the justices found that a separate law school denied Sweatt the opportunity to interact with whites, which, given Texas's majority white population, would be detrimental to a career in law. It is not a coincidence that at the same time the NAACP was fighting for equal educational opportunities for African Americans, Walter White was calling for the dignified depiction of black professionals (the lawyers and teachers that Sweatt and McLaurin hoped to become) in the movies. White pressed for everyday interactions between the races to be sensitively portrayed in American popular culture; the justices ruled that higher-education institutions should facilitate such interactions. Racial change would come about through challenging both the legal and institutional structures of racism and the prejudice in people's minds. Indeed, the waning of the latter may have had a direct influence on the former; Klarman argues that the decisions in 1948 and 1950 reflected in part the changing opinion of the justices, the "cultural elite," the white student body (in the university cases), and perhaps wider white society.[26] Thus if the NAACP's campaign in Hollywood could help to change attitudes, then the cultural strategy could play its part in the wider strategy for civil rights.

A film that suggested that a gap still existed between what White thought of as a sensitive portrayal of race and what the studios thought was acceptable was Daryl Zanuck's production *Pinky* (Twentieth-Century

Fox). Pinky, a "Negro" with light skin (played by Jeanne Crain, a white actress), had been living in the North as a white woman, training to be a nurse. At the start of the film she returns South to her grandmother Dicey (Ethel Waters), who asks her to look after an elderly white woman, Miss Em. Although Pinky resents it at first, she grows fond of her patient, and when Miss Em dies, she leaves Pinky her house. The will is challenged, but Pinky wins the case and turns the house into a clinic and nursery school for African Americans. When Pinky was living in the North she passed as white, and when she returns to the South she has difficulty adapting to being "Negro" again. During the course of the film, however, she learns to accept her race; she rejects her white fiancé and his offer to move North and pass as white and decides she wants to stay in the South and help her people.

The film script underwent countless rewrites, and in the process a number of the more outspoken black characters were removed, along with some of the radical ideas they expressed. Zanuck consulted with White on the script and asked the NAACP secretary and some of his acquaintances to look over it. White reported back that they were disappointed. He explained that if "the story been written around the turn of the century, it would have been novel and even revolutionary." However, in 1949 "it is dated, inaccurate both as to the thinking of Negroes and intelligent Southern whites, and even dangerous in its advocacy of the status quo. The story pictures every Negro who protests or otherwise attempts to correct injustice as being either a charlatan or a crook or a fool." Most of the black parts are close to stock characters; Dicey is a typical "Mammy" and Pinky a tragic mulatto. While, as with all good passing stories, the heroine learns to accept her race and take pride in her identity, this is brought about through interactions with whites and the status they afford her (through Miss Em's will). Her decisions to stay in the South, open a separate institution for blacks, and continue living within the rules of Jim Crow are all a tacit acceptance of the racial status quo.[27]

All this, however, was not apparent to the film's white producer. Zanuck was furious with White's response to his script. He sniped that White "disclose[s] no knowledge of the problems of motion picture production" and defended his record when it came to race in his pictures, claiming he had "stuck my neck out time and again." Zanuck pointed out to White that he had to balance his responsibilities to the stockholders and the public with the "truth" and success. He argued that movies could not have the same "militant propagandist attitude" as the NAACP: "A motion picture which deals with the Negro minority in the United States must be above all things non-propagandist. All it can hope to do, at its boldest, is to make the white majority experience emotionally the injustice and daily hurts suffered by colored people." He cautioned White, "You are not going to get everything you want all at once no matter how right the causes may be," and concluded that they would go ahead with the film whether the NAACP liked it or not.[28]

Zanuck was even more incensed when White criticized the film in the press. As the NAACP secretary (in fact, White was on a leave of absence from the association) explained to his readers, his "chief criticism of the film is that it accepts without visible objection the philosophy that the Negro has his 'place,' that he accepts that place, that all white people are united in agreement that colored people must forever stay in a position of inferiority." White claimed that he was not calling for a propaganda film but that he objected to the use of "wornout stereotypes." He finished by expressing his somewhat condescending belief that Zanuck would someday "do the picture he so much wants to do." Tellingly, White did not criticize the fact that Pinky was played by a white actress (just as he did not complain that the family in *Lost Boundaries* was played by whites); he was not concerned about opportunities for black actors. In a terse exchange of letters, Zanuck defended his film, telling White he should "be grateful to any producer who dares to invest his time, his energy and his money in an undertaking that is aimed in the right direction." Zanuck claimed that *Pinky* had helped "break down the barriers of prejudice in the deep South" and expressed his hope that "if we have enough pictures of this nature you will not need to devote all your time and life and work to your organization. Perhaps we won't even need such organizations. And when that day comes all Americans can be very happy and very proud." This last comment, in which Zanuck reflects on the power of the movies to eradicate racism, shows that the core premise of the NAACP's cultural strategy was shared by others. However, the exchange also highlights the gap between how the two sides continued to think about race and how it should be represented on film. The studios thought any film about racial passing was a daring move. Walter White increasingly wanted more from the movies: he wanted pictures that not only dealt with race but actually showed the need for a *change* in race relations.[29]

The NAACP might have been disappointed with the film, but White and his colleagues could see that it was at least a step in the right direction. When it was banned by local censors in the South, the organization came to the film's defense. Actually, they came to the defense of exhibitor W. L. Gelling, who defied a ban imposed by the self-appointed censorship board of Marshall, Texas. As White explained to the NAACP's legal department, "though the NAACP did not like 'Pinky' [an] important issue [is] at stake," and therefore they "should think about filing brief amicus." It worried White that "if so mild a picture dealing with anti-Negro bias in the deep South can be banned by arbitrary censorship, then all of the gains we have made over the period of the last 20 years can be lost or dramatically diminished."[30]

The film signaled a significant change in policy for the NAACP: in the past it had tried to use censorship to remove harmful images of the race from the screens. The more liberal films of the late 1940s caused it to reassess the situation. White was afraid that the studios would stop making films that dealt with racial issues if they encountered resistance from the censors. Previously, the NAACP had been the organization trying to persuade the censors to act, even though it knew that the tactic was problematic and that it lost the association potential allies. When the NAACP fought its bitter and protracted campaign against *The Birth of a Nation*, censorship had been its primary aim. Even as late as 1939 it continued to call for the film to be banned. In April that year Robert Allan, the owner of the Jewel Theater in Denver, Colorado, was arrested for screening the movie. The initial complaint against Allan had been made by the NAACP, and his defense in court was conducted by the American Civil Liberties Union (ACLU), a sometime ally of the NAACP that was extremely critical of the association's advocacy of censorship. Roger Baldwin of the ACLU wrote to White to express his concern about the "old difficulty" that had arisen. He assured White that he and his colleagues could "of course understand why Negroes generally bitterly oppose such a film," but he warned that "efforts to ban it are inevitably a boomerang. The precedent established will work against films favorable to Negroes, opposed by the other side."[31]

Ten years later Baldwin's warning came true, as some censors turned against Hollywood's more liberal depiction of race relations. In 1950 the NAACP found itself battling the censors over another of Zanuck's movies, *No Way Out*. Doctor Brooks (Sidney Poitier) is a black intern at a white hospital. After a white man dies during a procedure, there is racial unrest and rioting; the local African Americans defend themselves in their ghetto and fight back. Brooks, despite being shot by the dead man's brother, maintains his professional dignity and treats his assailant's wound. This time White had nothing but praise for Zanuck's production. "Having investigated more than forty lynchings and twelve race riots," he wrote to the studio, "I know from first-hand experience that the violence of human emotions on both sides of the racial fence is exactly as it is pictured in 'No Way Out.'" He praised the "courage which Twentieth Century Fox has demonstrated," which "indicates a maturation of the moving picture industry and establishes an example which I profoundly hope others will have the courage to follow." It is easy to see why White was so taken with the movie. Brooks is educated, professional, dignified, and honorable. When such men and the communities they represent are attacked by racist whites, it should surely shock middle-class white Americans. Indeed, White, in an echo of his strategy for antilynching culture in the 1930s, expressed his hope that the film could help to finally turn the nation against lynching. He told his readers that if they "dare to look on the unmasked face of violence and do something about it, America won't have to apologize any longer for lynchings and race riots which negate much of our devotion to freedom's cause." A few years earlier, in 1946, there had been an apparent upsurge in racial violence, with six reported lynchings, including a particularly shocking incident in Monroe, Georgia, and mob unrest in Tennessee. By 1950 the numbers had fallen again, and antilynching legislation, for largely practical reasons, had slipped down the NAACP's list of civil rights priorities. Nevertheless, as White's reaction to Zanuck's film suggests, activists had not given up their fight.[32]

Unsurprisingly, *No Way Out* was unpopular with some censors, including those in northern cities that had experienced their own share of racial tension and rioting. The film was banned in Chicago by the Police Commission, which felt it was "dangerous and may incite violence." The campaign against this decision was spearheaded by the NAACP's local branch, which, along with over thirty other organizations, lobbied the mayor. The national office weighed in too, firing off letters and telegrams and generating publicity over the issue. The ban was subsequently lifted, and the president of Twentieth-Century Fox wrote to White to thank this "friend" of the studio and his organization for their help. White and the NAACP appeared to have turned firmly against censorship. When censors in Maryland cut scenes from the film, White wrote to the Baltimore branch to set out why the organization opposed such actions. "There are two basic issues involved," he explained. "The first of these is that such censorship does a lot of harm by denying to moving picture audiences the tremendously powerful impact of the lesson which the film teaches." The other "is that if censors can get away with this kind of action, much of the work which Wendell Willkie and many of us have done in Hollywood will be lost because other picture makers will not carry on the progress we have made in recent years for fear of censor trouble." White was worried that the studios were not necessarily ideologically committed to these message movies; if they faced any threat to their profits, particularly in the form of censorship battles, then they would likely drop the whole project. Furthermore, he seemed to have decided that the principle of free speech needed defending in order for the message of these movies to reach the public. This was reflective of a broader trend, as censorship, already disliked by many in the early part of the century, increasingly fell out of favor in the postwar period. In 1952, in the so-called *Miracle* case, the Supreme Court would rule that the movie was a "significant medium for the communication of ideas" and so should be protected by the guarantees of freedom of speech.[33]

The Baltimore branch seemed to have taken no notice of White's missive on censorship, and the following year it came into conflict with the national office over the issue. Trouble flared over *The Well* (1951), a story about racial antagonism in a small town. The contentious element of the film within the NAACP was the use of racial epithets. White, having been persuaded by his daughter, defended their use in the film. He believed that context was important and that offensive words could be used to shock and to elicit sympathy from white viewers. It was acceptable when used in a racially liberal film such as *The Well* and against respectable African Americans by vicious white racists. White was, therefore, perturbed to find that the Baltimore branch had contacted the censors and asked for the word "nigger" to be cut from the film before it was shown in Maryland. Writing "as secretary" of the association, he "urge[d]" the chairman of the board of censors that "no deletions be made." He thought that the "moving story of how both white and Negroes succumbed to prejudice and fear" was "one of the most important motion pictures ever made in the United States." "Certain words like 'nigger,'" White explained, "which are objectionable in normal circumstances are used in the film completely within their proper context in demonstrating the basic prejudices of persons who use such epithets." He argued that to "remove them because of hypersensitivity would be the most regrettable step and one which would give falseness instead of truth to the film."[34]

The Baltimore branch was furious with the way in which White had undermined its actions, by writing directly to the censors "without consultation." The branch president, Carl Murphy, explained that for "many years" they had "protested the use of epithets applied to colored people in moving picture films," as well as "in newspapers, the radio, and on television." (So too, he might have pointed out, had the national office.) He said that while the national office "has a right to disagree with the local branch on this matter," White's telegram was "an unwarranted interference with our local affairs." A meeting of the NAACP's Board of Directors decided, however, that it was not a local issue. They felt that the branch's actions were wrong, that in "depicting a vicious person, the vicious person must use vicious language." In a statement that said much about the NAACP's organizational structure and the ways in which a cultural strategy was developed by the national office, it was found that any decision on how to proceed should be taken nationally. It is not surprising that the Baltimore branch was left confused by the national office's attitude toward censorship. At the same time that it was warning the branch not to be "hypersensitiv[e]" about racial epithets, it was in the middle of a skirmish to get a popular, groundbreaking all-black television program removed from the air.[35]

The show in question was *Amos 'n' Andy*, which had started out on the radio but was developed into a television program.[36] When it first aired on American screens in 1951, the NAACP launched a campaign against it. The national office and the branches lobbied the network and the show's sponsors, demanding that the program be removed. The consistency in the NAACP's attitude toward culture and racism is seen in the arguments made against the show: blacks are made to look foolish, lazy, and dishonest, and this cultural representation would have a damaging effect on how the race was seen and treated by white America. Perhaps the most disheartening aspect of the incident is that the reversion to censorship, so similar in many ways to the fight thirty-five years earlier against *The Birth of a Nation*, suggests that, despite some progress, the NAACP's options were still very limited. The issue of its reaction to *Amos 'n' Andy* is further complicated by the fact that not only did many whites object to the NAACP's methods, but so did many African Americans who were fans of the show.

Amos and Andy began life as Sam and Henry, a couple of characters devised by two white vaudeville entertainers, Charles Correll and Freeman Gosden, for their radio show in 1926. These characters were "Negro": Correll and Gosden used southern black dialect and accents in a form of oral blackface. When the show moved to television in the 1950s, all the characters were played by African Americans. The stories centered on Amos and Andy, two southerners who had moved north to seek their fortunes and opened a taxi company. They told of their trials and mishaps, loves and dreams. By the time the television program went into production, the most important character was actually Kingfish, a con man who was always trying to trick Andy out of his money. From the NAACP's perspective the world of *Amos 'n' Andy* was populated by African American stereotypes, from Sambo to Mammy.

There is nothing to suggest that the NAACP had any issue with the show while it was on the radio, nor when Correll and Gosden appeared in blackface as the characters in their movie *Check and Double Check* (1930). Other African Americans, however, were quicker to spot its dangers. In 1931 the *Pittsburgh Courier* launched a petition to demand that the Federal Radio Commission ban the show. But the results were mixed because many African Americans apparently enjoyed listening to the adventures of Amos and Andy. Among those who defended the radio program was Roy Wilkins, who was then editor of the *Kansas City Call.* He said it was "clean fun from beginning to end" and had "universal appeal."[37]

It was not until the program transferred to television in 1951 that the NAACP was prompted into action. Television, in the eyes of the NAACP leaders, was a new and dangerous medium, in much the same way that the motion picture had been thirty-five years earlier. The visual nature of the medium made it powerful: "'Amos 'n' Andy' on television is much worse than on radio because it is a *picture,* a living, talking, moving *picture* of Negroes, not merely a story in words over a radio loudspeaker."[38] The NAACP was convinced that seeing racial stereotypes had a much greater effect on people's prejudices than hearing them (or, indeed, reading them).

The association's arguments against shows such as *Amos 'n' Andy* and *Beulah* were much the same as they were against other forms of racial representation. *Beulah* was another program that had transferred from radio to television. It was based around a black maid and the white family for which she worked, and it ran on ABC between 1950 and 1953, with Ethel Waters and later Louise Beavers in the title role. The NAACP objected to the show's depiction of African Americans, but it concentrated its efforts on *Amos 'n' Andy.* According to the association, the depiction of "the Negro and other minority groups in a stereotyped and derogatory manner" served to "strengthen the conclusion among un-informed or prejudiced peoples that Negroes and other minorities are inferior, dumb and dishonest." *Amos 'n' Andy* was "a gross libel on the Negro and distortion of the truth," and it portrayed "Negroes as amoral, semi-literate, lazy, stupid, scheming and dishonest." The casting of black actors only made matters worse because the "vicious propaganda is more likely to be accepted as true." (Surely, however, the NAACP would have objected even more vociferously if the roles had been performed by whites in blackface.) The NAACP was worried about the effect of these degrading depictions of African Americans on racial prejudice. "Millions of whites will think the race is the same as on the show," and "millions of white children" would learn about the race from watching. The concern was that, as "most whites never meet Negroes personally," they would base their opinions on these representations. Walter White explained that such depictions upset African Americans because they were the only images of blacks to appear on television. If "Negroes [had] been permitted to appear more often in television as normal Americans with the same ambitions to achieve first class citizenship as others," then "we could take shows like 'Amos 'n' Andy' and 'Beulah' in our stride."[39]

One of the aspects of *Amos 'n' Andy* that most upset the NAACP was its depiction of the black middle class. For years the association had been calling for the inclusion of professional characters in popular culture, but this was hardly what it had in mind. The majority of the characters give the appearance of being middle class: they are well dressed and live in comfortable homes. Their "respectable" appearance is, however, subverted by their language and their actions, as in the case of Kingfish and Andy. Both these men speak with a heavy dialect many NAACP members would have associated with working-class blacks. Kingfish's attorney, "Lawyer" Calhoun, is as unscrupulous as his client. The show presented the members of his profession as "slippery cowards, ignorant of their profession and without ethics," and black doctors as "quacks and thieves," the NAACP complained. It is not surprising that, at a time when the black middle class was growing in number and visibility, the association's leaders were disgruntled by this mockery of their aspirations and achievements. Thomas Cripps argues that by focusing on the misrepresentation of the black middle class, Walter White "appeared to concede that the CBS show had been accurate in its depiction of the black lower classes." But, in fact, the NAACP criticized the portrayal of the whole of the race. It complained that the show "holds up 15,000,000 native Americans to public ridicule."[40]

Black public opinion was divided over *Amos 'n' Andy* on the television, as it had been when it first started on the radio. Many continued to follow their adventures and were bemused by or resented the NAACP's campaign. They thought it was humorous entertainment, and they enjoyed seeing black faces on television. The black scholar Henry Louis Gates Jr.

recalls watching the show as a child; "*everybody* loved *Amos 'n' Andy*," he remembers. "What was special to us was that their world was *all* colored just like ours." Billy Rowe, the show business columnist at the *Pittsburgh Courier* (the newspaper that had campaigned against the radio show), thought it a "cute and amusing show." An editorial in the *Los Angeles Sentinel* criticized the NAACP's campaign. It said the show was entertaining and enjoyed by black audiences. Furthermore, it provided jobs for "talented Negro actors who otherwise have too few outlets for their ability." Many black actors themselves, unsurprisingly, supported the show. Clarence Muse, White's old adversary, praised it as an "artistic" show that was based on "real Negroes you and I know." Actors hoped that the show would increase opportunities for other blacks in the profession. They resented the NAACP's interference, as they had in Hollywood in the previous decade. This controversy shows the NAACP's distance from the world of show business, both physically and in terms of attitude. Even more damning was the assertion of Almena Lomax in the *Los Angeles Tribune* that "Walter White has got the NAACP way out on the limb in this matter." The NAACP's cultural campaigns had long antagonized black actors, but now it seemed to have lost touch with the wider black community. Melvin Patrick Ely's research indicates that a person's class did not play a significant part in determining how they felt about the show. Middle-class blacks were just as likely to enjoy it as they were to complain. Furthermore, according to Adam Fairclough, by the 1940s the NAACP was no longer a middle-class organization in most major cities. The association appeared to have misjudged the mood of its own constituency.[41]

To the NAACP's mind the images in *Amos 'n' Andy* were a continuation of the harmful stereotypes it was committed to eradicating. By a strange coincidence the first broadcast of the television program took place during the NAACP's national convention in Atlanta, in June 1951. The convention's delegates sat together to watch the opening show. They were, for the most part, perturbed by what they saw and passed a resolution condemning shows such as *Amos 'n' Andy* and resolving "to utilize every means at its disposal to discourage the presentation of such shows." The resolution urged the branches to protest to the sponsors and radio and television stations. If necessary, it warned, they would resort to boycotts of those sponsors, stations, and networks. The national office immediately expressed its grievances to CBS and the show's sponsors, Blatz Brewing Company and its owner, Schenley Distillers. In a sign that the NAACP's threats were taken seriously, CBS sent Sig Mickelson to meet with White to discuss what could be done to resolve the issue. The NAACP secretary agreed to attend a screening, with officers from the NAACP and other black and white allies, including Edwin Lukas from the American Jewish Committee (AJC). Those from the NAACP decided that nothing could be done to improve the show. Henry Lee Moon, the association's director of public relations, found that the "root of the trouble" lay "in the established 'Amos 'n' Andy' pattern which in my mind can be no more cleaned up and made acceptable than, say, the word 'darky.'" To the NAACP, the complete removal of the program from the air was the only solution.[42]

The association's battle over *Amos 'n' Andy* had much in common with its campaign over three decades earlier against *The Birth of a Nation*. It was overseen by the national office, but with work done by the branches to tackle the issue at a local level. It used some of the same tactics: letters of protest, publicity for the cause, pressure on relevant bodies, and alliances with other groups. The ultimate goal was the same: the complete removal of the offending article from public view. It could not turn to censorship boards, but it did appeal to the network as the producer of the show. The greatest difference from the campaign in 1915 was that it also targeted the show's sponsor. It appealed to and threatened the company whose money lay behind the production. White warned Blatz's brewers, "No one of the fifteen million American Negroes who spend annually today in excess of twelve billion dollars which includes Blatz Beer and other Schenley products can fail to resent such libel" as appeared in *Amos 'n' Andy*. The mass boycott did not materialize, although in Milwaukee, the hometown of Blatz, the local branch formed an alliance with local businessmen and other organizations to boycott the product.[43]

The threatened boycott of Blatz Beer was indicative of the growing importance of African Americans as consumers. Radio stations had already identified blacks as a potentially valuable audience, and the assumption was that television would follow suit.[44] What is more, within a few years the increased economic power of African American communities would be a key tool in the civil rights movement, with boycotts in all areas, from public transport to restaurants and shops. Blacks' strengthening economic status gave the NAACP potential leverage to appeal to television's commercial interests, a tool that had not been open to White when he first tackled show business in the early 1940s. On the other hand, the increasingly complicated world of corporate interests made White's tactic of personal persuasion less effective. There was a whole range of parties to which he needed to appeal, which stretched the limits of even the NAACP secretary's talent for lobbying. However, the pragmatic approach of the NAACP continued to be an asset. It had always appealed to the self-interest or other considerations of the relevant parties, as well as making moral or ideological arguments. If the NAACP could not persuade someone of the justice of its argument, then it could always turn to expediency.

The NAACP's demand that the show be immediately removed from the air alienated some allies, as its blanket call for censorship had done in the fight against *Birth*. The ACLU agreed with the NAACP's concerns about the program, but it cautioned about the dangers of limiting free expression. In the atmosphere of the 1950s demands for censorship were, for many liberals, too close to the tactics of anti-Communists for comfort. The American Jewish Committee was also ideologically opposed to censorship. It had another reason to shy away from an all-out attack on *Amos 'n' Andy*. The president of the show's sponsor, Lewis Rosentiel, was Jewish and a major contributor to the AJC. The committee was therefore reluctant to criticize the program too strongly. Edwin Lukas urged White and his organization to accept a compromise and to work with CBS to make improvements to the script. The AJC went so far as the question whether the NAACP's attitude to the affair "border[ed] on anti-Semitism." It wondered whether "the failure of the Association to protest the show when it was on the radio and under gentile sponsorship," compared to its attitude toward the program on television, was proof of bias. White, of course, was quick to assure the committee that this was far from the case. Jewish organizations and individual Jews had long been allies of the NAACP. During his foray into Hollywood White had repeatedly turned to Jewish movie producers as sympathetic allies. However, this brief incident suggests that it was not always an easy alliance.[45]

CBS cancelled *Amos 'n' Andy* after the second series due to falling audience numbers and the withdrawal of sponsorship. It is not clear whether this was the result of pressure from the NAACP, as such achievements are difficult to measure. As was so often the case, the association was able to make a nuisance of itself; it caused a public relations headache for CBS and Blatz. But it did not have a mandate to carry out a sustained or successful campaign. In contrast to the fight against *The Birth of a Nation,* when the majority of African Americans and liberal whites shared the NAACP's disgust with and fear of the film, in the case of *Amos 'n' Andy* many whites and plenty of African Americans enjoyed the show. This disunity was a major flaw in the NAACP's campaign. As Ely argues, the NAACP "could not convincingly claim to represent an Afro-American consensus, and its threat of a boycott thus rang hollow."[46]

Any sense of pleasure at the show's cancellation would have been short-lived: CBS syndicated *Amos 'n' Andy* to hundreds of local television stations, and the program continued to be shown on televisions all over America until 1966. The NAACP had failed in its attempt to enforce the complete removal of the show. More important, it had not been able to convince the public, including large sections of the black community, that the program was harmful to the race's advancement. An unintended consequence of the controversy stirred up by the association over *Amos 'n' Andy* was that it would be 1965 before a network television series would again feature a black actor in a central role (Bill Cosby in *I Spy*). On the other hand, Ely suggests that the fact that images of blacks as comics and fools became too contentious for sponsors and networks marks a victory for the NAACP.[47] Certainly, the organization proved once again that African Americans would not take these cultural slights lying down.

In the same month that the association passed its resolution condemning *Amos 'n' Andy*, NAACP lawyers were in Topeka, Kansas, arguing *Brown v. Board of Education* before the district court. Again, the links between the NAACP's cultural work and its legal campaigns can be seen. The former, with its focus on highlighting the damaging effects of racial stereotyping and on challenging racist attitudes, was designed to complement the latter. Justin Lorts argues that the Supreme Court's decision in 1954 "vindicated" the NAACP's approach to *Amos 'n' Andy:* "At the core of the court's opinion was the finding that segregation in schools, like racist images on television, created a sense of inferiority that prevented blacks from attaining full equality in American society." Similarly, when rumors of a remake of *Birth of a Nation* reached the NAACP in 1954, it reacted to the news in the context of the current civil rights situation. At the meeting of the Board of Directors in November it was reported that there "are indications that some of the anti–civil rights forces in the South are interested in remaking the 'Birth of a Nation' or a similar film in opposition to implementation of the Supreme Court's decisions in the school cases." The film was seen as a potential weapon with which white supremacists could attack the recent civil rights gains. Thus any protest against such a revival or production (which, in the end, came to nothing) would be part of the NAACP's broader fight to secure the implementation of the court's ruling.[48]

The first half of the 1950s not only saw the legal campaign gaining momentum but also marked a period of transition within the NAACP. Walter White's controversial marriage to a white woman, Poppy Cannon, his ill heath, and his desire to move on to new challenges dampened his enthusiasm for his NAACP work.[49] Roy Wilkins took over the secretary's administrative duties and replaced White on his death in March 1955. White had been the one spearheading the efforts in Hollywood, and his demise marked the end of that chapter in the NAACP's cultural work. The decade prior to White's death, however, saw the NAACP largely continuing with its broad cultural strategy. As it had in previous decades, the association argued that cultural representations affected the social and political status of African Americans. White's campaign in Hollywood encountered difficulties: he clashed with black actors, his proposed Hollywood Bureau did not materialize, and anti-Communism threatened his progress. These setbacks suggest that there wasn't universal support for this approach, both within his organization and within the wider community. Nevertheless, White was able to maintain relationships with some of the key people in the industry, and he acted as a consultant on a number of films. He was rewarded with a spate of liberal films that dealt sympathetically with racial issues. Such movies were the exception rather than the rule: the majority of Hollywood films paid no attention to race. Nor were these films themselves without faults. However, they marked what must have been a satisfying culmination of White's campaign. Of course, he alone cannot take the credit for Hollywood's moment of relative enlightenment. He and his organization were just one of the many forces—which included the legacy of the Second World War, the liberal conscience of those in the industry, the small improvements in race relations more generally—that pushed Hollywood to this moment. Nevertheless, he was able to continue to exert pressure on the studios, and he acted as a constant reminder that African Americans were paying attention to how they were represented in American culture.

There are examples of the NAACP's engagement with other forms of culture during the postwar period. Its attempts to develop a radio strategy during these years were discussed briefly in the last chapter. The *Crisis* continued to include reviews of books, articles about artists and writers, and the occasional publication of poetry and short stories. However, by the 1950s, there was a noticeable decline in this type of content in the magazine from the heyday of the Du Bois era and even the period of Roy Wilkins's editorship (Wilkins was replaced by James W. Ivy in 1950). Indeed, even by the 1940s, art and literature had, in the minds of leaders like White, been usurped by film and later television. It was these latter forms of culture, with their mass appeal, that had the greatest potential impact on racial attitudes. Furthermore, in contrast to earlier decades, the NAACP now had increased access to their production. The notion of demonstrating the race's talent through the production of art and literature, or changing opinions through paintings and plays, thus had less currency than in earlier decades.

There were a number of positives to be taken from the NAACP's cultural campaigns by the 1950s. The film and television industries were beginning to take notice of African Americans, even if not always in ways of which the NAACP approved. The black community was becoming more visible in American life. It was also, from the point of view of these industries, growing in commercial and economic potential. This gave the NAACP a better bargaining position than it had ever had before. On the other hand, the NAACP's ongoing preoccupation with white-owned media meant that its influence was limited. The NAACP's cultural strategy had for a long time alienated many black actors. Its attitude toward actors who took what it considered to be harmful roles reflected a cultural elitism and a narrow view of how culture could be used in the struggle for equality. At the beginning of the 1950s the association found itself out of tune with many other blacks as well, including its middle-class constituency. When Walter White went to Hollywood in the 1940s, he had the backing of the wider black community, but this was not the case by the next decade. The NAACP's attitude toward *Amos 'n' Andy* betrayed an unsophisticated view of culture. It assumed that stereotypes must always be negative and that caricatures of the race would always have a detrimental effect on white attitudes. It did not consider the fact that the humanity and dignity of some of the characters could counteract the more offensive stereotypes or that an all-black television show could bring indirect benefits to not only individuals but also the race as a whole.

The NAACP's strategy really came unstuck when it came to censorship. It discovered that the principle could be used against black interests, and it found itself opposing the action of censorship boards across the country. In an era when free speech was under threat from the conservative forces sweeping across the country, censorship became an increasingly discredited notion in liberal circles. The problem the NAACP faced, however, was that it had still not found an effective way to deal with offensive stereotypes when they appeared in a new medium. When television introduced black characters, the association was forced to resort to its old tactic. Although it was careful not to refer to its campaign in such terms because it knew that it alienated many people and that it opened itself to charges of hypocrisy, its demands for the complete removal of programs such as *Beulah* and *Amos 'n' Andy* clearly amounted to censorship. This incident highlights the limitations of the NAACP's approach. The censorship issue was one through which the NAACP found it hard to plot a consistent path. It required a more sophisticated theory of culture than the association was able to deploy to fully explain all the factors at stake. After over thirty years of battling negative images of the race, it was back where it had started: complaining bitterly about a popular representation of African Americans that it believed retarded the advancement of the race. When a new form of media came along and an industry developed in which blacks had no stake or influence, the NAACP had to resort to protests after the fact. It was dishearteningly reminiscent of the fight against *The Birth of a Nation*. The NAACP's cultural strategy, it seemed, had come full circle.

## Conclusion

# "The true picture of America"

The NAACP's protest against *Amos 'n' Andy* seemed to bring the association back to where it had started, vigorously protesting what it saw as the demeaning portrayal of African Americans in "mainstream" white American culture. There were similarities between its campaign against *The Birth of a Nation* in 1915 and *Amos 'n' Andy* in 1951. On both occasions the association was faced with a new medium and a growing industry in which African Americans had no power. It was so worried about the potential harm of these depictions of the race that it could see no alternative but to call for their complete removal from public view. It had only very limited success in both cases: the film was banned in some places but usually only temporarily; the show was dropped by the national network but continued to be shown locally for another decade.

While the controversy over *Amos 'n' Andy* was the last time the NAACP waged a campaign on the same scale as the fight over *Birth,* its cultural work did continue after the death of Walter White in 1955, through the leadership of Roy Wilkins and beyond. One of the first examples of Wilkins engaging with the entertainment industry once he had become executive secretary was his meeting with film executives and black actors in Hollywood in October 1957. He reassured his audience that the NAACP did not "censor" films or television programs, but he warned them that it "reserves the right to criticize productions deemed racially offensive" and urged "the casting of Negro performers in a range of roles representative of the position of the Negro in American life today." In a clear echo of Walter White's statement fifteen years earlier, Wilkins claimed that his organization had "never advocated a ban against the use of Negroes in comic or servant roles," but it did "object to restricting them solely to such roles and to the perpetuation of the stereotype of the Negro as an illiterate, frightened buffoon." He told the film industry that it was "passing up an opportunity to render a service to America" by failing to "present the true

picture of America on the changing status of the Negro in American life."
Wilkins also linked the black image in popular culture to recent events in
the civil rights movement. "The dilemma in which American representatives abroad found themselves when the Little Rock crisis broke might
have been eased somewhat," he claimed, "had the peoples of those coun-
tries been informed of recent progress made in race relations in this country." Mary Dudziak notes the importance of Little Rock in how the rest of
the world viewed and judged American race relations. The US government
was particularly concerned that it was used as anti-American propaganda
by the Soviets. Hollywood, Wilkins told industry leaders, had the opportunity to improve America's image abroad.[1]

Five years later little progress had been made, and the NAACP believed that there was still important work to be done to improve the representation of the race. According to a resolution from the 1962 annual
convention, the "proper factual, complete and wholesome portrayal of the
Negro in newspapers, magazines, movies, television shows and in all other media has not yet been realized"; this was significant because "public
opinion and attitudes are greatly influenced" by this image. The following year the convention called on African Americans to "refrain from pur-
chasing the products of those who sponsor offensive television and radio
programs, ignore the presence and achievements of American Negroes, or
who refuse to give equal employment opportunities to Negroes." Branches
were urged to "organize protest demonstrations" at motion picture theaters and to challenge "the discrimination employment practices of motion
picture companies and trade unions" in the entertainment industries. The
association, then, was still taking a largely reactive approach to combating
negative depictions, and it was using some of the same methods, including boycotts and protests. However, its focus was beginning to change,
as it moved toward efforts to secure opportunities for African Americans
within the creative industries more broadly. According to a 1963 press
release, the association was engaged in "an all-out battle with the Hollywood craft unions over the almost total absence of Negro employment in
those unions." It had proposed "that one Negro in addition to the regular
crews be hired for each movie and TV show in production" but this had
been "curt[ly]" rejected by the unions. This change in direction was partly
a recognition that more African Americans working in the entertainment
industry might lead to more favorable depictions, perhaps suggesting that
the organization had finally become disillusioned with waiting for whites
to make improvements. It also highlighted, particularly as the decade pro-

gressed, the ways the NAACP hoped to use the victories of the civil rights movement in its cultural campaigns.[2]

Herbert Hill, the NAACP's labor secretary, spearheaded attempts to increase the employment of African Americans in the television and film industries. Hill and others wanted to file the complaints of black workers against industries and craft unions under Title VII of the Civil Rights Act of 1964, which prohibited employment discrimination based on race, color, religion, sex, or national origin. They made little progress in those areas "behind the scenes," such as production, writing, and technical crafts. Hill and NAACP staff from the Beverly Hills–Hollywood and Los Angeles branches found that much of the industry was a closed shop. Recruitment policies were not transparent, and most hiring was based on who you knew. Henry Scott, from Los Angeles, told Hill that "making a foray" into this area was "much like reaching into a barrel of eels. They are well equipped by nature to give you the slip." They had tried to test the industry by finding, preparing, and sending qualified applicants for jobs but were unsuccessful. Hill replied that they needed to get a formal complaint filed under Title VII as soon as possible. There had always been links between the NAACP's cultural campaigns and its legislative and legal strategy, but here the connection was explicit: the Civil Rights Act, it was hoped, could provide the legal basis for widening access to the entertainment industries, thus improving the black image in popular culture.[3]

By the 1960s there was growing evidence that the mass media could be used as a force for positive change. The importance of television in the civil rights movement has been acknowledged by historians, and it was recognized by contemporaries, including the NAACP.[4] Davis Roberts of the Beverly Hills–Hollywood branch suggested to Herbert Hill that the reporting on Birmingham, Oxford, and Selma was "primarily responsible" for the passage of civil rights legislation. As he wrote, "When the agonized faces and the clubs and the gas and the cattle prods and the horses and the dogs and the deputies and the sheriffs and the anger and the hate and the pain rushed into the living rooms . . . and the bars . . . across the nation, by the grace of television, we got action."[5] The NAACP tried to secure airtime and favorable coverage of its work, and it monitored those programs that dealt with civil rights issues, sending letters of congratulations or complaint. Its senior officers, especially Roy Wilkins, appeared regularly on television and radio to discuss civil rights.

The association continued to pursue a cultural agenda throughout the decade and beyond. In 1967 the Beverly Hills–Hollywood branch established the annual Image Awards to celebrate the achievements and contributions of African Americans in film and television. As a later article in the *Crisis* remembered, the awards were to "honor those people who worked to change the image of African-Americans." They "grew out of deep discontent and frustration" at stereotypes and barriers to employment. Over the years the remit has broadened to include contributions in literature and music, and the awards ceremony has become a star-studded, televised event. The inauguration of the awards was a continuation of the NAACP's policy of highlighting an issue and putting pressure on the industry through exposure. Harnessing celebrity and star status was a tactic of which Walter White would no doubt have approved. The focus on the lack of opportunities for blacks in the entertainment industry, and the subsequent effect this had on the type of work produced, continued. In 1999 NAACP president Kweisi Mfume complained that there was a "virtual whitewash" on national television. Then in 2003 the association published a report on the film and television industry that highlighted the lack of opportunities for ethnic minorities behind the scenes. The report argued that "when it comes to forming ideas, reinforcing stereotypes, establishing norms and shaping our thinking nothing affects us more than the images and concepts delivered into our lives on a daily basis by television and film." The principle that culture affected the social and political position of African Americans still guided the NAACP's work.[6]

One of the productions recognized by the NAACP's inaugural Image Awards was the television series *I Spy,* which ran between 1965 and 1968 and starred black actor Bill Cosby alongside a white character as a pair of secret agents. Cosby, according to Bogle, projected the image of "an educated, intelligent, articulate young man, able to function in and contribute to American society"—in other words, exactly the type of respectable character one might expect the NAACP, given its record, to praise. The show deliberately avoided dealing overtly with the topic of race (partly by setting many of the episodes abroad and therefore not having to show the color line at work), and Cosby himself had "created a career based on nonracial material." Comparing himself to civil rights activists, he said, "My way is to show white people that Negroes are human beings with the same aspirations and abilities that whites have." It was a comment that had much in common with the NAACP's own attitude toward the potential impact of culture. Cosby's role was particularly notable because it was the first central black character on network television since *Amos 'n' Andy.*[7]

There had, it seemed, been considerable improvements in representations of the race since the early 1950s, when the NAACP protested against what it saw as lazy, foolish, and scheming black characters. These changes were even more profound when compared to the popular image characterized by *The Birth of a Nation.* However, characters such as Cosby's or those of Sidney Poitier—who had made a career out of playing what Thomas Cripps calls the "lone Negro," a "not too black" figure who is "set down in a microcosmic company of whites (who would be the better for his having passed their way)"—remained the exception rather than the rule.[8] As the NAACP's continued efforts demonstrate, African Americans still remained largely invisible on the screen or confined to stereotypical parts. Nevertheless, the most overtly offensive racial images had largely disappeared. The most notable absence was the black man as uncontrolled beast and violent rapist. In Griffith's 1915 film blacks are presented as not only intellectually inferior but also dangerous, driven by a lust for sex and power. By the 1960s, African Americans had appeared as doctors, law students, brave soldiers, and government agents; issues such as discrimination, passing, and racial violence had been dealt with sympathetically. All of this was a far cry from *The Birth of a Nation*'s message of black savagery.

These improvements in the depiction of African Americans reflected, to some degree, the changing racial situation. The picture in 1967, the year of the first Image Awards, was much altered from when the association began its cultural campaign in the 1910s. There had been improvements in all areas of black life; the Civil Rights Act of 1964 had dismantled segregation in the South, and the Voting Rights Act of the following year had finally granted the franchise to African Americans. This is not to overstate the position of African Americans; indeed, as the decade drew to a close, the limitations of civil rights gains were becoming ever more obvious and divisive. Rather, it is to highlight the seismic changes that had taken place since the start of the century. This was significant because it meant the gradual opening of opportunity in American society, including the cultural industries. It was also important because racial representations had always reflected, in part, the wider social context. The segregation and racial violence of the early twentieth-century were shown in the racial stereotyping in *Birth;* the "New Negro" of the Harlem Renaissance spoke of a growing confidence and pride among African Americans; the belief in the links between culture and politics was, sometimes unwittingly, promoted by the New Deal and could be seen in the cultural production of the 1930s; the Second World War had a profound effect on the image of the African

American, just as anti-Communism and fear of challenging the status quo shaped representations in the postwar period; and finally, African Americans' ability to force the issue of civil rights onto the national conscience in the 1960s was reflected in a more sympathetic portrayal of the race on television and movie screens.

However, incremental civil rights gains alone were not responsible for the cultural image of the race; improvements in racial representations also suggested that the NAACP's campaign had been successful. During the 1940s Walter White was able to convince some movie producers to change the way their films portrayed blacks. He played a part in bringing the issue before the industry and the nation, maintaining pressure on the studios and trying to ensure that black interests (as he saw them) were upheld. Similarly, the association's campaign in the 1960s yielded some small improvements; it was reported that the number of black extras had risen by 100 percent over the summer of 1963, and there were accounts of individual gains in the hiring of blacks.[9] The NAACP was arguably more successful on those rarer occasions when it engaged with forms of culture that African Americans could create. Unsurprisingly the most sympathetic and therefore most useful (from the association's perspective) portrayals of the race were those produced by African Americans or supportive whites. For example, the compassionate art and literature of the antilynching campaign provided an important counter to the white supremacist vision. Similarly, the respectable and dignified images in the *Crisis* were a striking challenge to the fools and entertainers in the movie theaters. Of course, the final effect of these representations is very much up for debate, as discussed below. It is also important to note here that the NAACP was not the only group working to change cultural representations during the first half of the twentieth century. Other organizations, such as the National Urban League, engaged with the Harlem Renaissance and later tried to use radio to further their agenda. The black press consistently monitored and, where it felt necessary, critiqued the portrayal of African Americans in a wide range of media. Furthermore, there were countless individuals who expressed concerns and hopes about the black image on the page and screen. However, no other civil rights organization conducted such a lengthy, wide-ranging, or systematic campaign as the NAACP.

When looked at over fifty years, it becomes clear that the NAACP did not have one cultural strategy but many, although they were all underpinned by the same basic philosophy. The association did not respond to all forms of culture in the same way. The most striking difference was in its attitudes toward "high" and "popular" culture. Although it did not use these terms itself, a distinction can be seen between how it approached forms such as art and literature and others, including film and television. The former were, the NAACP believed, valued by middle-class whites. It encouraged and celebrated African Americans who created works of literature and art. The NAACP saw the creation of such culture as a sign of a group's civilization and as proof that African Americans should be treated as equals. In contrast, film and television were seen as having a great influence on public opinions but little artistic merit. Therefore, most black actors were not held in the same esteem as writers or painters. The NAACP, broadly speaking, gave greater freedom to these artists than it did to actors, whom it criticized for taking stereotypical roles.

The association could, at times, display an unsophisticated view of culture. For example, it did not seem to acknowledge any differences among genres. It did not recognize that *Amos 'n' Andy* was a comedy and therefore presented a lighthearted look at not only African Americans but life in general. In contrast, *The Birth of a Nation* claimed to be a historically accurate epic. The two thus presented African Americans in very different ways, but the NAACP failed to distinguish the differences and treated them the same way. In relation to film and television it followed a simplistic notion of what constituted a "negative" image or a "positive" image. Usually working-class equaled "bad" and middle-class "good." Jane Gaines is critical of the NAACP's very concept of challenging stereotypes. She argues that because stereotypical characters are not seen as "real," the inference is that there is an alternative "real" type. Those who argue they have been "misrepresented" actually "borrow the same ideological strategy used against themselves." She explains that "to argue that 'real people are not like that' is to answer one empirical claim (the self-evidence of racial characteristics) with another (the self-evidence of how black people really are)." The "positive" image offered as a substitute by the NAACP was an idealization and therefore also a stereotype.[10] The NAACP, in its campaigns for changing cultural representation, ended up advocating stereotypes of its own.

The way the NAACP approached and used culture changed during the fifty years between its formation and the late 1960s. During its first three decades, the association made use of cultural forms such as literature, fine art, and theater. By the 1940s the arts had largely dropped from its cultural agenda, although there remained a place for poems, for example, in the *Crisis* even in the 1960s. Instead, it increasingly focused on forms of culture with a mass audience, particularly motion pictures and television. This reflected the growing confidence of the organization and its desire to reach a national audience. Of course, ever since *The Birth of a Nation* it had been concerned about "popular" culture, but in 1915 it instigated a reactive campaign, whereas from the 1940s the NAACP was more proactive in its use of mass media. Moreover, African Americans as a group were becoming more visible, and their voices were beginning to be heard. The film and television industry began to take greater interest, and the NAACP wanted to exploit and monitor this opportunity.

It would be a mistake to assume that this large organization, from its senior officers to its membership base, held a unified view of culture and its use. Clear divisions between its leaders were seen during the Harlem Renaissance, just as the controversy over *Amos 'n' Andy* highlighted a difference of opinion between its leadership and much of its membership. Furthermore, the cultural strategy was largely the concern of the head office in New York. There were exceptions to this, most notably the campaign against *The Birth of a Nation,* when local members and branch officers were responsible for lobbying officials and asking for cuts in their city or state. The Los Angeles branch in particular was heavily involved in this battle and in monitoring Hollywood's portrayal of the race more generally (despite Walter White's best efforts to keep local blacks out of his negotiations with the studios). At other times the national office and the branches seemed to be at odds, as seen, for example, in the Baltimore branch's reaction to racial epithets in the film *The Well.* While examples of such direct conflict of opinion were rare, the impetus for a broad cultural campaign certainly seemed to come from the NAACP's national leaders. It was they who immersed themselves in the literature and art of the Renaissance, who commissioned antilynching dramas and artwork, and who traveled to Hollywood to liaise with film producers. Historians have explored the frequent tensions between local branches and the head office, arguing that they were the result of conflicts over priorities, finances, and politics. As Kevern Verney and Lee Sartain explain, policy was decided in New York, with the branches expected to implement those policies and to provide the money to help fund them. The cultural agenda was another example that was created and largely executed at the top, rather than the grassroots, of the organization. Similarly, the concern with popular culture and high art could seem very separate from the more pressing business of fighting Jim Crow laws. The voices of legal counsel Thurgood Marshall and Charles Hamilton Houston are largely missing from the discussion about culture.

The association's lawyers became involved when the cultural work raised legal matters, for example, when debating the NAACP's response to the Hollywood Ten or filing *amicus curiae* on behalf of the War Department's *Negro Soldier.* There was an apparent lack of interest in culture from those doing the heavy lifting of the association's work. This suggests that the cultural strategy, while not necessarily openly challenged as a waste of time or resources, was not a matter of importance to all members or leaders of the NAACP.[11]

The cultural campaigns reveal much about the NAACP as an organization and about the attitudes of its leadership toward racial inequality, class, strategies, and culture. The association has been accused by its critics of advocating assimilation, the complete integration of African Americans into white society. It might be expected that this assimilationism would be consistently applied to culture. David Levering Lewis argues that the NAACP, as "Talented Tenth" African Americans, "embraced an ideology of extreme cultural assimilationism."[12] Certainly, Walter White advocated a form of assimilation when in Hollywood. He wanted black characters to be incorporated into mainstream pictures. According to White, they should appear alongside white characters and thus depict the integrated American society for which the NAACP was striving. However, during the Harlem Renaissance, the NAACP, through the work of its senior officials and its magazine, embraced cultural pluralism. It celebrated what was unique in black literature and art, but at the same time it wanted black culture to be accepted by whites and find a place within the wider American culture. It did not support a separate black culture, but nor did it want black culture to lose its distinctiveness. This pluralism (as opposed to complete assimilation) reflects the NAACP's wider stance. Although there were some differences of opinion between individual officials over instances of voluntary segregation, the association rejected the social, economic, and political separation of the races and promoted a society in which African Americans could celebrate their identity and heritage and, at the same time, be accepted by white America.

Megan Williams writes that, "historically, the NAACP has worked to gain civil rights and achieve integration by . . . adopting the dominant culture's values of middle-class respectability and morality." This general statement is substantiated by its cultural campaigns. It encouraged the depiction of decent and reputable African Americans. Such images were considered to be more "American" and therefore more acceptable. They also challenged decades-old stereotypes of blacks as lazy and incompetent that were used to retard the race's economic and social advancement. As a number of scholars have shown, white supremacists deliberately wanted to halt the rise of a black middle class, and one way this was attempted was through cultural imagery. For example, Hale explains, advertisements often showed African Americans attempting to mimic white middle-class attire and behavior, with comical or ridiculous consequences. The adverts "addressed white fears of upwardly mobile blacks by insisting that African Americans could never integrate into middle-class society." The NAACP believed that more dignified images could help forge a place for a black middle class.[13]

The black sociologist E. Franklin Frazier in his scathing indictment of the "Black Bourgeoisie" argues that African Americans created the illusion of a prosperous middle class in order to be accepted by the white world. He claims that in the segregated cities after the First World War "a class structure emerged which was based upon social distinctions such as education and conventional behavior, rather than upon occupation and income."[14] Frazier suggests that African Americans could attain middle-class status by *appearing* middle class. The NAACP, which was preoccupied with the *image* of the race, wanted to show whites that African Americans could embody middle-class values and behavior. In other words, even if they were not economically middle class, they should be presented in the arts and popular culture as educated, professional, moral, and hardworking in order to be accepted by white America.

The NAACP thus pushed for images of middle-class blacks in the arts and popular culture. For example, in the *Crisis* Du Bois published a variety of depictions of African Americans who, while not always middle class, tended at least to embody the "middle-class values" of respectability, dignity, and hard work. This strategy suggests that the NAACP was an organization run by and for the black middle classes. Certainly, there is a sense that in adopting and encouraging such representations, the NAACP deliberately reflected its membership. When the membership broadened after the Second World War, it could be argued that it reflected the class and prejudices of those in the head office setting the cultural agenda. But the tactic was also implemented with the *white* middle class in mind. These were the people the association believed could be most readily persuaded that the race deserved full citizenship and who also had the power to facilitate black advancement. So the NAACP pushed for cultural representations that it felt would secure white support. For example, many of the antilynching plays included middle-class black characters in order to elicit sympathy from whites. Similarly, the NAACP wanted the inclusion of respectable black figures in motion pictures in order to stress the similarities between the two sections of American society. It also used those "high" cultural forms that it believed were most highly valued by the middle classes and therefore more likely to impress them. The use of art, literature, and theater in the antilynching campaign, for example, was a deliberate attempt to reach middle-class whites and persuade them to back antilynching legislation.

Although white America was often the target for the NAACP's cultural campaigns, much of this work reached and was intended to reach black Americans. During the Renaissance in particular, the creation and publication of black culture were intended to instill racial pride among African Americans. Du Bois published photographs, short stories, and sketches that featured black people. This helped forge a sense of a black collective identity, which was crucial in sustaining the fight for civil rights. The NAACP wanted the removal of derogatory stereotypes from American culture not only because of their effect on whites but also because of their impact on African Americans; degrading images of the race damaged black self-esteem. Black America needed to be motivated and ready for the battle for racial equality, and culture provided a way of raising morale, highlighting issues, and forging a common bond. It would be wrong, therefore, to characterize the NAACP as an organization solely concerned with white America; at its heart, in terms of leadership, membership, and focus, were African Americans.

At the core of the NAACP's cultural campaigns was the belief that representations of African Americans affected the attitude of whites toward the race and therefore impacted how blacks were treated. It hoped that in changing these cultural representations, it would therefore be able to alter the treatment and status of blacks in American society. This principle has been criticized by scholars. Writing about the NAACP's Image Awards, K. Anthony Appiah argues that "there's no guarantee . . . that a score of movies with good Negroes in them will change the mind of a single bigot."[15] The same could be said for "good Negroes" in books, drawings, television programs, or any other form of culture. The NAACP placed a lot of faith in the assumption that encountering examples of well-mannered, respectable blacks would eradicate racist attitudes. Similarly, it could be guilty of overvaluing cultural attainment. It put too much faith in the idea that racist whites could be dragged out of their ignorance by an appreciation of black artistic talent.

However, the NAACP was not alone in advocating such an approach. In her study of African Americans and radio during the Second World War, Barbara Savage explains that there is a long tradition among African Americans of believing that images can carry and reinforce political meanings. She claims that there is an "enduring and unrecognized strand of African American political thought that focuses on . . . the development of politically compelling images to advance black political and economic interests." Other groups also placed an emphasis on culture and cultural representations, as could be seen during the Harlem Renaissance and later the New Deal. Many on the Left, including in the Communist Party, shared the belief that culture could effect social change. Even the actions of HUAC affirmed a belief in the power of culture. During the 1960s civil rights activists, while attacking the structures of racism, continued to use black cultural forms as part of the political struggle. They used different forms, and they used them in different ways—for example, there was more emphasis on black empowerment through culture and little interest in using the arts to affect white opinion—but they continued a tradition that saw the political in the cultural. Appiah, then, may well be wrong to dismiss the NAACP's principle as simply including a few "good Negroes" in films. The NAACP's cultural strategy challenged white society's construction of African Americans. The association acknowledged that culture could be used as a political and social weapon. It was being used in such a way by white America to deny blacks their full civil rights, and therefore it was not misguided to hope that this trend could be reversed and have the opposite effect.[16]

However, the NAACP could be criticized for adopting what was a cautious and conservative tactic when conditions for African Americans during the first half of the twentieth century were so desperate. Art exhibitions, poetry anthologies, and a campaign to change the content of movies might have seemed like a triviality when blacks were being denied even the most basic of human rights on a daily basis. Furthermore, a change in cultural representations alone would not grant African Americans full equality. Indeed, the greatest flaw in the NAACP's cultural policy was the way it conceived of racism. It was based on a belief that racism was an anomaly that existed principally in people's minds, whereas racism is also structural and exists in the institutions of society, which is why African Americans increasingly targeted those institutions during the civil rights movement. The NAACP did also attack racism through the law courts and legislation. This was, arguably, the more successful strand of its work. Its lawyers saw victories against white primaries, segregation on interstate bus and rail travel, racially restrictive covenants, and segregated public education; its leaders helped pressure the government into establishing the FEPC, desegregating the armed forces, and passing civil rights laws. When measured against these accomplishments, an antilynching art exhibition or a movie with more black extras was of marginal significance.

This is not, however, to deny the importance and, at times, the effectiveness of the NAACP's cultural work. There were moments when it was granted considerable time and attention, and it was clearly of interest to figures such as Walter White, James Weldon Johnson, and W. E. B. Du Bois. These men and their colleagues had some success in shaping cultural representations; through pressure and encouragement they helped to remove some of the most offensive depictions and create images of the race that could help inspire African Americans and influence whites. Furthermore, it would be a mistake to separate this strand of the association's activism from the rest of its fight for civil rights. Its cultural campaigns were designed to complement the legal and political programs. The association knew that when it put cases before the courts, or lobbied politicians, its work was undermined by a culture that continually reasserted that blacks were inferior. In altering the way African Americans were represented, it forced white America to confront the truth about the racial situation. If offensive stereotypes were removed, whites could no longer hide behind culturally reinforced claims of black incompetence, savagery, or contentment to deny African Americans their civil rights. When viewed in this light, the cultural campaigns appear not only more understandable but also more significant.

The NAACP's long struggle for racial equality was a battle fought not just in the legislature and the courtroom but also in the movie theater and art gallery, on the stage and television screen. An examination of the NAACP's relationship to culture, therefore, allows us to appreciate more fully the reach and scope of this multifaceted organization. It also suggests that cultural representations had, and continue to have, social and political implications. Certainly, the NAACP was not prepared to let white America be the sole creator of the nation's cultural landscape, nor would it allow offensive depictions to go unchallenged. It believed that much was at stake in the image of the race. In 1926 W. E. B. Du Bois asked an audience of NAACP members how it was that their "fighting organization" could talk about art. As usual, the novelist, dramatist, editor, and civil rights activist answered his own question; it was, he explained, "part of the great fight we are carrying on and it represents a forward and an upward look—a pushing onward." For Du Bois, the arts could play an important role in uplifting the race, and he wanted African Americans to contribute to the beauty and wonder of the world. In fact, as this study has shown, the NAACP's cultural campaigns were more even than this; they were part of a "great fight" to secure a full and equal place for African Americans in the life of their nation.[17]

# Acknowledgments

This book would not have been possible without funding from the Arts and Humanities Research Council (AHRC). I was also lucky enough to be one of the first recipients of an AHRC–Library of Congress grant, which allowed me to spend three happy months as a fellow at the Kluge Center; many thanks to the staff at the center and to my fellow scholars for making my stay both productive and enjoyable. Also thanks to Claire Ogilvie for a home in DC. One of the great pleasures of historical research is spending time in the archives, an experience that is greatly enhanced by the expertise of the librarians. Thanks are due, therefore, to the staff at the British Library and the Cambridge University Library for putting up with my requests for endless microfilm reels of NAACP Papers; to the librarians in the Manuscript, Motion Picture and Television, and Microform Divisions of the Library of Congress; and to the staff of the Beinecke Rare Book and Manuscript Library at Yale.

This project began when I was based at the University of Nottingham. Special thanks go to John Fagg, Richard King, and Peter Ling, who offered their considerable wisdom and guidance. Thank you also to Sharon Monteith, for her feedback and her support of not only me but many young scholars, and to Celeste Marie Bernier for her insights. Thanks for encouragement of a different sort to Keith Nottle and Mark Storey, who always appreciated the finer points of my research methods. I have now crossed the river and have a new batch of colleagues at Nottingham Trent University to whom I must express my gratitude. Particular thanks to Amy Fuller, Kevin Gould, Nick Hayes, and Bill Niven.

There is a thriving American studies community in the UK, and this project has benefited from the questions and comments from many a conference paper. I am particularly grateful to Brian Ward, who provided excellent guidance and pointed me in the direction of the University Press of Kentucky. The editorial team at Kentucky has been wonderfully enthusiastic and extremely patient with this first-time author. The anonymous readers who read drafts of the book helped me to improve it while giving me the encouragement to carry on.

I am blessed with many wonderful friends who have been kind enough to at least pretend to be interested in how this book was progressing. Gemma Whiley and Ian Whiley deserve an extra thank you for providing me with pudding and a bed on so many occasions. I owe a debt of thanks I can never repay to my parents. And finally, thank you to Jon, who has supported me in every way.

# Notes



## Abbreviations

| | |
|---|---|
| JWJ | James Weldon Johnson |
| JWJ/MS | James Weldon Johnson and Grace Nail Johnson Papers, followed by box and folder |
| LOC | Library of Congress |
| MCN | May Childs Nerney |
| NAACP/MF | Records of the National Association for the Advancement of Colored People, Microfilm Collection, followed by part and reel |
| NAACP/LC | Records of the National Association for the Advancement of Colored People, Manuscript Division, Library of Congress, followed by group, series and box |
| RW | Roy Wilkins |
| WW | Walter White |
| WW/MS | Walter Francis White and Poppy Cannon Papers, followed by box and folder |
| WDBP | W. E. B. Du Bois Papers, Microfilm Collection, followed by reel |
| WDB | W. E. B. Du Bois |



## Introduction

1. WDB, "Criteria of Negro Art," *Crisis* (Oct. 1926): 290; JWJ, "Race Prejudice and the Negro Artist," *Harper's* (Nov. 1928): 769–76, JWJ/MS: 73, 376.

2. During its third annual conference, the association declared that African Americans are "the victim of race prejudice." "Report of Third Annual Conference," *Crisis* (May 1911): 24–25. Douglass quoted in Blight, "W. E. B. Du Bois and the Struggle," 52. Frederickson notes that *race prejudice* was the favored term in early works criticizing white supremacy and that *racism* did not come into general use in the United States until the 1960s. See Frederickson, *Racism,* 165, 167. Nevertheless, the term *racism* will be used throughout this study, alongside *race prejudice.*

3. WDB, "Editorial," *Crisis* (Dec. 1910): 16; Storey quoted in Zangrando, "Organized Negro," 149.

4. Frederickson, *Black Image in the White Mind,* chap. 1. See also Williamson, *Crucible of Race;* Hale, *Making Whiteness,* 7.

5. A review of the literature on images of blacks in American culture is beyond the scope of this introduction. In addition to those works referenced throughout this study, see, e.g., Toll, *Blacking Up;* Lott, *Love and Theft;* Van Deburg, *Slavery and Race in American Popular Culture;* Gossett, Uncle Tom's Cabin *and American Culture;* M. D. Harris, *Colored Pictures;* L. M. Anderson, *Mammies No More;* Boskin, *Sambo;* McElya, *Clinging to Mammy.*

6. Meier, *Negro Thought in America,* 265; WDB, "The Talented Tenth" (1903), in Meier, *Negro Problem,* 45.

7. Verney and Sartain, "NAACP in Historiographical Perspective," xx.

8. Walling quoted in Lewis, *W. E. B. Du Bois: Biography of a Race,* 389; Ovington, *Black and White Sat Down Together,* 57.

9. Kellogg, *NAACP,* 19–21.

10. Berg, *Ticket to Freedom,* 18.

11. Kellogg, *NAACP,* 137.

12. Schneider, *We Return Fighting,* 46.

13. A useful introduction to the historiography of the NAACP is provided in Verney and Sartain, *Long Is the Way.* This collection of essays also demonstrates the growing depth and breadth of academic research into the NAACP. On the national campaigns of the NAACP, see, e.g., Sullivan, *Lift Every Voice;* Kellogg, *NAACP;* Schneider, *We Return Fighting;* Zangrando, *NAACP Crusade against Lynching;* Tushnet, *NAACP's Legal Strategy against Segregated Education;* Goings, *NAACP Comes of Age;* Berg, *Ticket to Freedom.* A number of studies focus on the NAACP at the state level. See Reed, *Chicago NAACP;* Cortner, *Mob Intent on Death;* Bernstein, *First Waco Horror;* Sartain, *Invisible Activists.* Biographies of NAACP leaders include Lewis, *W. E. B. Du Bois: Biography of a Race;* Lewis, *W. E. B. Du Bois: The Fight for Equality;* Levy, *James Weldon Johnson;* and Janken, *Walter White.* The one monograph on the NAACP and culture is Arthur, *Black Images in the American Theatre.* However, the book is greatly limited because Arthur did not have access to the NAACP's extensive papers in his research. For an introduction to the NAACP's cultural strategy, see Woodley, "In Harlem and Hollywood," 15–27.

14. On the Black Arts Movement, see Smethurst, *Black Arts Movement;* Ongiri, *Spectacular Blackness;* Collins and Crawford, *New Thoughts on the Black Arts Movement;* Sklaroff, *Black Culture and the New Deal,* 6; Savage, *Broadcasting Freedom,* 10.

## 1. The Birth of a Cultural Strategy

1. Stokes, *D. W. Griffith's* The Birth of a Nation*;* Weinberger, *"Birth of a Nation,"* 92, 84. See also Cripps, *Slow Fade to Black.* For a detailed description

of the censorship of *Birth,* see Fleener-Marzec, *D. W. Griffith's* The Birth of a Nation. Studies that include a close consideration of the place of race and racism in the film include Staiger, *"Birth of a Nation,"* 195–213; Rogin, "Sword Became a Flashing Vision," 250–93; Rocchio, *Reel Racism;* Leab, *From Sambo to Super-spade;* Gaines, *Fire and Desire;* Taylor, "Re-Birth of the Aesthetic in Cinema," 15–37; Bogle, *Toms, Coons, Mulattoes;* Everett, *Returning the Gaze;* Gallagher, "Racist Ideology and Black Abnormality," 68–76; Dyer, "Into the Light," 165–76.

2. Stokes, *D. W. Griffith's* The Birth of a Nation, 3, 7.

3. WDB, "Editorial," *Crisis* (May 1915): 33; Board of Directors to Mayor Mitchel, Mar. 19, 1915, NAACP/MF: 11A, 32.

4. NAACP LA Branch to City Council, Feb. 2, 1915, NAACP/MF: 11A, 32.

5. E. Burton Ceruti to MCN, Feb. 3, 1915, NAACP/MF: 11A, 32; WW to Howard Butler, Sept. 2, 1930, NAACP/MF: 11A, 34. It was estimated that by 1946 over two hundred million people had seen Griffith's film. See Merritt, "Dixon, Griffith and the Southern Legend," 27.

6. Quoted in Staiger, *"Birth of a Nation,"* 202.

7. Notice the past tense. Quoted in Cripps, *Slow Fade to Black,* 64.

8. Griffith quoted in Rogin, "Sword Became a Flashing Vision," 279; D. W. Griffith to *New York Globe,* Apr. 10, 1915, in Lang, *Birth of a Nation,* 168–69; Pascoe, *What Comes Naturally,* 176.

9. Pascoe, *What Comes Naturally,* 175, 177.

10. Quoted in Rogin, "Sword Became a Flashing Vision," 278.

11. E. Burton Ceruti to MCN, Feb. 3, 1915, NAACP/MF: 11A, 32. In the end, the NAACP had to resort to these local fights.

12. On the NAACP and Progressivism, see Fairclough, *Better Day Coming,* 69; Meier and Bracey, "NAACP as a Reform Movement," 6; Zangrando, "Organized Negro," 153–54; Rosenbloom. "Between Reform and Regulation," 310; De Grazia and Newman, *Banned Films,* 7–12.

13. De Grazia and Newman, *Banned Films,* 6.

14. See NAACP/MF: 11A, 32–33; Stokes, *D. W. Griffith's* The Birth of a Nation, 134–40.

15. On the fight in Boston, see Stokes, *D. W. Griffith's* The Birth of a Nation, 142–48, and "Fighting a Vicious Film—Protest against *The Birth of a Nation,*" pamphlet published by the Boston Branch of the NAACP, 1915, LOC, Rare Books and Special Collections.

16. On the film in Chicago, see NAACP/MF: 11A, 32; Stokes, *D. W. Griffith's* The Birth of a Nation, 158.

17. Over one million people, 10 percent of the black population, left the South between 1910 and 1930. Over four hundred thousand left between 1910 and 1920. See Marks, "Black Workers," 148.

18. Stokes, *D. W. Griffith's* The Birth of a Nation, 157–59; Sullivan, *Lift Every Voice,* 53, chap. 2.

19. MCN to Mrs Henderson, Indianapolis, May 24, 1915, NAACP/MF: 11A, 32.

20. John Shillady, Oct. 10, 1918, NAACP/MF: 11A, 33. See Stokes for a similar argument about the context of the war: *D. W. Griffith's* The Birth of a Nation, 227–31.

21. NAACP press releases, May 7, 1921, Nov. 1921, NAACP/MF: 11A, 33.

22. Telegram to Governor of Kansas, June 8, 1923, and WW to C. Comegor, Chairman, Kansas City Branch, Dec. 17, 1923, both NAACP/MF: 11A, 34.

23. Stokes, *D. W. Griffith's* The Birth of a Nation, 235.

24. Cripps, *Slow Fade to Black,* 53; Stokes, *D. W. Griffith's* The Birth of a Nation, 133; Nerney and Du Bois quoted in Cripps, *Slow Fade to Black,* 58, 67; Gaines, *Fire and Desire,* 223.

25. *Mutual* ruling quoted in McEwan, "Lawyers, Bibliographies, and the Klan," 358; Menand, "Do Movies Have Rights?" 187–91.

26. Griffith quoted in Grieveson, *Policing Cinema,* 195; Cripps, *Slow Fade to Black,* 64.

27. Fleener, "Answering Film with Film," 401.

28. Fleener, "Answering Film with Film," 412.

29. Letter from Mary White Ovington, n.d., ca. June 1915, MCN to Dr. Charles Bentley, Chicago, May 11, 1915, MCN to supporters, June 10, 1915, all NAACP/MF: 11A, 32. Sterne had also contacted Tuskegee about a possible film, but this too came to nothing. Tuskegee was involved in *The Birth of a Race* (1918), but African Americans increasingly lost influence over it, and the final film had nothing to do with their original message or ideas. See Cripps, "Making of *The Birth of a Race.*"

30. Franklin, *"Birth of a Nation,"* 10–23; McEwan, "Lawyers, Bibliographies, and the Klan," 360. On historical facsimiles, see Gallagher, "Racist Ideology and Black Abnormality," 75; White, *"Birth of a Nation,"* 216–17; D. W. Griffith, *New York Globe,* Apr. 10, 1915, in Lang, *Birth of a Nation,* 168–69.

31. The historiography was dominated by the "Dunningite School" and included works by William A. Dunning, C. William Ramsdell, James G. de Roulhac Hamilton, and Walter Lynwood Fleming.

32. Moorfield Storey to editor of *Boston Herald,* n.d., in "Fighting a Vicious Film," 22; WDB, "Fighting Race Calumny," *Crisis* (June 1915): 87.

33. Thomas Dixon to *New York Globe,* Apr. 10, 1915, in Lang, *Birth of a Nation,* 166–67.

34. Blight, "W. E. B. Du Bois and the Struggle," 46; WDB, "Reconstruction and Its Benefits"; Lynch, *Facts of Reconstruction;* WDB, *Black Reconstruction in America* (1935).

35. Lewis, *W. E. B. Du Bois: Biography of a Race,* 509; see also 460–61.

36. Krasner, *Beautiful Pageant,* 89; "The Great Pageant," *Washington Bee,* Oct. 23, 1915, and *The Star of Ethiopia,* script, both WDBP: 87.

37. Stokes, *D. W. Griffith's* The Birth of a Nation, 167; Blight, *Race and Re-union,* 375–77; Du Bois quoted in Krasner, *Beautiful Pageant,* 82.

38. The pageant demonstrated that it was not always easy to reach a white audience. A review of the performance in Washington commented that "only a very few white persons came to see it." See "The Great Pageant," *Washington Bee,* Oct. 23, 1915, WDBP: 87.

39. Stokes, *D. W. Griffith's* The Birth of a Nation, 168, 227–41; Cripps, *Slow Fade to Black,* 57, 64–69.

40. Du Bois quoted in Stokes, *D. W. Griffith's* The Birth of a Nation, 169; Gaines, *Fire and Desire,* 263; Cripps, *Slow Fade to Black,* 63.

41. Stokes, *D. W. Griffith's* The Birth of a Nation, 169; Weinberger, *"Birth of a Nation,"* 80; Report of Chairman to Board of Directors, Jan. 1916, NAACP/MF: 1, 1; Gaines, *Fire and Desire,* 230.

42. Weinberger, *"Birth of a Nation,"* 79.

## 2. Representing the New Negro

1. JWJ, "Preface," in Johnson and Johnson, *Book of American Negro Spirituals* (1925), 49–50.

2. Du Bois quoted in Sullivan, *Lift Every Voice,* 138. There has been much scholarly work on the Harlem Renaissance, and a number of historians have considered the role that the NAACP and its leaders played in facilitating the outpouring of black culture during these decades. Kenneth Janken's biography of Walter White and David Levering Lewis's study of W. E. B. Du Bois are particularly useful, because they both examine how the artistic exploits of their respective subjects were linked to their civil rights work. See Janken, *Walter White;* Lewis, *W. E. B. Du Bois: The Fight for Equality.* See also Lewis, *When Harlem Was in Vogue;* G. Hutchinson, *Harlem Renaissance in Black and White;* Huggins, *Harlem Renaissance;* Schneider, *We Return Fighting.*

3. There exists some difference among historians as to the years that mark the perimeters of the Harlem Renaissance. For example, Steven Watson's timeline begins in 1920 and ends in 1930, with the publication of Langston Hughes's novel *Not Without Laughter,* whereas Nathan Huggins begins with the triumphant return in 1919 of the all-black 369th Regiment and ends with the Harlem riot of 1935. S. Watson, *Harlem Renaissance;* Huggins, *Harlem Renaissance;* Kornweibel, "Economic Profile of Black Life," 308–9; JWJ, *Black Manhattan,* 59.

4. Locke, "The New Negro," in Locke, *New Negro,* 15; JWJ, "Preface," in Johnson and Johnson, *Second Book of American Negro Spirituals* (1926), 19.

5. Rudwick and Meier, "Rise of the Black Secretariat," 94–127.

6. Schneider, *We Return Fighting,* chap. 2; Cortner, *Mob Intent on Death;* Sullivan, *Lift Every Voice,* 114.

7. Press release, Jan. 24, 1925, NAAC/MF: 1, 1.

8. JWJ to WW, Apr. 13, 1923, NAACP/MF: 2, 7; Kirschke, *Aaron Douglas,* 172; JWJ, *Book of American Negro Poetry,* 9.

9. See, e.g., Huggins, *Harlem Renaissance,* 27; Lewis, *W. E. B. Du Bois: The Fight for Equality,* 156; Carroll, *Word, Image, and the New Negro,* 7; Douglas, *Terrible Honesty,* 324.

10. Locke, *New Negro,* 15; Pearson, "Combating Racism with Art," 123–34; Charles S. Johnson, "An Opportunity for Negro Writers," *Opportunity* (Sept. 1924): 258; author unknown, "The Race Coming Back in Literature," *Negro World,* Oct. 11, 1924. See also Martin, *Literary Garveyism.*

11. Johnson used the narrator in his novel to test out some of the ideas he would later express as his own. See JWJ, *Autobiography of an Ex-Colored Man,* 40; JWJ, "American Music," *New York Age,* Jan. 13, 1916; JWJ, "Preface," in *Book of American Negro Poetry* (1st ed., 1922), 20.

12. WW, *Man Called White,* 180–85; Minutes of Spingarn Committee Meeting, Jan. 16, 1939, NAACP/MF: 11A, 6.

13. JWJ to Editor of the *Tribune,* Apr. 5, 1922, JWJ/MS: 12, 269.

14. JWJ, "Preface," in *Book of American Negro Poetry* (1st ed., 1922), 10–12, 16, 20; WDB, "The Social Origins of American Negro Art," *Modern Quarterly* (Autumn 1943), quoted in Turner, "W. E. B. Du Bois and the Theory," 78.

15. G. Hutchinson, *Harlem Renaissance in Black and White,* 145.

16. JWJ, "American Negro Spirituals," *Standard* (Jan. 1926): 155–57, JWJ/ MS: 67, 288; 1922 speech quoted in Sullivan, *Lift Every Voice,* 104.

17. George S. Schuyler, "The Negro Art Hokum," *Nation* 122 (June 16, 1926), reprinted in Mitchell, *Within the Circle,* 51–53.

18. Langston Hughes, "The Negro Artist and the Racial Mountain," *Nation* 122 (June 28, 1926), reprinted in Mitchell, *Within the Circle,* 55–59.

19. WDB, "The Younger Literary Movement," *Crisis* (Feb. 1924): 161; WDB, "Opinion," *Crisis* (June 1924): 56; WDB, "Opinion," *Crisis* (June 1921): 55–56.

20. WDB, "Krigwa, 1926," *Crisis* (Jan. 1926): 115.

21. WDB, "Criteria of Negro Art."

22. Byerman, *Seizing the Word.*

23. WDB, "Books," *Crisis* (Dec. 1926): 81–82.

24. JWJ, *Along This Way,* 381–82; JWJ to Richetta Randolph, Sept. 16, 1926, JWJ/MS: 16, 386; Wallace Thurman, "Stranger at the Gates," *Messenger* (Sept. 1926): 279.

25. WDB, "The Browsing Reader," *Crisis* (June 1928): 202.

26. WDB, "The Negro in Art: How Shall He Be Portrayed?" *Crisis* (Mar. 1926): 219.

27. WDB, "The Negro in Art," *Crisis* (Mar. 1926): 291, (Apr. 1926): 280.

28. WDB, "The Negro in Art," *Crisis* (Aug. 1926): 194, (Apr. 1926): 278.

29. Charles S. Johnson, "American Negro Art," *Opportunity* (Aug. 1926): 238–39; Alain Locke, "Art or Propaganda?" *Harlem* 1, no. 1 (1928), 12.

30. WDB, "The Negro in Art," *Crisis* (April 1926): 279 (emphasis in original), (June 1926): 71–72, and (Mar. 1926): 220.

31. WDB, "The Negro in Art," *Crisis* (Apr. 1926): 279–80.

32. JWJ, *Along This Way,* 374, 382.

33. A circular sent out to advertise Johnson's autobiography offered discounts for bulk orders and payment to the branch for sales; the branch received between $1.16 and $1.40 for every copy sold. See NAACP/MF: 11A, 12.

34. Levy, *James Weldon Johnson,* 311.

35. Countee Cullen to WW, June 20, 1925, NAACP/MF: 2, 9.

36. WW to Claude McKay, May 20, 1925, NAACP/MF: 2, 19. There is no reference in any of this correspondence to the name of the novel. Most scholars believe that it was *Color Scheme,* McKay's first attempt at a novel, which was never published. See, e.g., Scruggs, "Alain Locke and Walter White," 95, 96; WW to McKay, July 8, 1925, NAACP/MF: 2, 9. See also Waldron, *Walter White and the Harlem Renaissance,* 137–45.

37. McKay, *Long Way from Home,* 111; Sterling Brown to JWJ, Nov. 30, 1931, JWJ/MS: 4, 66.

38. The others identified by Lewis were Jessie Fauset, Charles Johnson, Alain Locke, and Casper Holstein, a West Indian businessman who ran a lucrative betting enterprise and donated money to *Opportunity.* See Lewis, *When Harlem Was in Vogue,* 120; Wintz, *Black Culture,* 102–3; Janken, *Walter White,* 91.

39. Lewis, *When Harlem Was in Vogue,* 136; Hughes, *Big Sea,* 191; JWJ, *Along This Way,* 378.

40. Boyle, *Arc of Justice.*

41. Raymond McKelvey to JWJ, Dec. 17, 1928, NAACP/MF: 2, 2; WW to Alain Locke, June 28, 1924, NAACP/MF: 2, 7; Konrad Bercovici, "The Rhythm of Harlem," *Survey Graphic,* "Harlem Number" (Mar. 1925): 679.

42. Harold Cruse is particularly critical of white control of the Harlem Renaissance; he claims this is the primary reason why it failed. See Cruse, *Crisis of the Negro Intellectual.*

43. Lewis, *When Harlem Was in Vogue,* 135.

44. JWJ, "Negro Authors and White Publishers," *Crisis* (July 1929): 228–29.

45. WDB, "Postscript," *Crisis* (April 1927): 70; WDB to Amy Spingarn, Jan. 19, 1928, in Aptheker, *Correspondence of W. E. B. Du Bois,* 372.

46. Hughes, *Big Sea,* 178; Huggins, *Harlem Renaissance,* 303; Lewis, *When Harlem Was in Vogue,* 305.

47. Langston Hughes quoted in Wintz, *Black Culture,* 227; Carroll, *Word, Image, and the New Negro;* Huggins, *Harlem Renaissance,* 303–4; Kellogg, *NAACP,* 240; WW, *Man Called White,* 50–51.

48. Committee evidence quoted in Sullivan, *Lift Every Voice,* 97; JWJ, "Race Prejudice and the Negro Artist."

## 3. Du Bois's *Crisis* and the Black Image on the Page

1. See, e.g., Huggins, *Harlem Renaissance,* 30; Johnson and Johnson, *Propaganda and Aesthetics,* 37; Rampersad, *Art and Imagination,* 201; Lewis, *W. E. B. Du Bois: The Fight for Equality,* 163.

2. Kirschke, *Art in Crisis*; Carroll, *Word, Image, and the New Negro.*

3. WDB, *Dusk of Dawn,* 248, 258. In 1919 there were 56,345 members, whereas circulation of the *Crisis* peaked in June that year with one hundred thousand copies sold. See Kellogg, *NAACP,* 136, 153. It is reasonable to speculate that the readership was even greater still, given that one copy of a magazine would often be seen by many. See WDB, "Editorial," *Crisis* (Mar. 1917): 218.

4. Lewis, *When Harlem Was in Vogue,* 7; WDB, "Editing 'The Crisis,'" *Crisis* (Mar. 1951): 150; Marable, *W. E. B. Du Bois,* 77; Kellogg, *NAACP,* 137, 150.

5. Her contribution to the Harlem Renaissance has not always been acknowledged, and she has often been evaluated on the basis of her novels rather than her literary editorship of the *Crisis.* Notable exceptions are A. Johnson, "Literary Midwife," 143, and Sylvander, *Jessie Redmon Fauset.*

6. WDB, "Opinion," *Crisis* (Nov. 1922): 7, and (May 1925): 8.

7. Figures taken from data in Yellin, "Index of Literary Materials," 453–65; Lewis, *W. E. B. Du Bois: The Fight for Equality,* 180.

8. JWJ, *Book of American Negro Poetry,* 9; "Krigwa," *Crisis* (Oct. 1926): 105–6.

9. WDB, "The Amy Spingarn Prizes for Literature and Art," *Crisis* (Oct. 1924): 244. A "competition" was first mentioned in the *Crisis* in 1912, but it was not so much a competition as a call for submissions of work. See "Short Story Competition," *Crisis* (Aug. 1912): 189: WDB; "Krigwa," *Crisis* (Oct. 1925): 275–78.

10. WDB, "Krigwa," *Crisis* (Dec. 1926): 70–71; WDB, "Proposed Rules of the Competition," *Crisis* (May 1931): 157; WDB, "The Annual Du Bois Literary Prize of One Thousand Dollars," and WDB, "Postscript," both *Crisis* (Apr. 1934): 117, 137.

11. WDB, "Krigwa," *Crisis* (Dec. 1926): 71.

12. Lewis, *When Harlem Was in Vogue,* 97; S. Watson, *Harlem Renaissance,* 25; advertisement for "*Opportunity*'s Second Annual Contest for Negro Writers," *Opportunity* (Oct. 1925); Locke quoted in Johnson and Johnson, *Propaganda and Aesthetics,* 51.

13. Randolph and Owen quoted in Johnson and Johnson, *Propaganda and Aesthetics,* 58. Two hundred twenty-six poems were published in *Messenger,* compared to 194 in the *Crisis* and 202 in *Opportunity.* See Kornweibel, *No Crystal Stair,* 126, 106. Kornweibel has underestimated the number of poems in the *Crisis;* 253 poems were printed during this period. The figure is from Yellin, "Index of Literary Materials."

14. Douglas, *Terrible Honesty,* 83; Carroll, *Word, Image, and the New Negro,* 191.

15. Kirschke, *Art in Crisis.*

16. WDB, "Opinion," *Crisis* (Oct. 1920): 263–64 (emphasis in original).

17. WDB, *Dusk to Dawn,* 271.

18. Kirschke, *Art in Crisis,* 131; Aaron Douglas, *Invincible Music: The Spirit of Africa, Crisis* (Feb. 1926): 169.

19. Langston Hughes, "The Negro," *Crisis* (Jan. 1922): 113.

20. "The Muslim Priest and the Heathen," adapted by A. O. Stafford, *Crisis* (Nov. 1913): 345–46; "How the Spider Won and Lost Nzambi's Daughter," from the collection by Monroe Work, *Crisis* (Oct. 1915): 301–2: Fenton Johnson, "Black Fairy," *Crisis* (Oct. 1913): 292–94.

21. G. Hutchinson, *Harlem Renaissance in Black and White,* 145–46.

22. Williams, "*Crisis* Cover Girl," 200–218.

23. Anonymous, "Octoroon," *Crisis* (Nov. 1913): cover; John Henry Adams, untitled, *Crisis* (Mar. 1922): cover; Sherrard-Johnson, *Portraits of the New Negro Woman,* 10. For examples of passing stories, see Edith Manuel Durham, "Deepening Dusk," *Crisis* (Jan. 1931): 12–14, (Feb. 1931): 49–52; Ottie B. Graham, "Holiday," *Crisis* (May 1923): 12–17; Rudolph Fisher, "High Yaller," *Crisis* (Oct. 1925): 281–86, (Nov. 1925): 33–38; Sherrard-Johnson, *Portraits of the New Negro Woman,* 4.

24. Aaron Douglas, *The Burden of Black Womanhood, Crisis* (Sept. 1927): cover.

25. Anonymous, "Woman to the Rescue," *Crisis* (May 1916): 43; J. B. Watson, untitled, *Crisis* (Feb. 1933): cover.

26. Richard Brown, *Dark Easter, Crisis* (April 1929): cover; Allan Freelon, *A Jungle Nymph, Crisis* (June 1928): cover; Kirschke, *Art in Crisis,* 160.

27. Rampersad, *Art and Imagination,* 208.

28. WDB, "The Browsing Reader," *Crisis* (June 1928): 202.

29. Mrs. Paul Lawrence [*sic*] Dunbar, "Hope Deferred," *Crisis* (Sept. 1914): 238–42.

30. "Social Life of Colored America," *Crisis* (Feb. 1912): 154–55; "Colored Los Angeles Greets THE CRISIS in Its Own Motor Cars," *Crisis* (Aug. 1913): 182–83.

31. John Henry Adams, *The Christmas Reckoning, Crisis* (Dec. 1910): 18–19.

32. Edwin Drummond Sheen, "The Death Game," *Crisis* (Jan. 1927): 134–37, (Feb. 1927): 198–202.

33. On Du Bois and labor, see Lewis, *W. E. B. Du Bois: The Fight for Equality,* 305–10; Heba Jannath, "Black Man," *Crisis* (May 1930): 163. Not all the pieces celebrating black life were written by African Americans. Heba Jannath was the pen name of Josephine Cogdell, the white wife of the black literary critic and *Messenger* editor George Schuyler.

34. J. E. Dodd, *The Black Miner, Crisis* (Nov. 1933): cover.

35. S. Watson, *Harlem Renaissance,* 158.

36. H. F. V. Edward, "Job-Hunters," *Crisis* (Dec. 1931): 417–20.

37. On Fauset, see McDowell, "Introduction," xii–xiii. On Du Bois, see Wilkerson and Zamir, "Du Bois and the 'New Negro,'" 74.

38. Kirschke, *Art in Crisis,* 137.

39. Fenton Johnson, "The Servant," *Crisis* (Aug. 1912): 189–90.

40. Vincent, *Keep Cool,* 171, 169, 172.

41. For an account of Du Bois's battle with Villard, see Rudwick, "W. E. B. Du Bois in the Role," 218–24. On Du Bois and the war, see WDB, "Close Ranks," *Crisis* (July 1918): 111; Henry Davis Middleton, "The Ragtime Regiment," *Crisis* (Sept. 1917): 252–55; William Edward Scott, "At Bay," *Crisis* (Nov. 1918): cover. On African Americans during the Depression, see Badger, *New Deal,* 25–26. On the board and the *Crisis,* see NAACP/LC: I F 2.

42. WDB, "Segregation," *Crisis* (Jan. 1934): 20; WW to Joel Spingarn, Jan. 15, 1934, NAACP/MF: 11A, 30; WDB, "Segregation in the North," *Crisis* (Apr. 1934): 115–17; "The Board of Directors on Segregation," *Crisis* (May 1934): 149; Minutes of Board of Directors Meeting, May 14, 1934, NAACP/MF: 1, 2.

43. Roy Wilkins, "Memorandum to the chairman of the Committee on the Future Plan and Program of the NAACP," July 1934, NAACP/MF: 16A, 8; Roy Wilkins, "The Crisis, 1934–49," *Crisis* (Mar. 1951): 156.

44. G. Hutchinson, *Harlem Renaissance in Black and White,* 145.

45. Schneider, *We Return Fighting,* 399.

## 4. "A union of art and propaganda"

1. Moorfield Storey, NAACP Conference, June 1922, NAACP/MF: 1, 8.

2. WW to Mrs Harry Payne Whitney, Dec. 13, 1934, NAACP/MF: 7B, 2.

3. Dray, *At the Hands of Persons Unknown,* viii; Zangrando, *NAACP Crusade against Lynching,* 4; WW, *Rope and Faggot,* 82. For a discussion of lynching, sexuality, and patriarchy, see Hall, *Revolt against Chivalry,* 145–47.

4. WW, *Rope and Faggot,* 112; address of Moorfield Storey, Annual Conference, 1921, NAACP/MF: 1, 8.

5. Zangrando, *NAACP Crusade against Lynching,* 51–71, 114–15.

6. Angelina Weld Grimké quoted in Krasner, *Beautiful Pageant,* 105; Hale, *Making Whiteness;* Wood, *Lynching and Spectacle.* See also Patterson, *Rituals in Blood;* and Markovitz, *Legacies of Lynching.*

7. For example, George Wright, in his study of lynching in Kentucky, found that at least 353 people were lynched there, compared to the figure of 205 in most sources. He suggests that there was likely to be a similar disparity in other southern states. See Wright, *Racial Violence in Kentucky,* 5.

8. Stephens, "Lynching Dramas and Women: History and Critical Context," in Perkins and Stephens, *Strange Fruit,* 3. Perkins and Stephens helped focus scholarly attention on lynching dramas in the 1990s and were among those who "rediscovered" plays that had fallen from view.

9. Program quoted in *Washington Evening Star,* extract in *Crisis* (Apr. 1916): 284; Hatch, "Introduction," in Hatch and Hamalian, *Lost Plays of the Harlem Renaissance,* 12; Hull, *Color, Sex and Poetry,* 118.

10. Angelina Weld Grimké, *Rachel,* in Perkins and Stephens, *Strange Fruit,* 27, 42.

11. Angelina Weld Grimké, "'Rachel,' The Play of the Month: The Reason and Synopsis by the Author," in Hatch and Hamalian, *Lost Plays of the Harlem Renaissance,* 424–25; *Courier* and *Catholic World* quoted in Hull, *Color, Sex and Poetry,* 122; Hatch and Shine, *Black Theatre USA,* 134.

12. Alice Dunbar-Nelson, *Mine Eyes Have Seen, Crisis* (Apr. 1918): 271–74.

13. Myrtle Smith Livingston, *For Unborn Children, Crisis* (July 1926): 123–24; Omodele, "For Us," 62.

14. Georgia Douglas Johnson, *A Sunday Morning in the South,* in Hatch and Shine, *Black Theatre USA,* 233–37; Georgia Douglas Johnson, *Safe,* in Perkins and Stephens, *Strange Fruit,* 110–15. Johnson almost certainly deliberately chose a name close to that of Sam Hose, a black man who was brutally tortured and killed in Georgia in 1899. This was a lynching that had a particular resonance for African Americans. Du Bois often recounted how he was walking down a street in Atlanta when he learned Hose's knuckles were for sale in a nearby shop. See, for example, Dray, *At the Hands of Persons Unknown,* 3–16; Georgia Douglas Johnson, *Blue-Eyed Black Boy,* in Perkins and Stephens, *Strange Fruit,* 116–20.

15. WW to Georgia Douglas Johnson, Jan. 18, 1937, Georgia Douglas Johnson, *A Bill to Be Passed,* ca. 1938, Juanita Jackson to Georgia Douglas Johnson, Feb. 7, 1938, and Georgia Douglas Johnson to Juanita Jackson, Jan. 7, 1938, all NAACP/LC: I C 299. There is no evidence in the NAACP papers that it was used in this way.

16. Juanita Jackson to Georgia Douglas Johnson, Feb. 7, 1938.

17. Livingston, *For Unborn Children,* 122; Grimke, "'Rachel,' The Play of the Month," 425; Johnson, *Sunday Morning,* 233.

18. *Aftermath* was published in 1919 and performed by the New York Krigwa Players in 1928. In it a black man returns from the war in France to discover his father has been lynched. See Perkins and Stephens, *Strange Fruit,* 79–91.

19. T. Harris, "Before the Strength, the Pain," 32.

20. Zangrando, *NAACP Crusade against Lynching,* 101 (league quote at 112); letter from WW, Jan. 12, 1934, NAACP/MF: 7B, 4; WW to Heywood Broun, Dec. 5, 1933, NAACP/MF: 7B, 4.

21. Quoted in Arnold, "Erskine Caldwell and Judge Lynch," 198.

22. Examples include Theodore Dreiser, "Nigger Jeff" (1918); Sutton Griggs, *The Hindered Hand* (1905); Claude McKay, "The Lynching" (1922); and Richard Wright, "Big Boy Leaves Home," from *Uncle Tom's Children* (1938). NAACP members themselves produced work that included or dealt with incidents of racial violence. Walter White's *The Fire in the Flint* (1924) depicts two lynchings;

branch secretary Robert Bagnall wrote a short story about the effect of lynching on whites ("The Unquenchable Fire," 1924); the protagonist of James Weldon Johnson's *Autobiography of an Ex-Colored Man* (1912) witnesses a mob killing, and Johnson writes of it in his poem "Brothers" (1916).

23. T. Harris, *Exorcising Blackness,* 28.

24. See Hughes, "Home" (1934), 37–45; Robert Bagnall, "The Unquenchable Fire" (1924), in Rice, *Witnessing Lynching,* 240–46; Caldwell, *Trouble in July* (1940; reprint, 1948). In the latter two white women also become victims of a patriarchal and racist society.

25. "The Work of a Mob," *Crisis* (Sept. 1918): 221–23.

26. Angelina Weld Grimké, "Goldie" (1920), in Rice, *Witnessing Lynching,* 203. Another response is Anne Spencer's poem "White Things" (originally published in *Crisis* [Mar. 1923]), in Rice, *Witnessing Lynching,* 236. Barbara Foley draws the comparison between Turner's death and the lynching Kabnis hears of in Jean Toomer's *Cane.* See Foley, "In the Land of Cotton," 184.

27. See "The Lynching of Claude Neal," NAACP/MF: 7A, 4; WW to WLAL members, Dec. 24, 1934, NAACP/MF: 7B, 4.

28. George Schuyler, "Scripture for Lynchers," *Crisis* (Jan. 1935): 12.

29. WW, *Man Called White,* 167.

30. See Apel, *Imagery of Lynching,* and Wood, *Lynching and Spectacle,* for further analysis of the construction and power of lynching photographs and the ways in which they were used by both apologists and activists. See "The Waco Horror," *Crisis* (July 1916): 6. See also Bernstein, *First Waco Horror.*

31. Apel, *Imagery of Lynching,* 40. See also NAACP/MF: 7A, 9.

32. Langa, "Two Antilynching Art Exhibitions," 10–39; Park, "Lynching and Antilynching," 311–65; Vendryes, "Hanging on Their Walls," 154–76. See also Kirschke's discussion of lynching imagery in the *Crisis* (*Art in Crisis*).

33. WW to Mrs Harry Payne Whitney, Dec. 13, 1934, WW to Suzanne La Follette, Dec. 13, 1934, and Erskine Caldwell, "A Note," *An Art Commentary on Lynching Catalogue,* all NAACP/MF: 7B, 2.

34. NAACP press release, Feb. 7, 1935, WW to Julius Bloch, Dec. 20, 1934, WW to Hugo Gellet of the *New Masses,* Jan. 16, 1935, and Caldwell, "Note," all NAACP/MF: 7B, 2.

35. The black artists were Samuel Brown, E. Simms Campbell, Henry Bannern, Allan Freelon, Wilmer Jennings, Malvin Grey Johnson, William Mosby, and Hale Woodruff. There are some disparities between the pieces and artists discussed in the secondary literature. I have based my discussion on those who are listed in the NAACP's catalog and whose appearance has been corroborated by Apel, Langa, Park, or Vendryes.

36. Apel, *Imagery of Lynching,* 87; Langa, "Two Antilynching Art Exhibitions," 22.

37. Apel, *Imagery of Lynching,* 91.

38. Langa, "Two Antilynching Art Exhibitions," 28; Vendryes, "Hanging on Their Walls," 168. White artists also used religious symbolism; for examples, see Prentiss Taylor's *Christ in Alabama* (1932) and Julius Bloch's *The Lynching* (1932), which shows a black man in a crucifix position.

39. Allan Freelon to WW, Feb. 2, 1935, NAACP/MF: 7B, 2.

40. *Brooklyn Daily Eagle,* Feb. 15, 1935, NAACP/MF: 7B, 3; *Times* quoted in Apel, *Imagery of Lynching,* 95; *New York Post,* Feb. 15, 1935, NAACP/MF: 7B, 3; *World-Telegram* quoted in the *Crisis* (Apr. 1935): 106.

41. WW to William Mosby, Feb. 26, 1935, NAACP/MF: 7B, 2.

42. WW to Charles Alston, Mar. 1, 1935, and press release, Feb. 12, 1935, both NAACP/MF: 7B, 2; *New York Amsterdam News,* quoted in Park, "Lynching and Antilynching," 327. The CP Bill was meant only as a symbolic gesture because the Communists believed lynching could not be stopped by legislation but only ended through revolution.

43. Quoted in Apel, *Imagery of Lynching,* 122.

44. The artists who appeared in both shows were Aaron J. Goodelman, Noguchi, Orozco, Becker, and Sternberg. See Hemingway, *Artists on the Left,* 64.

45. On the images in the Communist show, see Langa, "Two Antilynching Art Exhibitions," 14–15, 12. Alexander quoted in Apel, *Imagery of Lynching,* 119.

46. On the NAACP and the black working class, see Sullivan, *Lift Every Voice,* 203, 191.

47. See Record, *Negro and the Communist Party,* 292; Record, *Race and Radicalism;* Cruse, *Crisis of the Negro Intellectual,* 187, 148–51; Young, *Black Writers of the Thirties,* 180; Bone, *Negro Novel in America,* 116.

48. Naison, *Communists in Harlem during the Depression;* Foley, *Radical Representations;* Mullen, *Popular Fronts;* Maxwell, *New Negro, Old Left.* Important in this scholarly reassessment of the Left and culture is Denning's *The Cultural Front.* Denning provides a broader understanding of Popular Front influence, which lasted longer and was farther reaching than had been assumed.

49. On *New Masses,* see Hemingway, *Artists on the Left,* 8–20; Naison, *Communists in Harlem during the Depression,* 207–8 (emphasis in original).

50. Sklaroff, *Black Culture and the New Deal,* 5 (Ickes quote at 33); JWJ, *Book of American Negro Poetry,* 9.

51. WW to Sherwood Anderson, Apr. 20, 1938, WW to Sidney Howard, Apr. 23, 1938, and letters between RW and Emmet Lavery, Apr. 11, Apr. 14, Apr. 15, 1938, all NAACP/MF: 10, 8; Sklaroff, *Black Culture and the New Deal,* 6.

52. Lynching figures from Zangrando, *NAACP Crusade against Lynching,* 6–7; Gallup Brian Search Results are at http://brain.gallup.com/search/results.asp x?SearchTypeAll=lynching&SearchConType=1 (accessed Apr. 26, 2012).

53. Tolnay and Beck argue that migration brought a reduction in lynchings because it economically affected the white southern elite (*Festival of Violence,* 255).

54. WW, *Rope and Faggot,* 181; Dray, *At the Hands of Persons Unknown,* 461.

55. Rice, *Witnessing Lynching,* 23.

56. Definition drawn up at conference of antilynching activists in 1940, quoted in Ames, *Changing Character of Lynching,* 29.

57. Zangrando, *NAACP Crusade against Lynching,* 146; Sklaroff, *Black Culture and the New Deal,* 5.

58. Quoted in Margolick, *Strange Fruit,* 74.

59. "Anti-lynching Film Is Hit in New York," *Crisis* (July 1936): 212; Cripps, *Slow Fade to Black,* 295.

## 5. White in Hollywood

1. In 1930 a synchronized version of *Birth* incorporating the musical score and sound effects was released. Caught between the old dilemma of not wanting to inadvertently assist the film by fanning the flames of controversy and the fear of leaving it uncontested, the national office instructed the branches to quietly exert pressure on the local authorities. See "Hallelujah," *Crisis* (Oc. 1929): 355; Bogle, *Toms, Coons, Mullatoes,* 36; Chauncey Townsend, "Out of the Kitchen," *Crisis* (Jan. 1935): 15, 29.

2. WW to Joseph Breen, Motion Picture Producers Association, July 27, 1942, NAACP/LC: II A 275.

3. WW, *Man Called White,* 199; press release, July 27, 1942, NAACP/LC: II A 275.

4. Report on study in Arthur Kellogg, "Minds Made by Movies," *Survey Graphic,* May 1933; Edgar Dale, "The Movies and Race Relations," *Crisis* (Oct. 1937): 294–96. On the black press, see Everett, *Returning the Gaze;* Widener, *Black Arts West,* chap. 1.

5. WW to Peter Furst, editor, *PM,* Sept. 23, 1942, NAACP/LC: II A 275.

6. WW to Edwin Embree, Mar. 4, 1943, NAACP/LC: II A 279.

7. WW to Sara Boynoff, *Los Angeles Daily News,* Mar. 12, 1942, NAACP/LC: II A 275.

8. Cripps, *Making Movies Black,* chap. 2; Janken, *Walter White,* chap. 9; Sklaroff, *Black Culture and the New Deal,* 204.

9. George Schuyler, "Not Gone with the Wind," *Crisis* (July 1937): 205–6.

10. Leff, "David Selznick's *Gone with the Wind,*" 149–51.

11. WW to David Selznick, June 26, 1938, NAACP/LC: II L 15.

12. See Butsch, "American Movie Audiences of the 1930s," 106–20.

13. RW to Alfred Duckett, secretary of Brooklyn branch, Jan. 31, 1940, NAACP/LC: II A 277; WW to Selznick, June 7, 1938, and Selznick to WW, June 20, 1938, both NAACP/LC: II L 15. There were two historical advisers on the set, both white southerners. Although there was some discussion of black advisors— Selznick thought of the choir leader Hall Johnson, while the NAACP suggested

the dean of Howard University, Charles Wesley—one never materialized. See RW to Selznick, July 25, 1938, NAACP/LC: II L 15.

14. WW to Selznick, June 26, 1938, NAACP/LC: II L 15.

15. On pressure from the black community, see Watts, *Hattie McDaniel*, 157; Cripps, "Winds of Change," 139.

16. Breen quoted in Leff, "David Selznick's *Gone with the Wind*," 152; story editor quoted in Watts, *Hattie McDaniel*, 154, 158.

17. Tolson quoted in Watts, *Hattie McDaniel*, 174–75; Du Bois quoted in Cripps, *Slow Fade to Black*, 364; William L. Patterson, "*Gone with the Wind:* A Review," *Chicago Defender*, Jan. 6, 1940.

18. Roy Wilkins, "Editorial," *Crisis* (Jan. 1940): 17.

19. RW to Alfred Duckett, Jan. 31, 1940, NAACP/LC: II A 277.

20. WW to Selznick, Mar. 26, 1940, NAACP/LC: II A 280.

21. Leff, "David Selznick's *Gone with the Wind*," 155.

22. FDR quoted in Winkler, *Politics of Propaganda,* 57; Koppes and Black, *Hollywood Goes to War,* 66.

23. Koppes and Black, "Blacks, Loyalty and Motion-Picture Propaganda," 385; Koppes and Black, *Hollywood Goes to War,* 179.

24. RW to WW, memo, Mar. 23, 1942, and memo by RW for OFF, "Improving Negro Morale with White People," Apr. 3, 1942, both NAACP/LC: II A 607.

25. See letters in NAACP/LC: VIII 458.

26. Janken, *Walter White,* 252; WW to John Holley, Nov. 25, 1941, NAACP/LC: II A 280.

27. WW, *Man Called White,* 199.

28. Letter from Eleanor Roosevelt, Feb. 17, 1942, NAACP/LC: II A 275; WW to RW, Feb. 23, 1942, NAACP/LC: II A 607.

29. WW to Sara Boynoff, *Los Angeles Daily News,* Mar. 12, 1942, NAACP/LC: II A 274.

30. WW to Boynoff and Report of Secretary for April 1942 Meeting of Board of Directors, both NAACP/LC: II A 144.

31. Guest list, July 18, 1942, and press release, July 27, 1942, both NAACP/LC: II A 275.

32. Press release, Aug. 21, 1942, NAACP/LC: II A 275.

33. E. J. Mannix to Office of Darryl Zanuck, July 21, 1942, NAACP/LC: II A 275.

34. Breen to WW, Aug. 3, 1942, NAACP/LC: II A 275.

35. WW to Peter Furst, June 9, 1943, NAACP/LC: II A 277. The NAACP had always counted American Jews among its friends. Indeed, a number of its founders and its early financiers, leaders, and attorneys were Jewish. See Weiss, "Long-Distance Runners." It was not necessarily an easy alliance, however, and sympathy for African Americans' plight was not always able to overcome the industry leaders' financial and pragmatic concerns. See Cripps, "African Americans and Jews in Hollywood."

36. Cripps, *Making Movies Black,* 69–70.

37. WW to Louis Mayer, Aug. 3, 1942, Mayer to WW, Aug. 19, 1942, and WW to Lowell Mellet, Aug. 17, 1942, all NAACP/LC: II A 277.

38. Howard Dietz to WW, Sept. 14, 1942, and copy of letter from Nelson Poynter, Aug. 28, 1942, both NAACP/LC: II A 277.

39. Cripps, "Movies, Race and World War II," 64–65; Mellet quoted in Dietz to WW, Dec. 2, 1942, NAACP/LC: II A 277; WW to Dietz, Nov. 27, 1942, NAACP/LC: II A 277.

40. WW to Philip Van Doren Stern, Sept. 25, 1942, NAACP/LC: II A 275; Earl Conrad, "Review," *Journal of Negro History* 27 (Oct. 1942): 463–65; WW to John Woodburn, editor at Doubleday Doran Co., Aug. 24, 1942, NAACP/LC: VIII 455.

41. WW to Stern, Sept. 25, 1942, NAACP/LC: II A 275; copy of Board of Directors minutes, Sept. 14, 1942, NAACP/LC: II A 277; Cripps, "Movies, Race and World War II," 65.

42. WW to Wendell Willkie, Apr. 17, 1943, NAACP/LC: II A 275.

43. Cripps, *Making Movies Black,* 74; WW quote for MGM publicity, NAACP/LC: II A 275.

44. Press release, Feb. 1, 1944, NAACP/LC: II A 275.

45. Review quoted in RW to William Goetz, Feb. 17, 1944, NAACP/LC: II A 275; Jason Joy to RW, Mar. 31, 1944, NAACP/LC: II A 275.

46. Julia Baxter (Apr. 16), memo, quoted in WW to Harry Warner, Apr. 28, 1943, NAACP/LC: II A 275; press release, Apr. 30, 1943, NAACP/LC: II A 275. It took its protest further when it complained about Universal's *Scrub Me Mama with a Boogie Beat* (1941). It objected to screenings of the cartoon in 1948 and, together with the Jewish Labor Committee, was able to exert enough pressure for the studio to withdraw the picture. See correspondence in NAACP/LC: II A 280.

47. Langston Hughes, "Here's a Film Everyone Should See," *Chicago Defender,* Feb. 26, 1944; Wynn, *Afro-American and the Second World War,* 30.

48. Report of Secretary for May 1944, Meeting of Board of Directors, NAACP/LC: II A 144; Letter to Committee on Military Affairs, Apr. 1944, RW to Jack Goldberg, Negro Marches On Inc., Apr. 27, 1944, and "Court Records: Motion for Leave to File Brief *Amicus Curiae* by NAACP," all NAACP/LC: II A 278; Cripps, *Making Movies Black,* 114–15. See also Cripps and Culbert, "*Negro Soldier,*" 616–40.

49. WW, *Rising Wind;* soldier quoted in Wynn, *Afro-American and the Second World War,* 30.

50. Savage, *Broadcasting Freedom,* 107, 11, 74, 78, 84.

51. On the relationship to radio, see NAACP/LC: II A498; Ward, *Radio and the Struggle for Civil Rights,* 38, 42, 153–54.

52. WW to Edwin Embree, Mar. 4, 1943, NAACP/LC: II A 279; Bogle, *Toms, Coons, Mulattoes,* 131; Sklaroff, *Black Culture and the New Deal,* 211.

53. Strub, "Black and White and Banned All Over," 689; "Negroes Ask for Better Shade in Pix," *Variety,* June 17, 1942, NAACP/LC: II A 275.

54. Berg, *Ticket to Freedom*, 94, 110.

55. Winkler, *Politics of Propaganda,* 36; Barnes quoted in Koppes and Black, "Blacks, Loyalty and Motion-Picture Propaganda," 389.

56. Koppes and Black, *Hollywood Goes to War,* 179–80.

57. Koppes and Black, *Hollywood Goes to War,* 184.

58. Janken, *Walter White,* 272; Watts, *Hattie McDaniel,* 226.

## 6. Blacks, Reds, White

1. 42nd Annual Convention, resolution, June 1951, NAACP/LC: II A 498.

2. For an entertaining account of Black Hollywood, see Bogle, *Bright Boulevards, Bold Dreams.* Photograph of McDaniel, *Crisis* (Apr. 1940): cover.

3. Cripps, *Making Movies Black,* 46; White's article (which appeared in May 1943) is quoted in Watts, *Hattie McDaniel,* 227.

4. Walter White was even accused by his own colleague, W. E. B. Du Bois, of preferring the company of whites rather than his own race. See Janken, *Walter White,* 189–91; Clarence Muse, "The Trial of 'Uncle Tom' NAACP and William Pickens Purge: As Hollywood Views it," *Pittsburgh Courier,* Sept. 12, 1942, NAACP/LC: II A 276. The first half of Muse's article is an angry denouncement of what he saw as the NAACP board's unfair treatment of William Pickens, who had clashed with the association over its policy during the war, particularly over the issue of segregated training grounds. See Avery, *Up from Washington,* chap. 8.

5. Hattie McDaniel's letter, dated July 26, 1945, enclosed in Leslie Perry to WW, Aug. 2, 1945, NAACP/LC: II A 502.

6. WW to Lena Horne, June 16, 1944, NAACP/LC: II A 303; WW, *Man Called White,* 202.

7. WW to NAACP supporters, Dec. 26, 1945, NAACP/LC: II A 275; Julia Baxter to WW, memo, Oct. 11, 1945, NAACP/LC: II A 277. On the NAACP's other work during this period, see Sullivan, *Lift Every Voice,* 300; *Crisis* (July 1945).

8. WW to Arthur Hays, Oct. 17, 1945, NAACP/LC: II A 277; Watts, *Hattie McDaniel,* 243. On the Los Angeles branch, see J. Watson, "NAACP in California," 185–200.

9. WW to RW, Jan. 25, 1946, NAACP/LC: II A 277.

10. Hattie McDaniel to T. L. Griffith, Jan. 20, 1946, NAACP/LC: II A 502. On the Screen Actors Guild and black actors' formation of the Hollywood Fair Play Committee, see Watts, *Hattie McDaniel,* 223, 227.

11. WW to Sterling Brown, Feb. 20, 1946, and draft of statement regarding NAACP's establishment of Hollywood bureau by WW, Feb. 18, 1946, both NAACP/LC: II A 277.

12. Cripps, "Walter's Thing," 116–25.

13. Quoted in Bogle, *Toms, Coons, Mulattoes,* 82.

14. Cripps, *Making Movies Black,* 175; Hope Spingarn to WW, memo, Nov. 23, 1946, and press release, Nov. 21, 1946, both NAACP/LC: II A 280.

15. Julia Baxter to RW, memo, May 17, 1947, NAACP/LC: II A 275.

16. Cripps, *Making Movies Black,* 208; correspondence between *Ebony* and WW, Oct. 1, 1947, NAACP/LC: II A 275.

17. Marable, *Race, Reform, and Rebellion,* 32; Horne, *Black and Red,* 57; C. Anderson, *Eyes Off the Prize,* 167 (emphasis in original). See also Plummer, *Rising Wind,* 188; Berg, *Ticket to Freedom,* 118, 138–39.

18. Marshall to RW, memo, Oct. 30, 1947, NAACP/LC: II A 274.

19. Telegram to J. Parnell Thomas, Oct. 16, 1947, NAACP/LC: II A 274. Over half of the "Hollywood Ten" (those who continued to resist HUAC's demands to give evidence) were Jewish. See WW to Nicholas Schenck, Samuel Goldwyn, MGM, Nov. 7, 1947, NAACP/LC: II A 274.

20. Perry means *The House I Live In* (1945), a short in which Frank Sinatra's title song preaches a message of tolerance. Leslie Perry to WW, Nov. 11, 1947, NAACP/LC: II A 274.

21. WW to Arthur Spingarn, Nov. 13, 1947, and WW to Perry, telegram, Nov. 14, 1947, both NAACP/LC: II A 274.

22. Walter White's column, *Herald Tribune,* May 13, 1949, NAACP/LC: II A 276.

23. WW to Louis de Rochemont, RD-DR Corp., Feb. 25, 1949, and May 23, 1949, both NAACP/LC: II A 277; White's syndicated column, June 23, 1949, WW/MS: 23, 210. On the ban, see McGehee, "Disturbing the Peace," 23–51.

24. Typescript for White's *Chicago Defender* column, Jan. 7, 1950, WW/MS: 22, 198.

25. Klarman, *From Jim Crow to Civil Rights,* 215–16.

26. Klarman, *From Jim Crow to Civil Rights,* 207.

27. Cripps, *Making Movies Black,* 232–39; WW to Daryl Zanuck, Sept. 5, 1948, NAACP/LC: II A 279; Bogle, *Blacks in American Films and Television,* 165.

28. Zanuck to WW, Sept. 21, 1948, NAACP/LC: II A 279.

29. Typescript for White's *Chicago Defender* column, n.d., WW/MS: 22, 197; Daryl Zanuck to WW, Nov. 1, 1949, and Nov. 18, 1949, both WW/MS: 8, 240.

30. Gelling's case eventually went to the Supreme Court, which in June 1952 ruled against the censors' ordinance. Bogle, *Blacks in American Films and Television,* 166; McGehee, "Disturbing the Peace," 42; WW to Legal Department, memo, n.d., NAACP/LC: II A 279.

31. Roger Baldwin to WW, Apr. 25, 1939, NAACP/MF: 11A, 34; Stokes, *D. W. Griffith's* The Birth of a Nation, 247.

32. WW to Malcolm Ross, Twentieth-Century Fox, July 26, 1950, NAACP/LC: II A 278; White's syndicated column, Aug. 3, 1950, WW/MS: 23, 216.

33. NAACP press releases, Aug. 24, Aug. 31, 1950, Nelson Willis, president

of Chicago branch, to WW, Sept. 5, 1950, Spyros Skouras to WW, Sept. 5, 1950, and WW to Sidney Hollander, Baltimore branch, Oct. 20, 1950, all NAACP/LC: II A 278. On *Miracle,* see De Grazia and Newman, *Banned Films,* 84.

34. WW to Chairman, Maryland Board of Motion Picture Censors, telegram, Nov. 12, 1951, NAACP/LC: II A 276.

35. Carl Murphy to Dr. Louis Wright, Board of Directors, Dec. 4, 1951, and Copy of Minutes of Board of Directors meeting, Dec. 10, 1951, both NAACP/LC: II A 276.

36. The fullest account of *Amos 'n' Andy* on radio and television is Ely, *Adventures of Amos 'n' Andy.* On black protests against the show, see Cripps, "*Amos 'n' Andy,*" 25–40; Lorts, "Black Laughter/Black Protest." On Amos and Andy on the radio, see also Barlow, *Voice Over,* chap. 2.

37. Barlow, *Voice Over,* 41–43; Wilkins quoted in Ely, *Adventures of Amos 'n' Andy,* 170–71.

38. Letter to branches, Aug. 15, 1951, NAACP/LC: II A 498 (emphasis in original).

39. On *Beulah,* see WW to Walter Lancaster, Apr. 30, 1952, NAACP/LC: II A 499; Resolution, 42nd Annual Convention, Atlanta, June 1951, WW to Blatz Brewing Company, telegram, July 6, 1951, fact sheet on why the NAACP opposes *Amos 'n' Andy,* n.d., letter to branches, Aug. 15, 1951, and WW to Harriet Van Horne, July 30, 1951, all NAACP/LC: II A 498.

40. Letter to branches, Aug. 15, 1951, NAACP/LC: II A 498; Cripps, "*Amos 'n' Andy,*" 33; NAACP advertising copy, sent with letter, Sept. 10, 1951, NAACP/LC: II A 498.

41. Gates, *Colored People,* 22 (emphasis in original); Rowe quoted in Ely, *Adventures of Amos 'n' Andy,* 217; clipping, *Los Angeles Sentinel,* Aug. 23, 1951, NAACP/LC: II A 499; Muse quoted in Cripps, "*Amos 'n' Andy,*" 33; *Courier* and *Tribune* quoted in Ely, *Adventures of Amos 'n' Andy,* 217, 221; Fairclough, *Better Day Coming,* 184.

42. Resolution, 42nd Annual Convention, June 1951, NAACP/LC: II A 498; Moon quoted in memo from WW, July 10, 1951, NAACP/LC: II A 499.

43. WW to Blatz Brewing Company, telegram, July 6, 1951. See also correspondence between national office and Milwaukee branch. Both NAACP/LC: II A 498.

44. Cripps, "*Amos 'n' Andy,*" 29.

45. On the ACLU, see Lorts, "Black Laughter/Black Protest," 118; Gloster B. Current to Pearl Mitchell, July 17, 1951, NAACP/LC: II A 498.

46. Ely, *Adventures of Amos 'n' Andy,* 226.

47. Ely, *Adventures of Amos 'n' Andy,* 240.

48. Lorts, "Black Laughter/Black Protest," 138; Report to the Board, Nov. 1954, NAACP/MF: 16B, 20.

49. Janken, *Walter White,* chap. 11.

## Conclusion

1. Report of the Secretary for Oct. 1957, NAACP/MF: 16 (supplement, 1956–1965), 10; "Along the Battlefront," *Crisis* (Dec. 1957), 624; Dudziak, *Cold War Civil Rights,* chap. 4.

2. Resolutions, 53rd Annual Convention, July 2–8, 1962, NAACP/MF: 1 (supplement, 1961–1965), 4; press release, July 13, 1963, NAACP/MF: 24A, 25; press release, Aug. 3, 1963, NAACP/MF: 13, 3.

3. Correspondence between Davis Roberts and Herbert Hill, Apr. 1965, and press release, Apr. 30, 1965, both NAACP/MF: 13, 3; Henry Scott to Herbert Hill, July 22, 1965, and reply, Aug. 4, 1965, both NAACP/MF: 13, 14.

4. Two useful starting points are Torres, *Black, White, and in Color;* and Ward, *Media, Culture.*

5. Davis Roberts to Herbert Hill, May 11, 1965, NAACP/MF: 13, 3.

6. "25th NAACP Image Awards," *Crisis* (Nov.–Dec. 1992): 9; Mfume quoted in Torres, *Black, White, and in Color,* 68; NAACP, "Out of Focus, Out of Sync: A Report on the Film and Television Industry," 2003, http://www.naacpimageawards.net/hollywoodbur.html, 3.

7. For information on the Image Awards, see "NAACP: A Century in the Fight for Freedom," 2009, www.loc.gov; Bogle, *Primetime Blues,* 123.

8. Cripps, *Making Movies Black,* 68.

9. Sieving, *Soul Searching,* 18.

10. Gaines, *Fire and Desire,* 260–61.

11. Verney and Sartain, *Long Is the Way,* xxi. For further discussions on the relationship between the head office and the branches, see essays in the same collection by Flack, Fearnley, and Kirk.

12. Lewis, "Parallels and Divergences," 543.

13. Williams, "*Crisis* Cover Girl," 201; Hale, *Making Whiteness,* 156–57. See also Goings, *Mammy,* 14; M. D. Harris, *Colored Pictures,* 62–63.

14. Frazier, *Black Bourgeoisie,* 23.

15. Appiah, "No Bad Nigger," 84.

16. Savage, *Broadcasting Freedom,* 10. On black culture and politics in the 1960s, see, for example, Street, *Culture War in the Civil Rights Movement.*

17. WDB, "Criteria of Negro Art," 290.

# Bibliography

## Primary Sources

### Manuscript Collections

W. E. B. Du Bois Papers. Microfilm Collection, Manuscript Division, Library of Congress, Washington, DC.

James Weldon Johnson and Grace Nail Johnson Papers, Yale Collection of American Literature, Beinecke Rare Book and Manuscript Library.

Records of the National Association for the Advancement of Colored People, Manuscript Division, Library of Congress, Washington, DC.

Records of the National Association for the Advancement of Colored People, Microfilm Collection, British Library, London and Cambridge University Library, UK.

Walter Francis White and Poppy Cannon Papers, Yale Collection of American Literature, Beinecke Rare Book and Manuscript Library.

### Journals and Periodicals

*The Crisis: A Record of the Darker Races,* 1910–1992
*Harlem,* 1928
*The Messenger,* 1917–1928
*Negro World,* 1923–1924
*Opportunity: Journal of Negro Life,* 1923–1930
*Survey Graphic,* 1925

### Films

*Bataan,* 1943
*The Birth of a Nation,* 1915
*Cabin in the Sky,* 1943
*Crash Dive,* 1943
*Duel in the Sun,* 1946
*Gone with the Wind,* 1939
*Hallelujah,* 1929
*Hearts in Dixie,* 1929
*Home of the Brave,* 1949
*Imitation of Life,* 1934
*Intruder in the Dust,* 1949

*Lost Boundaries,* 1949
*The Negro Soldier,* 1944
*No Way Out,* 1950
*Pinky,* 1949
*Sahara,* 1943
*Song of the South,* 1946
*Stormy Weather,* 1943
*The Well,* 1951

### Books and Articles

Caldwell, Erskine. *Trouble in July.* 1940. Reprint, London: Falcon Press, 1948.

Conrad, Earl. "Review." *Journal of Negro History* 27 (October 1942): 463–65.

Du Bois, W. E. B. *Black Reconstruction in America: An Essay toward a History of the Part Which Black Folk Played in the Attempt to Reconstruct Democracy in America.* New York: Harcourt Brace, 1935.

———. *Dusk of Dawn: An Essay toward an Autobiography of a Race Concept.* 1940. Reprint, Millwood, NY: Kraus-Thomson Organization, 1975.

———. "Reconstruction and Its Benefits." *American Historical Review* 15 (1910): 781–99.

Fauset, Jessie Redmon. *Plum Bun: A Novel without a Moral.* 1929. Reprinted with an introduction by Deborah E. McDowell. Boston: Beacon Press, 1990.

Hughes, Langston. *The Big Sea.* 1940. Reprinted in *The Collected Works of Langston Hughes,* Vol. 13, edited by Joseph McLaren. Columbia: University of Missouri Press, 2002.

———. "Home." 1934. In *The Collected Works of Langston Hughes.* Vol. 15, *The Short Stories,* edited by R. Baxter Miller, 37–45. Columbia: University of Missouri Press, 2002.

Johnson, James Weldon. *Along This Way: The Autobiography of James Weldon Johnson.* 1933. Reprint, New York: Da Capo Press, 2000.

———. *The Autobiography of an Ex-Colored Man.* 1912. Reprint, New York: Dover, 1995.

———. *Black Manhattan.* 1930. Reprint, New York: Atheneum, 1968.

———. *The Book of American Negro Poetry.* 1922. Reprint, New York: Harcourt, Brace and World, 1958.

Johnson, James Weldon, and J. Rosamond Johnson. *The Books of American Negro Spirituals.* 1925. 1926. Reprint, New York: Viking, 1966.

Locke, Alain, ed. *The New Negro.* 1925. Reprint, New York: Touchstone, 1997.

McKay, Claude. *Home to Harlem.* New York: Harper and Brothers, 1928.

———. *A Long Way from Home.* 1937. Reprint, New York: Arno Press, 1969.

Van Vechten, Carl. *Nigger Heaven.* 1926. Reprint, New York: Harper & Row, 1971.

White, Walter F. *The Fire in the Flint.* 1924. Reprint, Athens: University of Georgia Press, 1996.

———. *A Man Called White.* New York: Viking Press, 1948.

———. *A Rising Wind.* New York: Doubleday Doran, 1945.

———. *Rope and Faggot: A Biography of Judge Lynch.* New York: Alfred A Knopf, 1929.

## Secondary Sources

Allen, James. *Without Sanctuary: Lynching Photography in America.* Santa Fe: Twin Palms, 2000.

Ames, Jessie Daniel. *The Changing Character of Lynching.* 1942. Reprint, New York: AMS Press, 1973.

Anderson, Carol. *Eyes Off the Prize: The United Nations and the African American Struggle for Human Rights, 1944–1955.* Cambridge: Cambridge University Press, 2003.

Anderson, Lisa M. *Mammies No More: The Changing Image of Black Women on Stage and Screen.* Lanham, MD: Rowman & Littlefield, 1997.

Apel, Dora. *Imagery of Lynching: Black Men, White Women and the Mob.* New Brunswick, NJ: Rutgers University Press, 2004.

Appiah, K. Anthony. "'No Bad Nigger': Blacks as the Ethical Principle in the Movies." In *Media Spectacles,* edited by Marjorie Garber, Jann Matlock, and Rebecca L. Walkowitz, 77–90. New York: Routledge, 1993.

Aptheker, Herbert, ed. *The Correspondence of W. E. B. Du Bois.* Vol. 1, *1877–1934.* Amherst: University of Massachusetts Press, 1973.

Arnold, Edwin T. "Erskine Caldwell and Judge Lynch: Caldwell's Role in the Anti-Lynching Campaigns of the 1930s." In *Reading Erskine Caldwell: New Essays,* edited by Robert L. McDonald, 183–202. Jefferson, NC: McFarland & Company, 2006.

Arthur, Leonard C. *Black Images in the American Theatre: NAACP Protest Campaigns—Stage, Screen, Radio and Television.* New York: Pageant-Poseidon, 1973.

Avery, Sheldon. *Up from Washington: William Pickens and the Negro Struggle for Equality, 1900–1954.* Newark: University of Delaware, 1989.

Badger, Anthony J. *The New Deal: The Depression Years, 1933–1940.* New York: Noonday Press, 1989.

Barlow, William. *Voice Over: The Making of Black Radio.* Philadelphia: Temple University Press, 1999.

Berg, Manfred. *The Ticket to Freedom: The NAACP and the Struggle for Black Political Integration.* Gainesville: University Press of Florida, 2005.

Bernardi, Daniel, ed. *The Birth of Whiteness: Race and the Emergence of U.S. Cinema.* New Brunswick, NJ: Rutgers University Press, 1996.

———. "The Voice of Whiteness: D. W. Griffith's Biograph Films (1908–1913)." In Bernardi, *Birth of Whiteness,* 103–28.

Bernstein, Patricia. *The First Waco Horror: The Lynching of Jesse Washington and the Rise of the NAACP.* College Station: Texas A&M University Press, 2005.

Blight, David W. *Race and Reunion: The Civil War in American Memory.* Cambridge: Belknap, 2001.

———. "W. E. B. Du Bois and the Struggle for American Historical Memory." In *History and Memory in African-American Culture,* edited by Geneviève Fabre and Robert O'Meally, 45–71. Oxford: Oxford University Press, 1994.

Bogle, Donald. *Blacks in American Films and Television: An Encyclopaedia.* New York: Simon and Schuster, 1989.

———. *Bright Boulevards, Bold Dreams: The Story of Black Hollywood.* New York: Random House, 2005.

———. *Primetime Blues: African Americans on Network Television.* New York: Farrar, Straus and Giroux, 2001.

———. *Toms, Coons, Mulattoes, Mammies and Bucks: An Interpretive History of Blacks in American Films.* New York: Continuum, 2001.

Bone, Robert. *The Negro Novel in America.* 1958. Reprint, New Haven, CT: Yale University Press, 1973.

Boskin, Joseph. *Sambo: The Rise and Demise of an American Jester.* Oxford: Oxford University Press, 1986.

Boyle, Kevin. *Arc of Justice: A Saga of Race, Civil Rights, and Murder in the Jazz Age.* New York: Henry Holt, 2005.

Brundage, W. Fitzhugh. *Lynching in the New South: Georgia and Virginia, 1880–1930.* Urbana: University of Illinois Press, 1993.

Butsch, Richard. "American Movie Audiences of the 1930s." *International Labor and Working Class History* 59 (2001): 106–20.

Byerman, Keith E. *Seizing the Word: History, Art, and Self in the Work of W. E. B. Du Bois.* Athens: University of Georgia Press, 1994.

Carroll, Anne Elizabeth. *Word, Image, and the New Negro: Representation and Identity in the Harlem Renaissance.* Bloomington: Indiana University Press, 2005.

Carter, Dan. *Scottsboro: A Tragedy of the American South.* Baton Rouge: Louisiana State University Press, 1969.

Collins, Lisa Gail, and Margo Natalie Crawford, eds. *New Thoughts on the Black Arts Movement.* Piscataway, NJ: Rutgers University Press, 2006.

Cortner, Richard C. *A Mob Intent on Death: The NAACP and the Arkansas Riot Cases.* Middletown, CT: Wesleyan University Press, 1988.

Cripps, Thomas. "African Americans and Jews in Hollywood: Antagonistic Allies." In Salzman and West, *Struggles in the Promised Land,* 257–74.

———. "*Amos 'n' Andy* and the Debate over American Racial Integration." In *Critiquing the Sitcom: A Reader,* edited by Joanne Morreale, 25–40. Syracuse, NY: Syracuse University Press, 2003.

———. *Making Movies Black: The Hollywood Message Movie from World War II to the Civil Rights Era.* Oxford: Oxford University Press, 1993.

———. "The Making of *The Birth of a Race:* The Emerging Politics of Identity in Silent Movies." In Bernardi, *Birth of Whiteness,* 38–55.

———. "Movies, Race and World War II: *Tennessee Johnson* as an Anticipation of the Strategies of the Civil Rights Movement." *Prologue* 14, no. 2 (1982): 49–67.

———. *Slow Fade to Black: The Negro in American Film, 1900–1942.* Oxford: Oxford University Press, 1977.

———. "'Walter's Thing': The NAACP's Hollywood Bureau of 1946—A Cautionary Tale." *Journal of Popular Film and Television* (Summer 2005): 116–25.

———. "Winds of Change: *Gone with the Wind* and Racism as a National Issue." In Pyron, *Recasting* Gone with the Wind, 137–52.

Cripps, Thomas, and David Culbert. "*The Negro Soldier:* Film Propaganda in Black and White." *American Quarterly* 31 (Winter 1979): 616–40.

Cruse, Harold. *The Crisis of the Negro Intellectual: A Historical Analysis of the Failure of Black Leadership.* 1967. Reprint, New York: New York Review of Books, 2005.

De Grazia, Edward, and Roger K. Newman. *Banned Films: Movies, Censors and the First Amendment.* New York: Bowker, 1982.

Denning, Michael. *The Cultural Front: The Laboring of American Culture in the Twentieth Century.* London: Verso, 1997.

Diner, Hasia R. *In the Almost Promised Land: American Jews and Blacks, 1915–1935.* Baltimore: Johns Hopkins University Press, 1995.

Douglas, Ann. *Terrible Honesty: Mongrel Manhattan in the 1920s.* New York: Farrar, Strauss and Giroux, 1995.

Dray, Phillip. *At the Hands of Persons Unknown: The Lynching of Black America.* New York: Modern Library, 2003.

Dudziak, Mary L. *Cold War Civil Rights: Race and the Image of American Democracy.* Princeton, NJ: Princeton University Press, 2002.

Dyer, Richard. "Into the Light: The Whiteness of the South in *The Birth of a Nation.*" In *Dixie Debates: Perspective on Southern Cultures,* edited by Richard H. King and Helen Taylor, 165–76. London: Pluto, 1996.

Ellis, Mark. "'Closing Ranks' and 'Seeking Honors': W. E. B. Du Bois in World War I." *Journal of American History* 79 (June 1992): 96–124.

Ely, Melvin Patrick. *The Adventures of Amos 'n' Andy: A Social History of an American Phenomenon.* 2nd edition. Charlottesville: University Press of Virginia, 2001.

Everett, Anna. *Returning the Gaze: A Genealogy of Black Film Criticism, 1909–1949.* Durham, NC: Duke University Press, 2001.

Fairclough, Adam. *Better Day Coming: Blacks and Equality, 1890–2000.* New York: Penguin, 2002.

Fleener, Nickie. "Answering Film with Film: The Hampton Epilogue, a Positive Alternative to the Negative Stereotypes Presented in *The Birth of a Nation*." *Journal of Popular Film and Television* 7, no. 4 (1980): 400–425.

Fleener-Marzec, Nickieann. *D. W. Griffith's* The Birth of a Nation: *Controversy, Suppression, and the First Amendment as It Applies to Filmic Expression, 1915–1973*. New York: Arno Press, 1980.

Foley, Barbara. "'In the Land of Cotton': Economics and Violence in Jean Toomer's *Cane*." *African American Review* 32, no. 2 (Summer 1998): 181–98.

———. *Radical Representations: Politics and Form in U.S. Proletarian Fiction, 1929–1941*. Durham, NC: Duke University Press, 1993.

Franklin, John Hope. "*The Birth of a Nation*: Propaganda as History." In *Race and History: Selected Essays, 1938–1988*, 10–23. Baton Rouge: Louisiana State Press, 1989.

Frazier, E. Franklin. *Black Bourgeoisie: The Rise of a New Middle Class in the United States*. New York: Collier, 1962.

Frederickson, George M. *The Black Image in the White Mind: The Debate on Afro-American Character and Destiny, 1817–1914*. New York: Harper and Row, 1972.

———. *Racism: A Short History*. Princeton, NJ: Princeton University Press, 2002.

Gaines, Jane M. *Fire and Desire: Mixed-Race Movies in the Silent Era*. Chicago: University of Chicago Press, 2001.

Gallagher, Brian. "Racist Ideology and Black Abnormality in *The Birth of a Nation*." *Phylon* 43, no. 1 (1982): 68–76.

Gans, Herbert J. *Popular Culture and High Culture: An Analysis and Evaluation of Taste*. New York: Basic Books, 1974.

Gates, Henry Louis, Jr. *Colored People: A Memoir*. New York: Knopf, 1994.

Goings, Kenneth W. *Mammy and Uncle Mose: Black Collectibles and American Stereotyping*. Bloomington: Indiana University Press, 1994.

———. *The NAACP Comes of Age: The Defeat of Judge John J. Parker*. Bloomington: Indiana University Press, 1990.

Goodman, James. *Stories of Scottsboro*. New York: Vintage, 1995.

Gossett, Thomas F. Uncle Tom's Cabin *and American Culture*. Dallas: Southern Methodist University Press, 1985.

Grieveson, Lee. *Policing Cinema: Movies and Censorship in Early-Twentieth-Century America*. Berkeley: University of California Press, 2004.

Hale, Grace Elizabeth. *Making Whiteness: The Culture of Segregation in the South, 1890–1940*. New York: Pantheon Books, 1998.

Hall, Jacquelyn Dowd. *Revolt against Chivalry: Jesse Daniel Ames and the Women's Campaign against Lynching*. New York: Columbia University Press, 1979.

Harris, Michael D. *Colored Pictures: Race and Visual Representation*. Chapel Hill: University of North Carolina Press, 2003.

Harris, Trudier. "Before the Strength, the Pain: Portraits of Elderly Black Women in Early Twentieth-Century Anti-Lynching Plays." In *Black Women Playwrights: Visions on the American Stage,* edited by Carol P. Marsh-Lockett, 25–42. New York: Garland, 1999.

———. *Exorcising Blackness: Historical and Literary Lynching and Burning Rituals.* Bloomington: Indiana University Press, 1984.

Hatch, James V., and Leo Hamalian, eds. *Lost Plays of the Harlem Renaissance, 1920–1940.* Detroit: Wayne State University Press, 1996.

Hatch, James V., and Ted Shine, eds. *Black Theatre USA: Plays by African Americans. The Early Period, 1847–1938.* New York: Free Press, 1996.

Hemingway, Andrew. *Artists on the Left: American Artists and the Communist Movement, 1926–1956.* New Haven, CT: Yale University Press, 2002.

Horne, Gerald. *Black and Red: W. E. B. Du Bois and the Afro-American Response to the Cold War, 1944–1963.* Albany: State University of New York Press, 1986.

Huggins, Nathan Irvin. *Harlem Renaissance.* 1971. Reprint, Oxford: Oxford University Press, 2007.

Hull, Gloria T. *Color, Sex and Poetry: Three Women Writers of the Harlem Renaissance.* Bloomington: Indiana University Press, 1987.

Hutchinson, Earl Ofari. *Blacks and Reds: Race and Class in Conflict, 1919–1990.* East Lansing: Michigan State University Press, 1995.

Hutchinson, George. *The Harlem Renaissance in Black and White.* Cambridge: Belknap Press, 1995.

Janken, Kenneth. *Walter White: Mr. NAACP.* Chapel Hill: University of North Carolina Press, 2006.

Johnson, Abby Arthur. "Literary Midwife: Jessie Redmon Fauset and the Harlem Renaissance." *Phylon* 39, no. 2 (1978): 143–53.

Johnson, Abby Arthur, and Ronald Maberry Johnson. *Propaganda and Aesthetics: The Literary Politics of Afro-American Magazines in the Twentieth Century.* Amherst: University of Massachusetts Press, 1979.

Kelley, Robin D. G. *Hammer and Hoe: Alabama Communists During the Great Depression.* Chapel Hill: University of North Carolina Press, 1990.

Kellogg, Charles Flint. *NAACP: A History of the National Association for the Advancement of Colored People.* Vol. 1, *1909–1920.* Baltimore: Johns Hopkins University Press, 1967.

Kirschke, Amy Helene. *Aaron Douglas: Art, Race and the Harlem Renaissance.* Jackson: University Press of Mississippi, 1995.

———. *Art in Crisis: W. E. B. Du Bois and the Struggle for African American Identity and Memory.* Bloomington: Indiana University Press, 2007.

Klarman, Michael J. *From Jim Crow to Civil Rights: The Supreme Court and the Struggle for Racial Equality.* Oxford: Oxford University Press, 2004.

Koppes, Clayton R., and Gregory D. Black. "Blacks, Loyalty and Motion-Picture Propaganda in World War II." *Journal of American History* 73, no. 2 (September 1986): 383–406.

———. *Hollywood Goes to War: How Politics, Profits and Propaganda Shaped World War II Movies.* London: I. B. Tauris and Co., 1987.

Kornweibel, Theodore. "An Economic Profile of Black Life in the Twenties." *Journal of Black Studies* 6, no. 4 (June 1976): 307–20.

———. *No Crystal Stair: Black Life and the Messenger.* Westport, CT: Greenwood Press, 1975.

Krasner, David. *A Beautiful Pageant: African American Theatre, Drama, and Performance in the Harlem Renaissance, 1910–1927.* New York: Palgrave Macmillan, 2002.

Lang, Robert, ed. *The Birth of a Nation.* New Brunswick, NJ: Rutgers University Press, 1994.

Langa, Helen. "Two Antilynching Art Exhibitions: Politicized View Points, Racial Perspectives, Gendered Constraints." *American Art* 13, no. 1 (Spring 1999): 10–39.

Leab, Daniel J. *From Sambo to Superspade: The Black Experience in Motion Pictures.* London: Secker and Warburg, 1973.

Leff, Leonard J. "David Selznick's *Gone with the Wind:* 'The Negro Problem.'" *Georgia Review* 38, no. 1 (1984): 146–64.

Lehman, Christopher P. *The Colored Cartoon: Black Representation in American Animated Short Films, 1907–1954.* Amherst: University of Massachusetts Press, 2007.

Levine, Lawrence W. *Highbrow/Lowbrow: The Emergence of Cultural Hierarchy in America.* Cambridge, MA: Harvard University Press, 1988.

Levy, Eugene. *James Weldon Johnson: Black Leader, Black Voice.* Chicago: University of Chicago Press, 1973.

Lewis, David Levering. "Parallels and Divergences: Assimilationist Strategies of Afro-American and Jewish Elites from 1910 to the Early 1930s." *Journal of American History* 71, no. 3. (December 1984): 543–64.

———. *W. E. B. Du Bois: Biography of a Race, 1868–1919.* New York: Henry Holt, 1993.

———. *W. E. B. Du Bois: The Fight for Equality and the American Century, 1919–1963.* New York: Henry Holt, 2000.

———. *When Harlem Was in Vogue.* 1981. Reprint, New York: Penguin, 1997.

Lorts, Justin T. "Black Laughter/Black Protest: Civil Rights, Respectability, and the Cultural Politics of African American Comedy, 1934–1968." PhD diss., Rutgers University, 2008.

Lott, Eric. *Love and Theft: Blackface Minstrelsy and the American Working Class.* New York: Oxford University Press, 1993.

Lynch, John Roy. *The Facts of Reconstruction.* New York: Neale Publishing, 1913.

Marable, Manning. *Race, Reform, and Rebellion: The Second Reconstruction in Black America, 1945–1990.* 2nd edition. Jackson: University Press of Mississippi, 1991.

————. *W. E. B. Du Bois: Black Radical Democrat.* Boulder, CO: Paradigm Publishers, 2005.

Margolick, David. *Strange Fruit: Billie Holiday, Café Society, and an Early Cry for Civil Rights.* Philadelphia: Running Press, 2000.

Markovitz, Jonathan. *Legacies of Lynching.* Minneapolis: University of Minnesota Press, 2004.

Marks, Carole. "Black Workers and the Great Migration North." *Phylon* 46, no. 2 (1985): 148–61.

Martin, Tony. *Literary Garveyism: Garvey, Black Arts and the Harlem Renaissance.* Dover, MA: Majority Press, 1983.

Maxwell, William J. *New Negro, Old Left: African-American Writing and Communism between the Wars.* New York: Columbia University Press, 1999.

McDowell, Deborah E. "Introduction." In *Plum Bun: A Novel without a Moral,* by Jessie Redmon Fauset. 1929. Reprint Boston: Beacon Press, 1990.

McElya, Micki. *Clinging to Mammy: The Faithful Slave in Twentieth-Century America.* Cambridge, MA: Harvard University Press, 2007.

McEwan, Paul. "Lawyers, Bibliographies, and the Klan: Griffith's Resources in the Censorship Battle over *The Birth of a Nation* in Ohio." *Film History* 20 (2008): 357–66.

McGehee, Margaret T. "Disturbing the Peace: *Lost Boundaries, Pinky,* and Censorship in Atlanta, Georgia, 1949–1952." *Cinema Journal* 46, no. 1 (Autumn 2006): 23–51.

Meier, August. *The Negro Problem.* New York: Arno Press, 1969.

————. *Negro Thought in America, 1880–1915: Racial Ideologies in the Age of Booker T. Washington.* Ann Arbor: University of Michigan Press, 1963.

Meier, August, and John Bracey Jr. "The NAACP as a Reform Movement, 1909–1965: 'To Reach the Conscience of America.'" *Journal of Southern History* 59, no. 1 (February 1993): 3–30.

Menand, Louis. "Do Movies Have Rights?" In *Thomas Dixon and the Birth of Modern America,* edited by Michele K. Gillespie and Randall Hall, 187–91. Baton Rouge: Louisiana State University Press, 2006.

Merritt, Russell. "Dixon, Griffith and the Southern Legend." *Cinema Journal* 12, no. 1 (Autumn 1972): 26–45.

Miller, James A. *Remembering Scottsboro: The Legacy of an Infamous Trial.* Princeton, NJ: Princeton University Press, 2009.

Mitchell, Angelyn, ed. *Within the Circle: An Anthology of African American Literary Criticism from the Harlem Renaissance to the Present.* Durham, NC: Duke University Press, 1994.

Mullen, Bill. *Popular Fronts: Chicago and African-American Cultural Politics, 1935–46.* Urbana: University of Illinois Press, 1999.

Murray, Hugh T. "The NAACP versus the Communist Party: The Scottsboro Rape Cases." *Phylon* 28 (1967): 276–87.

Naison, Mark. *Communists in Harlem during the Depression.* 1983. Reprint, Urbana: University of Illinois Press, 2005.

Ochillo, Yvonne. "The Race-Consciousness of Alain Locke." *Phylon* 47, no. 3 (1986): 173–81.

Omodele, Remi. "'For Us, about Us, near Us and by Us': American Women Playwrights and the Making of NAACP–Du Bois's Edutainment Agenda." *Women's History Review* 11, no. 1 (2002): 49–69.

Ongiri, Amy Abugo. *Spectacular Blackness: The Cultural Politics of the Black Power Movement and the Search for a Black Aesthetic.* Charlottesville: University of Virginia Press, 2010.

Ovington, Mary White. *Black and White Sat Down Together: The Reminiscences of an NAACP Founder.* New York: Feminist Press, 1995.

Park, Marlene. "Lynching and Antilynching: Art and Politics in the 1930s." *Prospects: An Annual of American Cultural Studies* 18 (1993): 311–65.

Pascoe, Peggy. *What Comes Naturally: Miscegenation Law and the Making of Race in America.* Oxford: Oxford University Press, 2009.

Patterson, Orlando. *Rituals in Blood: Consequences of Slavery in Two American Centuries.* New York: Basic Civitas, 1998.

Pearson, Ralph. "Combating Racism with Art: Charles S. Johnson and the Harlem Renaissance." *American Studies* 18, no. 1 (1977): 123–34.

Perkins, Kathy A., and Judith L. Stephens, eds. *Strange Fruit: Plays on Lynching by American Women.* Bloomington: Indiana University Press, 1998.

Plummer, Brenda Gayle. *Rising Wind: Black Americans and U.S. Foreign Affairs, 1935–1960.* Chapel Hill: University of North Carolina Press, 1996.

Pyron, Darden Asbury, ed. *Recasting* Gone with the Wind *in American Culture.* Miami: University Presses of Florida, 1983.

Rampersad, Arnold. *The Art and Imagination of W. E. B. Du Bois.* Cambridge, MA: Harvard University Press, 1976.

Record, Wilson. *The Negro and the Communist Party.* 1951. Reprint, New York: Atheneum, 1971.

———. *Race and Radicalism: The NAACP and the Communist Party in Conflict.* Ithaca, NY: Cornell University Press, 1964.

Reed, Robert Christopher. *The Chicago NAACP and the Rise of Black Professional Leadership, 1910–1966.* Bloomington: Indiana University Press, 1997.

Rice, Anne P., ed. *Witnessing Lynching: American Writers Respond.* New Brunswick, NJ: Rutgers University Press, 2003.

Rocchio, Vincent. *Reel Racism: Confronting Hollywood's Construction of Afro-American Culture.* Boulder, CO: Westview, 2000.

Rogin, Michael Paul. *Blackface, White Noise: Jewish Immigrants in the Hollywood Melting Pot.* Berkeley: University of California Press, 1996.

———. "'The Sword Became a Flashing Vision': D.W. Griffith's *The Birth of a Nation.*" In Lang, *Birth of a Nation,* 250–93.

Rosenbloom, Nancy J. "Between Reform and Regulation: The Struggle over Film Censorship in Progressive America, 1909–1922." *Film History* 1, no. 4 (1987): 307–25.

Ross, B. Joyce *J. E. Spingarn and the Rise of the NAACP, 1911–1972.* New York: Atheneum, 1972.

Rudwick, Elliott. "W. E. B. Du Bois in the Role of *Crisis* Editor." *Journal of Negro History* 43, no. 3 (July 1958): 214–40.

Rudwick, Elliott, and August Meier. "The Rise of the Black Secretariat in the NAACP, 1909–35." In *Along the Color Line: Explorations in the Black Experience,* 94–127. 1976. Reprint, Urbana: University of Illinois Press, 2002.

Salzman, Jack, and Cornel West, eds. *Struggles in the Promised Land: Toward a History of Black-Jewish Relations in the United States.* Oxford: Oxford University Press, 1997.

Sartain, Lee. *Invisible Activists: Women of the Louisiana NAACP and the Struggle for Civil Rights, 1915–1945.* Baton Rouge: Louisiana State University Press, 2007.

Savage, Barbara Dianne. *Broadcasting Freedom: Radio, War and the Politics of Race, 1938–1948.* Chapel Hill: University of North Carolina Press, 1999.

Schneider, Mark Robert. *We Return Fighting: Civil Rights in the Jazz Age.* Boston: Northeastern University Press, 2002.

Scruggs, Charles. "Alain Locke and Walter White: Their Struggle for Control of the Harlem Renaissance." *Black Literature Forum* 14, no. 3 (Autumn 1980): 91–99.

Shapiro, Herbert. *White Violence and Black Response: From Reconstruction to Montgomery.* Amherst: University of Massachusetts Press, 1988.

Sherrard-Johnson, Cherene. *Portraits of the New Negro Woman: Visual and Literary Culture in the Harlem Renaissance.* New Brunswick, NJ: Rutgers University Press, 2007.

Sieving, Christopher. *Soul Searching: Black-Themed Cinema from the March on Washington to the Rise of Blaxploitation.* Middletown, CT: Wesleyan University Press, 2011.

Sklaroff, Lauren Rebecca. *Black Culture and the New Deal: The Quest for Civil Rights in the Roosevelt Era.* Chapel Hill: University of North Carolina Press, 2009.

Smethurst, James Edward. *The Black Arts Movement: Literary Nationalism in the 1960s and 1970s.* Chapel Hill: University of North Carolina Press, 2005.

Staiger, Janet. "*The Birth of a Nation:* Reconsidering Its Reception." In Lang, *Birth of a Nation,* 195–213.

Stokes, Melvyn. *D. W. Griffith's* The Birth of a Nation: *A History of "The Most Controversial Motion Picture of All Time."* Oxford: Oxford University Press, 2007.

Street, Joe. *The Culture War in the Civil Rights Movement.* Gainesville: University Press of Florida, 2007.

Strub, Whitney. "Black and White and Banned All Over: Race, Censorship and Obscenity in Postwar Memphis." *Journal of Social History* 40, no. 3 (Spring 2007): 685–715.

Sullivan, Patricia. *Lift Every Voice: The NAACP and the Making of the Civil Rights Movement.* New York: New Press, 2009.

Sylvander, Carolyn Wedin. *Jessie Redmon Fauset, Black American Writer.* Troy, NY: Whitston Publishing Company, 1981.

Taylor, Clyde. "The Re-Birth of the Aesthetic in Cinema." In Bernardi, *Birth of Whiteness,* 15–37.

Toll, Robert C. *Blacking Up: The Minstrel Show in Nineteenth-Century America.* New York: Oxford University Press, 1974.

Tolnay, S. E., and E. M. Beck. *A Festival of Violence: An Analysis of Southern Lynchings, 1882–1930.* Urbana: University of Illinois Press, 1995.

Torres, Sasha. *Black, White, and in Color: Television and Black Civil Rights.* Princeton, NJ: Princeton University Press, 2003.

Turner, Darwin. "W. E. B. Du Bois and the Theory of a Black Aesthetic." In *Critical Essays on W. E. B. Du Bois,* edited by William L. Andrews, 73–92. Boston: G. K. Hall and Co., 1985.

Tushnet, Mark V. *The NAACP's Legal Strategy against Segregated Education, 1925–1950.* Chapel Hill: University of North Carolina Press, 1987.

Van Deburg, William L. *Slavery and Race in American Popular Culture.* Madison: University of Wisconsin Press, 1984.

Vendryes, Margaret Rose. "Hanging on Their Walls: An Art Commentary on Lynching, the Forgotten 1935 Art Exhibition." In *Race Consciousness: African-American Studies for the New Century,* edited by Judith Fossett and Jeffrey Tucker, 54–176. New York: New York University Press 1997.

Verney, Kevern, and Lee Sartain, eds. *Long Is the Way and Hard: One Hundred Years of the NAACP.* Fayetteville: University of Arkansas Press, 2009.

———. "The NAACP in Historiographical Perspective." In Verney and Sartain, *Long Is the Way and Hard,* xv–xxviii.

Vincent, Ted. *Keep Cool: The Black Activists Who Built the Jazz Age.* London: Pluto, 1995.

Waldrep, Christopher. *The Many Faces of Judge Lynch: Extralegal Violence and Punishment in America.* New York: Palgrave Macmillan, 2002.

Waldron, Edward. *Walter White and the Harlem Renaissance.* New York: Kennihat Press, 1978.

Ward, Brian, ed. *Media, Culture, and the Modern African American Freedom Struggle.* Gainesville: University Press of Florida, 2001.

———. *Radio and the Struggle for Civil Rights in the South.* Gainesville: University Press of Florida, 2004.

Watson, Jonathan. "The NAACP in California, 1914–1950." In Verney and Sartain, *Long Is the Way and Hard,* 185–200.

Watson, Steven. *The Harlem Renaissance: Hub of African-American Culture, 1920–1930.* New York: Pantheon Books, 1995.

Watts, Jill. *Hattie McDaniel: Black Ambition, White Hollywood.* New York: HarperCollins, 2005.

Weinberger, Stephen. "*The Birth of a Nation* and the Making of the NAACP." *Journal of American Studies* 45, no. 1 (February 2011): 77–93.

Weiss, Nancy J. "Long-Distance Runners of the Civil Rights Movement: The Contribution of Jews to the NAACP and the National Urban League in the Early Twentieth Century." In Salzman and West, *Struggles in the Promised Land,* 123–52.

White, Mimi. "*The Birth of a Nation:* History as Pretext." In Lang, *Birth of a Nation,* 214–24.

Widener, Daniel. *Black Arts West: Culture and Struggle in Postwar Los Angeles.* Durham, NC: Duke University Press, 2010.

Wilkerson, Carmiele Y., and Shamoon Zamir. "Du Bois and the 'New Negro.'" In *The Cambridge Companion to W. E. B. Du Bois,* edited by Shamoon Zamir, 64–75. Cambridge: Cambridge University Press, 2008.

Williams, Megan E. "*The Crisis* Cover Girl: Lena Horne, the NAACP, and Representations of African American Femininity, 1941–1945." *Journal of History, Criticism, and Bibliography* 16, no. 2 (2006): 200–218.

Williamson, Joel. *The Crucible of Race: Black-White Relations in the American South since Emancipation.* Oxford: Oxford University Press, 1984.

Winkler, Allan. *The Politics of Propaganda: The Office of War Information, 1942–1945.* New Haven, CT: Yale University Press, 1978.

Wintz, Cary D. *Black Culture and the Harlem Renaissance.* Houston: Rice University Press, 1988.

Wolters, Raymond. *Du Bois and His Rivals.* Columbia: University of Missouri Press, 2001.

Wood, Amy Louise. *Lynching and Spectacle: Witnessing Racial Violence in America, 1890–1940.* Chapel Hill: University of North Carolina Press, 2009.

Woodley, Jenny. "In Harlem and Hollywood: The Cultural Campaigns of the NAACP, 1910–1950." In Verney and Sartain, *Long Is the Way and Hard,* 15–27.

Wright, George C. *Racial Violence in Kentucky, 1865–1940: Lynchings, Mob Rule and "Legal Lynchings."* Baton Rouge: Louisiana State University Press, 1990.

Wynn, Neil A. *The Afro-American and the Second World War.* London: Paul Elek, 1976.

Yellin, Jean Fagan. "An Index of Literary Materials in *The Crisis,* 1910–1934: Articles, Belles Lettres, and Book Reviews." *CLA Journal* 14 (June 1971): 453–65.

Young, James O. *Black Writers of the Thirties.* Baton Rouge: Louisiana State University Press, 1973.

Zangrando, Robert L. *The NAACP Crusade against Lynching, 1909–1950.* Philadelphia: Temple University Press, 1980.

———. "'The Organized Negro': The National Association for the Advancement of Colored People and Civil Rights." In *The Black Experience in America: Selected Essays,* edited by James C. Curtis and Lewis L. Gould, 145–71. Austin: University of Texas Press, 1970.

Zelden, Charles L. *The Battle for the Black Ballot:* Smith v. Allwright *and the Defeat of the Texas All-White Primary.* Lawrence: University Press of Kansas, 2004.

# Index

Page numbers set in *italics* refer to illustrations.

abolitionist movement, 146
Abyssinian Baptist Church (Harlem, NY), 56
ACA Gallery (New York, NY), 117–18
Adams, John Henry, 76, *78,* 86, *87,* 90
Africa: *Crisis* and, 73–75
African Americans: all-black military units, 211n3; all-black theater projects, 121; *Birth of a Nation* portrayals of, 12, 14–18; as consumers, 184; disenfranchisement of, 60; as filmmakers, 31; Great Depression and, 88–90; Great Migration of, 21, 32, 36, 98, 209n17; Hollywood employment opportunities, 192–93; internal divisions among, 31; Jews and, 144; lynching as means of control of, 98, 100; lynching records kept by, 101; political affiliations of, 123–24; political power of, 171; unemployment rates of, 88, 92–93; visual imagery as viewed by, 202; WWII propaganda efforts and, 139–40
African Americans, racial stereotypes of: in *Birth of a Nation,* 14; in *Crisis,* 76; "darky" stereotype, 73, 135, 136; Du Bois and challenges to, 44, 48, 63, 65, 72, 79, 81, 86, 92; "entertainer" stereotype, 156, 157–58; films and reinforcement of, 127, 128, 129, 162; jazz and, 92; "Jezebel" stereotype, 79; lynching dramas and, 106; "Mammy" stereotype, 79, 106, 132, 162, 175; in music, 40; racism as ideology and, 3–4; "savage" stereotype, 148; servant stereotype, 128, 136, 157, 162, 166, 168, 191
*Aftermath* (Burrill), 106–7, 217n18
Alexander, Stephen, 118
Allan, Robert, 177
American Civil Liberties Union (ACLU), 163, 177, 185
*American Dilemma, The* (Myrdal), 167
American Jewish Committee, 184, 185
Ames, Jessie, 99
*Amos 'n' Andy* (radio program), 154, 180–81
*Amos 'n' Andy* (TV program), 180–81, 182–83, 186
*Amos 'n' Andy* (TV program), NAACP campaign against: African American cultural representation denounced in, 159, 180, 181–82, 188; anti-*Birth of a Nation* campaign compared to, 184, 185–86; black middle class and, 182; black public opinion of, 182–83; censorship and, 33; failure of, 186; medium and, 154, 180, 181; NAACP cultural view and, 188, 197; NAACP internal divisions about, 198; sponsor boycott threatened, 183–84; White's lobby tactics and, 184–85

Anderson, Carol, 169
Anderson, Charles W., 19
Anderson, Marian, 40–41
Anderson, Sherwood, 108, 113, 121
*And Yet They Paused* (G. Johnson),
    105–6
anticommunism, 159, 166, 168–71,
    224n19
antilynching legislation: Costigan-
    Wagner Bill (1934, 1935), 99, 108,
    113–14, 117, 118, 120; Dyer Bill
    (1919), 99; NAACP support for,
    127, 178; public support for, 122;
    Wagner-Van Nuys-Gavagan bill
    (1938), 105
antilynching movement, 99. See also
    *Art Commentary on Lynching*
    exhibition (New York, NY; 1935);
    NAACP antilynching campaign;
    Writers' League Against Lynching
    (WLAL)
anti-Prohibition movement, 113
anti-Semitism, 141, 170, 185
Apel, Dora, 114, 218n35
Appiah, K. Anthony, 201, 202
*Art Commentary on Lynching*
    exhibition (New York, NY; 1935):
    art as propaganda in, 117; artworks
    featured in, 114; black vs. white
    contributions, 114–15, 218n35,
    219n38; competing Communist
    exhibition, 117–19, 120; goals
    of, 113, 116–17; organizing of,
    127; press reviews of, 116, 124;
    scholarship on, 112–13; sponsors
    of, 113; timing of, 113–14
Arthur U. Newman Galleries (New
    York, NY), 117
*Art in Crisis* (Kirschke), 66
artistic freedom, 46, 50, 51
Artists' Committee of Action (ACA),
    118

Artists' Union, 118
assimilation, 6, 42, 57, 59, 65, 131, 199
Association of Southern Women for
    the Prevention of Lynching, 99
Atherton, Gertrude, 108
Atlanta (GA), 183
Atlantic City (NJ), 21
*At the End of a Rope* (linocut;
    Jennings), 115
*Autobiography of an Ex-Colored
    Man* (J. W. Johnson), 39–40, 52,
    213n33, 218n22

Bagnall, Robert, 8, 71, 218n22
Baldwin, Roger, 177
Baltimore (MD), 86
Baltimore (MD) NAACP branch,
    178–80, 198
Bannern, Henry, 218n35
*Barbecue: American Style* (painting;
    Freelon), 115, 117
Barnes, George, 157
*Bataan* (film; 1943), 147, 148, 149,
    155, 156
Baxter, Julia, 128–29, 151
Beavers, Louise, 128, 164, 167, 181
Beck, E. M., 219n53
Becker, Sam, 219n44
Beeston, Fred, 143
Bellows, George, 114
Bennett, Gwendolyn, 70, 72
Bercovici, Konrad, 56–57
Berg, Manfred, 169
*Beulah* (TV program), 159, 181, 182
Beverly Hills–Hollywood NAACP
    branch, 193–94
"Big Boy Leaves Home" (Wright),
    217n22
Bill for Negro Rights, 117, 118,
    219n42
*Bill to Be Passed, A* (G. Johnson),
    105–6

Birmingham (AL), 193
*Birth of a Nation, The* (film; 1915): artistic merits of, 13, 27–28; bannings of, 21, 23, 28, 177; blacks as portrayed in, 12–13, 14–18, 195; cuts made in, 19; epilogue added to, 26; film proposed to counteract, 26–27; historical accuracy of, 27–29, 134; intermarriage as portrayed in, 15–16; length of, 12; lynching as glorified in, 17, 100, 125; psychological/educational effect of, 129–30; release of (1915), 17; remaking rumors, 186; revival of, 137; synchronized version of, 220n1; as white supremacist tract, 13–14, 32
*Birth of a Nation, The* (film; 1915), NAACP campaign against, 5, 8, 10; ACLU criticism of, 163; anti-*Amos 'n' Andy* campaign compared to, 191; censorship and, 11, 18–21, 24–26, 33, 163, 177, 185; cultural response, 26–27, 29–31, 102; direct action tactics, 20, 23, 184, 198; film industry opposition, 20–21, 25; fundraising problems, 27; historical accuracy challenged, 28–29; KKK and, 23–24; reasons for, 12–13; scholarship on, 11; significance of, 31–34, 125, 133, 137; strategy behind, 17, 18; successes, 21, 133; WWI and, 22–23, 33
*Birth of a Race, The* (film; 1918), 210n29
Black, Gregory D., 157
black actors: employment opportunities of, 164–65, 176; Hollywood Bureau proposal opposed by, 163–67; NAACP cultural elitism and, 197; prejudices of, 166–67; TV casting of, 181–82, 186; union of, 157; White's relations with, 158, 159–62, 165, 166–67, 176, 187; in WWII-era films, 156, 157–58
Black Arts Movement, 9
blackface, 181, 182
"Black Fairy" (F. Johnson), 75
black intelligentsia, 71–72
black lower classes, 86–90, *87, 89,* 95
black magazines, 70–72. See also *Crisis* (NAACP magazine)
"Black Man" (poem; Jannath), 88
black middle class: Communist Party and, 118–19; *Crisis* representations of, 65, 85–86, 95; Depression impact on, 93; growth of, 182; as illusion, 200; in lynching dramas, 201–2; NAACP cultural strategy and, 130–31, 197, 200; TV portrayals of, 182
*Black Miner, The* (*Crisis* cover art; Dodd), 88, *89*
black music, 40–41, 92
black patriotism, 23, 92
black press, 135, 136, 160, 168, 196. *See also specific newspaper*
*Black Reconstruction in America* (Du Bois), 29, 134
black soldiers, 147–53, 156
black women, cultural representations of, 63, *64,* 75–85, *77–78, 80, 82–84,* 95, 106, 175
Blatz Brewing Company, 183–84, 185
Blight, David, 29, 207n2
Bloch, Julius, 219n38
*Blue-Eyed Black Boy* (G. Johnson), 104
*Body and Soul* (film; 1947), 168, 170
Bogart, Humphrey, 148
Bogle, Donald, 128, 155, 194

Bontemps, Arna, 69, 70, 72
*Book of American Negro Poetry* (ed. J. W. Johnson), 1, 38, 52
*Book of American Negro Spirituals, The* (ed. J. W. Johnson), 35
Boston (MA), *Birth of a Nation* protested in, 19–20
*Boston Guardian,* 19
*Boston Herald,* 28
boycotts, 183–84, 192
Boynoff, Sara, 141
*Boy with the Green Hair, The* (film; 1947), 168
Breen, Joseph, 135, 143–44
*Broken Banjo, The* (Richardson), 69
Brooklyn (NY) NAACP branch, 136
Brooklyn Citizens Club, 19
*Brooklyn Daily Eagle,* 116
Brooks, William, 7
Brooks County (GA), 109
Brotherhood of Sleeping Car Porters, 39, 71
"Brothers" (J. W. Johnson), 218n22
Brown, Richard, 81, *83*
Brown, Samuel, 115, 117, 218n35
Brown, Sterling, 54, 108, 153, 165
*Brown v. Board of Education,* 9, 186
*Buffalo Courier,* 103
*Burden of Black Womanhood, The* (*Crisis* illustration; Douglas), 79, *80*
Bureau of Motion Pictures (BMP), 138–39, 145, 146, 147, 156
Burrill, Mary, 106–7, 217n18
Byerman, Keith, 46
*By Parties Unknown* (print; Woodruff), 115

"Cabaret" (poem; Hughes), 47
*Cabin in the Sky* (film; 1943), 155
Cagney, James, 141
cakewalk, 40

Caldwell, Erskine, 108
*California Eagle,* 136
Caliver, Ambrose, 153
Calloway, Cab, 41
Campbell, E. Simms, 115, 218n35
*Cane* (Toomer), 58, 218n26
Cannon, Poppy, 187
Capitol Theater (New York, NY), 23
Capra, Frank, 142, 151
Carroll, Anne, 60, 66, 71–72
Carter, Ben, 147
*Casablanca* (film; 1943), 156, 162
castrations, 17, 114
*Catholic World,* 103
CBS, 182, 183–84, 185, 186
censorship, 6; of all-black/message movies, in South, 155, 176–77; black movie roles and, 165; controversy over, 33, 159, 177–80; in *Crisis,* 65, 90; Hollywood Bureau proposal and, 163, 166; NAACP advocacy of, in anti-*Amos 'n' Andy* campaign, 185; NAACP advocacy of, in anti-*Birth of a Nation* campaign, 11–12, 24–26, 33; NAACP withdrawal from use of, 131; self-censorship, in movie industry, 18–19, 135, 139; Supreme Court cases involving, 224n30
Ceruti, E., 13, 18
Chesnutt, Charles, 68, 69
Chicago (IL): *Birth of a Nation* protested in, 20–21; Du Bois NAACP speech in (1926), 1, 45–46, 203–4; film censorship in, 179; race riots in (1919), 37
*Chicago Defender,* 136, 160–61
Chicago Police Commission, 179
*Chicago Tribune,* 41
*Christ in Alabama* (lithograph; Taylor), 219n38

*Christmas Reckoning, The* (*Crisis* illustration; Adams), 86, *87,* 90
civil rights, 171–72
Civil Rights Act (1964), 193, 195
civil rights movement, 192, 193, 195, 196, 202–3
civil rights organizations, 71, 165
Civil War, 146
*Clansman, The* (Dixon), 12
class struggle, 118
Cleveland (OH) NAACP branch, 21
"Close Ranks" (editorial; Du Bois), 93
*Coal Black and de Sebben Dwarfs* (cartoon short; 1943), 150–51
Cobb, James, 60
Cogdell, Josephine. *See* Jannath, Heba
Cohen, Octavus Roy, 121
Cold War, 171, 174
*Color* (Cullen), 53
"Colored Los Angeles Greets *THE CRISIS* in Its Own Motor Cars" (photograph), 86
*Color Scheme* (unpublished novel; McKay), 213n36
Columbia Pictures, 147, 149
Columbia University, 157
Commission on Interracial Cooperation, 99
Communist Party, 107, 117–20, 144–45, 169–71, 202, 219n42
Connelly, Marc, 142
Correll, Charles, 180–81
Cosby, Bill, 186, 194, 195
Costigan, Edward, 99, 108
Costigan-Wagner Bill (1934, 1935), 99, 108, 113–14, 117, 118, 120
Crain, Jeanne, 175
*Crash Dive* (film; 1943), 147–48, 156, 162
Cripps, Thomas, 24, 25, 31, 32, 131, 135, 147, 166, 168, 195
*Crisis* (NAACP magazine): African influence on, 73–75, 91; antilynching literature in, 103–4, 110–11; black actor successes celebrated in, 160; black lower classes as portrayed in, 86–90, *87, 89,* 95; black middle class as portrayed in, 65, 85–86, 95; black women as portrayed in, 63, *64,* 75–85, *77–78, 80, 82–84,* 95; book reviews in, 46–47; "Children's" issue, 72; competing magazines, 70–72; cultural agenda of, 8, 10, 94, 96, 154; as culturally elitist, 91–92; Du Bois as editor of, 10, 37, 65–67, 68, 81–86, 90–93, 94; Du Bois resigns from, 93–94; Du Bois's censorship in, 65, 90; editorials in, 68; "Education" issue, 72–73, 85; establishment of, 5, 34; Fauset as literary editor of, 67–68, 90–91, 94, 214n5; film reviews in, 128, 132, 136–37; finances of, 66–67, 93, 94; first issue of, 66; Harlem Renaissance and, 68; on Image Awards, 194; Ivy as editor of, 187; letters to the editor, 72; lighter-skinned cover girls in, *64,* 65, 75–79, *77–78,* 95; literary competitions of, 58, 69–70, 87, 104, 214n9; literary content of, 67–69, 73–75, 94, 197, 214n9; lynchings recorded in, 101, 109, 112; "Men of the Month" column, 73, 85–86; NAACP cultural campaigns and, 2, 31, 63–65, 69, 94–96, 196; "Negro in Art" questionnaire/responses in, 49; racial pride highlighted in, 31, 34, 65, 72, 94–95; readership of, 67, 69, 72, 92, 94, 214n3; scholarship on, 65–66; significance of, 61, 94–96; subscriptions to, 93; visual

*Crisis (cont.)*
imagery in, 72–73, *74,* 110–11,
196; white contributions to,
215n33; white patrons of, 58; on
white publishers, 57–58; Wilkins
as editor of, 94, 187
"Criteria of Negro Art," 90
*Crucifixion, The* (painting; M.
Johnson), 115
Cruse, Harold, 213n42
Cullen, Countee: as antilynching
art exhibition sponsor, 113; art
vs. propaganda debate and, 49;
correspondence of, 52, 53, 54; as
*Crisis* award winner, 69; Du Bois
and, 44; Fauset as "discoverer"
of, 68; as *Fire!!* contributor, 72;
*Opportunity* contributions of, 70;
as WLAL member, 108; writings
of, 53, 69
cultural elitism, 6, 91–92, 166, 188,
197
*Cultural Front, The* (Denning),
219n48
cultural pluralism, 6, 42, 199
Curley, James, 19–20

Dabney, Virginius, 108
*Daily Worker,* 144–45
*Dark Easter (Crisis* cover art; Brown),
81, *83*
"darky" stereotype, 73, 135, 136
Darrow, Clarence, 56
Davis, Elmer, 138, 157
Davis, Jonathan M., 23
*Death* (sculpture; Noguchi), 114, 116
"Death Game, The" (Sheen), 86–87,
90
Democratic Party, 99, 123–24
Denning, Michael, 219n48
Denver (CO), 177
Dietz, Howard, 145, 146–47

disenfranchisement, 3, 27, 34, 60
Disney, Walt, 167–68
Dixon, Thomas, 12, 13–14, 15–16, 27,
28, 29
*Documentary History of
Reconstruction* (Fleming), 28
Dodd, J. E., 88, *89*
"Double Victory" campaign, 138, 149
Douglas, Aaron, 53, 68, 70, 71, 72, 73,
*74,* 79, *80*
Douglas, Ann, 71
Douglas, Melvyn, 141
Douglass, Frederick, 2, 146
Dray, Philip, 122
Dreiser, Theodore, 108, 217n22
*Drums of Morning, The* (Stern),
146–47
Du Bois, W. E. B.: antilynching
activism of, 111, 112; art vs.
propaganda debate and, 43–51,
71–72; biography of, 211n2;
book reviews written by, 46–47;
Chicago NAACP speech of (1926),
1, 45–46, 203–4; correspondence
of, 58; as *Crisis* editor, 10, 37,
58–59, 65–67, 68, 73, 81–86,
90–93, 94; "Criteria of Negro
Art," 90; cultural pluralism and,
41–42; Harlem Renaissance
and, 36–37, 39, 58–59, 68, 95;
influence on NAACP cultural
model, 43–44; literary prize in
name of, 69; on NAACP early
history, 35; as NAACP publicity/
research director, 7–8; "Negro in
Art" questionnaire of, 48–51; race
prejudice as viewed by, 3; as radio
advisor, 153; resignation of, as
*Crisis* editor, 93–94, 128; speaking
tours of, 22; on Talented Tenth,
5; theatrical project of, 69; visual
imagery in antilynching campaign

and, 111; White and, 93, 223n4;
white patronage and, 57, 58, 61;
as women's rights advocate, 81;
writings of, 29–31, 134, 211n38
"Du Bois Literary Prize," 69
Dudziak, Mary, 192
*Duel in the Sun* (film; 1946), 168
Dunbar-Nelson, Alice, 103
Dunning, William A., 210n31
Dunning School, 29, 210n31
Dyer, Leonidas, 99

educational inequality, 3
Educational Research Committee
(Payne Fund), 129–30
Egyptian iconography, 73, 91
Ellington, Duke, 41
Ely, Melvin Patrick, 183, 185–86
"entertainer" stereotype, 156, 157–58
Executive Order 8802, 138

Fairclough, Adam, 183
Fair Employment Practices Committee
(FEPC), 163
fascism, 118, 128, 148
Faulkner, William, 173
Fauset, Jessie: art vs. propaganda
debate and, 50–51; *Crisis*
contributions by, 68; as *Crisis*
literary editor, 8, 67–68, 90–91, 94,
214n5; Du Bois and, 44; Harlem
Renaissance and, 36, 39, 213n38,
214n5; writings of, 44, 58
Federal Theater Project, 121
Federal Writers Project, 121
film industry. *See* motion picture
industry; White, Walter,
Hollywood campaign of
*Fire!!* (race journal), 71–72
*Fire in the Flint, The* (White), 49, 109,
217–18n22
Fisher, Rudolph, 52–53, 69

Fitzgerald, Ella, 41
Fleming, Walter Lynwood, 28, 210n31
Foley, Barbara, 218n26
*Foreign Mail* (Spence), 69
*For Unborn Children* (Livingston),
103, 104, 106
*Foxes of Harrow, The* (film; 1947), 168
Franklin, John Hope, 27
Frazier, E. Franklin, 108, 200
Frederickson, George, 2, 207n2
*Freedom's People* (NBC radio series),
153
Freelon, Allan, 81, *84,* 115, 117,
218n35
Freeman, Elisabeth, 56, 112
*Fury* (film; 1936), 125

Gaines, Jane, 24, 31, 197
Gallup Poll, 122
Garvey, Marcus, 39, 104
Gary (IN), 21
Gates, Henry Louis, Jr., 182–83
Gavagan antilynching bill, 140
Gelling, W. L., 177, 224n30
Georgia, lynchings in, 217n14
Goetz, William, 142
"Goldie" (Grimké), 109–10
*Gone with the Wind* (film; 1939),
132–37, 160, 220–21n13
*Gone with the Wind* (Mitchell), 132, 133
Goodelman, Aaron J., 219n44
Gosden, Freeman, 180–81
"Government Information Manual
for the Motion Picture Industry"
(OWI), 139
Great Depression, 59, 88–90, 92–93,
107, 127
Griffith, D. W., 11, 13, 15–16, 25,
27–29. See also *Birth of a Nation,
The* (film; 1915); *Birth of a
Nation, The* (film; 1915), NAACP
campaign against

Griffith, Tom, 164
Griggs, Sutton, 217n22
Grimké, Angelina Weld, 99–100,
    101–3, 106–7, 109–10, 124
*Guinn v. the United States,* 15
Guinzburg, Harold, 53, 57

Hale, Grace Elizabeth, 3, 100, 200
*Hallelujah* (film; 1929), 128
Hamilton, James G. de Roulhac,
    210n31
Hampton Epilogue, 26
Hampton Institute, 26
Harlem (NY), 36, 47, 55–57, 172–73
Harlem Renaissance, 1, 213n38,
    214n5; art vs. propaganda
    debate during, 39, 43–51; black
    magazines and, 70–72; black
    theater projects and, 128; *Crisis*
    and, 68, 70, 95; duration of, 36,
    211n3; limitations of, 59, 96;
    NAACP involvement with, 2, 8,
    10, 31, 36–37, 40, 59–61, 127,
    154, 160, 199; NAACP officers
    as mentors to, 51–54; "Negro" vs.
    "American" cultural debate during,
    36, 42–43; "New Negro" during,
    36, 51–52; racial pride highlighted
    during, 31, 34, 195, 201; radio
    advisors from, 153; scholarship
    on, 54, 211nn2–3; significance of,
    59–61; white control of, 51, 54–55,
    57–59, 61, 213n42
Harlem riot (1935), 211n3
Harmon, William E., 57
Harmon Foundation, 57
Harris, Trudier, 106–7, 109
Hayes, Roland, 40
Hays, Will H., 135, 142
Hays Office. *See* Motion Pictures
    Producers Association (MPPA)
*Hearts in Dixie* (film; 1929), 128

*Henderson v. United States,* 174
Hernandez, Juano, 172
Herndon, Angelo, 118
"High Yaller" (Fisher), 69
Hill, Herbert, 193
*Hindered Hand, The* (Griggs), 217n22
*History of the American People*
    (Wilson), 28
Holliday, Billie, 125
Hollywood. *See* motion picture
    industry; motion pictures; White,
    Walter, Hollywood campaign of
Hollywood Bureau proposal, 162–67,
    187
Hollywood Ten, 199, 224n19
Holstein, Casper, 213n38
*Home of the Brave* (film; 1949), 149,
    171–72
*Home to Harlem* (McKay), 48, 58, 85
Horne, Gerald, 169
Horne, Lena, 160
Hose, Sam, 217n14
House Committee on Un-American
    Activities (HUAC), 169–70,
    224n19
*House I Live In, The* (film; 1945), 170
housing discrimination, 203
Houston, Charles Hamilton, 198
Howard, Sidney, 121, 133, 134
Howard Players, 103
Howe, Frederic, 19
Huggins, Nathan, 59, 60, 211n3
Hughes, Langston: art vs. propaganda
    debate and, 49; on black artist,
    43, 50; correspondence of, 52,
    54; *Crisis* contributions by, 68,
    73–75, 90; Du Bois and, 39, 44,
    90; as *Fire!!* co-founder, 71; as
    *Fire!!* contributor, 72; on Harlem
    Renaissance limitations, 59–61;
    *Opportunity* contributions of, 70;
    poetry of, 47; Schuyler vs., 43, 50;

on White, 55; white patrons of, 57;
writings of, 211n3
Hurston, Zora Neale, 54, 57, 70, 71
Hutchinson, George, 42, 75, 94–95

Ickes, Harold, 120–21
*Imitation of Life* (film; 1934), 128
*Independent* (newspaper), 6, 7
Ingram, Rex, 148–49
intermarriage, 15–17, 104
International Labor Defense (ILD),
118
*Intruder in the Dust* (Faulkner), 173
*Intruder in the Dust* (film; 1949),
171–72, 173
*Invincible Music* (*Crisis* illustration;
Douglas), 73, *74*
*I Passed Along This Way* (drawing;
Campbell), 115
*I Spy* (TV show), 186, 194, 195
Ivy, James W., 187

Jackson County (FL), 110
Jacques Seligmann Galeries (New
York, NY), 117
Janken, Kenneth, 54, 131, 158, 211n2
Jannath, Heba, 88, 215n33
jazz, 40, 92, 124–25
Jennings, Wilmer, 115, 218n35
Jewel Theater (Denver, CO), 177
Jewish Labor Committee, 222n46
Jews, 144, 221n35, 224n19
"Jezebel" stereotype, 79
"Job Hunter" (one-act play), 88–90
John Reed Club, 117, 119
Johnson, Andrew, 144–45, 146
Johnson, Charles S., 38–39, 49–50,
54, 70, 153, 213n38
Johnson, Fenton, 75, 91
Johnson, Georgia Douglas, 44, 68, 71,
104–6, 217n14
Johnson, Hall, 220n13

Johnson, James Weldon: on
art approach, 1–2, 38, 69;
autobiography of, 39–40, 52,
213n33, 218n22; on black artistic
achievements, 39–40, 121;
black music as viewed by, 41;
congressional testimony of, 60;
correspondence of, 38, 52–53,
54, 56; *Crisis* contributions by,
57–58; as first black NAACP
executive secretary, 1, 8, 35, 37,
52, 54, 55; Harlem Renaissance
and, 8, 36–37, 39, 51–53, 59;
as Harlem "tour guide," 56;
interracial socializing of, 55;
reputation of, 55; temperament
of, 54; Van Vechten defended by,
47; white publishers and, 54–55,
57–58, 61; writings of, 35, 38,
39–40, 52
Johnson, Malvin Gray, 115, 218n35
Johnson, Rosamond, 35
Joy, Jason, 150
*Jungle Nymph, A* (*Crisis* cover art;
Freelon), 81, *84*

Kansas, 23–24
Kansas City (KS) NAACP branch, 23
Kelley, Florence, 7
Kellogg, Charles, 67, 92
Kentucky, lynching in, 216n7
Kirschke, Amy, 38, 66, 72, 81, 91
Klarman, Michael, 174
Knopf, Alfred, 49, 55, 57
Koppes, Clayton R., 157
Kornweibel, Theodore, 71, 214n9
Krehbiel, H. E., 41
"Krigwa" competition (1926), 87
Krigwa Players' Negro Theater, 69,
217n18
Ku Klux Klan, 12, 17–18, 23–24, 133,
137

Langa, Helen, 113, 114, 118, 218n35
Larsen, Nella, 52–53, 58
Lavery, Emmet, 121
*Law Is Too Slow, The* (lithograph; Bellows), 114
Lawson, John Howard, 170
League of Struggle for Negro Rights, 117–18
Lee, Canada, 150, 168, 170
Leff, Leonard, 137
Left (political faction), 96, 107, 202, 219n48. *See also* Communist Party
legal inequality, 3, 22
Levy, Eugene, 52
Lewis, David Levering, 54, 55, 59, 68, 70, 199, 211n2, 213n38
Lewis, Sinclair, 108
Lewis, Theophilis, 71
Lichtman, Al, 143
*Lifeboat* (film; 1944), 150
*Lincoln's Dream* (unfinished film), 26–27
Little Rock (AR), school desegregation crisis in (1957), 192
Livingston, Myrtle Smith, 103, 104, 106
Locke, Alain, 36, 38–39, 50, 54, 70–71, 103, 108, 153, 213n38
Lomax, Almena, 183
Longview (TX), 37
Lorts, Justin, 186
Los Angeles (CA), 30
Los Angeles (CA) NAACP branch, 13, 18, 160, 161, 163–64, 193, 198
*Los Angeles Daily News,* 141
*Los Angeles Sentinel,* 183
*Los Angeles Tribune,* 183
*Lost Boundaries* (film; 1949), 171–73, 176
Lowndes County (GA), 109
Lukas, Edwin, 184, 185
lynching: brutality of, 109–10, 122;
Communist Party view of, 219n42; defined, 98; federal intervention in, 171; film portrayals of, 17, 27, 100, 125; literary portrayals of, 133, 201–2, 217–18n18, 218n26 (*see also* lynching dramas); narrative of, 5, 99–101, 108–9, 111, 123; numbers of, 98, 101, 122, 216n7, 219n53; photographs of, 111–12; post-WWII upsurge in, 178; purpose of, 98, 100; ritual/spectacle nature of, 100; southern movement against, 99; white attitudes toward, 97, 98–99. *See also* antilynching legislation; NAACP antilynching campaign
"Lynching, The" (McKay), 217n22
*Lynching, The* (painting; Bloch), 219n38
*Lynching, The* (painting; Brown), 115, 117
lynching dramas, 101–7, 201–2, 216n8, 217n14

MacLeish, Archibald, 138
Maltz, Albert, 170
"Mammy" stereotype, 79, 106, 132, 162, 175
Mannix, E. J., 142
Marable, Manning, 67, 169
March on Washington Movement, 138
Marsh, Reginald, 110–11, 115
Marshall (TX), 177
Marshall, Thurgood, 169–70, 171, 198
Mason, Charlotte Osgood, 57
Matheus, John F., 69
Matthews, Mrs. E. R., 69
Mayer, Louis, 145–46
McDaniel, Hattie, 136, 157, 160, 161–62, 164, 166, 167
McKay, Claude: autobiography of, 54; correspondence of, 52, 54; *Crisis*

contributions by, 90; Du Bois and, 44, 48, 85, 90; Johnson (J. W.) and, 54; lynchings in works of, 217n22; White and, 53; writings of, 48, 58, 85, 213n36, 217n22
McKelvey, Raymond, 56
*McLaurin v. Oklahoma,* 174
McQueen, Butterfly, 168
Meeropol, Abel, 125
Meier, August, 5
Mellett, Lowell, 138, 140, 145, 156
Memphis (TN), 155
Menand, Louis, 25
Mencken, H. L., 49, 57
"message movies," 159, 171–73, 174–77
*Messenger* (Brotherhood of Sleeping Car Porters magazine), 39, 71, 215n33
Mfume, Kweisi, 194
MGM, 125, 141, 142, 143, 144–47, 155, 172
Micheaux, Oscar, 31
Mid-Winter Assembly (Baltimore; 1912), 86
Milwaukee (WI) NAACP branch, 184
*Mine Eyes Have Seen* (Dunbar-Nelson), 103
Minneapolis (MN), 21
Minnesota, 23
minstrelsy, 40
*Miracle* case (*Burstyn v. Wilson*), 179
miscegenation, 15–17
miscegenation laws, 34
Mitchel, John, 19
Mitchell, Margaret, 132, 133
Monroe (GA), 178
Moore, Fred, 19
Mosby, William, 218n35
Moskowitz, Henry, 7
motion picture industry: African American employment in, 192–93; anticommunist investigations into, 169–71, 224n19; Jewish moguls in, 221n35; NAACP alliance with, 156–57; profit motive of, 157; racism in, 29, 125; self-censorship by, 19, 135; Senate investigations of, 141; Wilkins and, 191–92; WWII propaganda and, 138–40. *See also* White, Walter, Hollywood campaign of
Motion Picture Research Council, 129–30
motion pictures, 10; all-Negro, 131, 155; censorship of, 18–19; liberalization of, 172; "message movies," 159, 171–73, 174–77; NAACP cultural elitism and, 160, 197; NAACP inclusion strategy toward, 141–42; propaganda films, 138–39, 142; psychological/educational effect of, 129–30, 131–32, 168; racial attitudes influenced by, 187–88
Motion Pictures Producers Association (MPPA), 134, 141–42, 143
Muir, Jean, 141
mulattos/mulattas, 15, 79, 81, 175
Murphy, Carl, 179–80
Muse, Clarence, 161, 164, 167, 183, 223n4
*Mutual Film Corp. v. Industrial Commission of Ohio,* 25
Myrdal, Gunnar, 167

NAACP antilynching campaign, 34; anti-*Birth of a Nation* campaign and, 17; art as propaganda in, 10, 97–98, 101–7, 122, 124–25; effectiveness of, 122–25; fundraising for, 108; investigations, 52, 101, 109, 112; lobbying efforts, 99; local-level responses

NAACP antilynching campaign *(cont.)* to, 22; lynching photographs and, 111–12; WLAL and, 107–11. See also *Art Commentary on Lynching* exhibition (New York, NY; 1935)

NAACP cultural strategy: for anti-*Birth of a Nation* campaign, 22, 177; art approach, 1–2, 5–6, 37–38, 40–42, 59, 154; art as propaganda in, 117, 191–92; censorship, 177, 188–89; in *Crisis,* 2, 31, 63–65, 69, 94–96; as elitist, 124–25, 130–31, 197; in Hollywood, 130–31, 137, 141–42 (*see also under* White, Walter, Hollywood campaign of); legal campaigns vs., 166; NAACP leaders and, 8; national vs. local executions of, 198; objectives of, 6; philosophy underpinning, 196–97; radio and, 187–88; scholarship on, 9–10, 211n2; significance of, 203–4; strengths of, 188, 196; weaknesses of, 124–25, 166, 188–89, 197. *See also* censorship; propaganda

NAACP Image Awards, 194, 195

Naison, Mark, 120

*Nation,* 42–43

National Association for the Advancement of Colored People (NAACP): American Jews and, 221n35; Annual Convention (1922), 97; Annual Convention (1951), 159, 160, 183; Annual Convention (1962), 192; anticommunism and, 169–71; assimilationist tendencies of, 57, 65, 72, 76–79, 131; black leadership of, 1, 7–8, 35, 37; Board of Directors, 12, 93, 142, 186; as bourgeois organization, 86; Communist Party vs., 117–20; as culturally elitist, 92, 160, 166; Drama Committee, 102, 103; Du Bois speech before (1926), 1, 203–4; founding of, 6–7, 18; fundraising problems, 107, 125, 127; Harlem Renaissance and, 36–37, 40, 51–52, 59–61, 154, 160, 199; historical research on, 8–9; Image Awards, 194, 195; Information Division, 128–29; internal divisions in, 93–94, 198; interracial socializing of, 55–56; legal campaigns of, 3, 8–9, 21–22, 33–34, 37, 56, 167, 173–74, 186–87, 199, 202–3; lynching records kept by, 101; magazine of (*see Crisis* (NAACP magazine); membership building efforts, 22, 32, 156; membership of, 93, 201, 214n3; miscegenation laws and, 16–17; race problem as viewed by, 2–5, 32–33; radio and, 153–54; relations with local branches, 163–64, 198; reputation of, 6; Spingarn medal, 40; Spingarn (Amy) prize, 44; white leadership of, 7–8, 22, 33; Youth Council, 105. See also *Amos 'n' Andy* (TV program), NAACP campaign against; *Birth of a Nation, The* (film; 1915), NAACP campaign against; NAACP antilynching campaign; NAACP cultural strategy; *specific officer*

National Board of Censorship of Motion Pictures, 18–19

National Negro Conference (New York, NY; 1909), 7

National Service Bureau, 121

National Urban League, 38, 70–71, 196

Native Americans, 168

Nazism, 148
NBC, 153
Neal, Claude, 110
"Negro, The" (poem; Hughes), 73–75
"Negro in Art" questionnaire, 48–51
Negro Marches On Inc., 151–52
*Negro Soldier, The* (documentary film;
    1944), 151–53, 155, 199
*Negro World* (journal), 39
Nerney, May Childs, 7, 8, 18, 19, 22,
    24, 26
Newark (NJ) Negro Unit, 121
New Deal, 61, 120–24, 140, 159, 195,
    202
"New Era, The" (*Birth of a Nation*
    epilogue; "Hampton Epilogue"),
    26
New Haven (CT), 21
*New Masses* (radical magazine), 118,
    119–20
"New Negro," the, 36, 51–52, 195. *See
    also* Harlem Renaissance
*New Negro, The* (ed. Locke), 36
*New Orleans* (film; 1947), 168
New York (NY), *Birth of a Nation*
    protested in, 19, 23
*New York Age,* 19, 52
New York Krigwa Players, 217n18
*New York Times,* 116
*New York World-Telegram,* 116
"nigger" epithet, 135, 179
*Nigger Heaven* (Van Vechten), 46–48
"Nigger Jeff" (Dreiser), 217n22
Noguchi, Isamu, 114, 116, 219n44
*Not Without Laughter* (Hughes),
    211n3
*No Way Out* (film; 1950), 177–79

"Octoroon" (photograph; anon.), 76
Omedele, Remi, 104
O'Neill, Eugene, 69
Oppenheimer, George, 53, 57

*Opportunity* (National Urban League
    magazine), 38, 39, 70–71, 213n38
Oregon, 23
Orozco, José Clemente, 219n44
Ovington, Mary White, 6–7, 19, 26,
    51, 92
Owen, Chandler, 71
*Ox Bow Incident, The* (film; 1943),
    156
Oxford (MS), 193

pan-Africanism, 75
Paramount Studios, 142
Park, Marlene, 113, 218n35
Parker, Dorothy, 113
Parker, John, 127
Pascoe, Peggy, 16, 17
passing (racial), 175–76
Payne Fund, 129–30
People's Institute, 18
Perkins, Kathy, 101, 216n8
Perry, Leslie, 170, 171
Philadelphia (PA), 30
Phillips County (AR), 37
Pickens, William, 8, 60, 223n4
*Pictures Can Fight!* (exhibition
    catalog; Herndon), 118
Pike, James S., 28
*Pinky* (film; 1949), 171–72, 174–77,
    224n30
*Pittsburgh Courier,* 138, 183
plantation nostalgia, 12
Platt, David, 144–45
Poitier, Sidney, 177, 195
police brutality, 22
Popular Front, 119
Poynter, Nelson, 138, 140, 145, 156
President's Committee on Civil
    Rights, 171
Production Code Administration
    (PCA), 135, 143
Progressives/Progressive Era, 18–19, 25

propaganda, 6; art and, 36, 43–51;
artistic freedom and, 70–71; in
*Birth of a Nation,* 23, 27–28;
Communist use of, 120, 192;
controversy over, 175–76; Du Bois
and, 39, 43–51; in *Gone with the
Wind,* 132; musical, 125; NAACP
antilynching art exhibition and,
117, 120; Senate investigations of,
141; during WWII, 138, 139, 142,
157
propaganda films, 138–39, 142
*Prostrate South, The* (Pike), 28
Providence (RI), 21
Public Works Administration (PWA),
120–21

race journals, 70–72. See also *Crisis*
(NAACP magazine)
race prejudice, 2–3, 4, 32–33, 129–30,
207n2. *See also* racism
race riots, 6, 37, 52, 60
*Rachel* (Grimké), 101–3, 106–7, 124
racial epithets, 179–80, 198
racism: anti-*Birth of a Nation*
campaign and, 25–26;
historiography of, 2; as ideology,
2–5, 97; institutional, 202; in
motion pictures, 125, 129–30;
NAACP cultural strategy and, 201;
use of term, 207n2; WWII and
international awareness of, 167.
*See also* African Americans, racial
stereotypes of
radio, 153–54, 184, 196
ragtime, 40, 41
Rampersad, Arnold, 85
Ramsdell, C. William, 210n31
Randolph, A. Philip, 71, 138, 169
RD-DR Corp, 172–73
Reconstruction Era: film portrayals of,
12–13, 26, 28, 132–33, 134, 145;

historical consensus on, 28, 29,
210n31
Red Summer (1919), 37, 60
religious symbolism, 219n38
Republican Party, 99
restrictive covenants, 173–74, 203
Rhode Island, 23
Rice, Anne P., 123
Richardson, Willis, 53, 69
"Rise and Fall of Free Speech, The"
(pamphlet; Griffith), 25
*Rising Wind, A* (White), 152
Roberts, Davis, 193
Robinson, Bill ("Bojangles"), 41
Roosevelt, Eleanor, 141
Roosevelt, Franklin D., 108, 138–39, 140
*Rope and Faggot* (White), 114
Rosenbloom, Nancy, 19
Rosentiel, Lewis, 185
Rossen, Robert, 170
Rowe, Billy, 183
Russell, Charles Edward, 7

*Saboteur* (film; 1942), 155
*Safe* (G. Johnson), 104, 217n14
*Sahara* (film; 1943), 147, 148–49,
156, 162, 170
Sartain, Lee, 198
Savage, Barbara, 9–10, 153, 154, 202
savage stereotype, 148
Schenley Distillers, 183–84
Schneider, Mark, 96
Schomburg, Arthur, 53
school segregation, 203
Schuyler, George S., 42–43, 47–48,
50, 71, 110, 132, 215n33
Scott, Henry, 193
Scottsboro Boys, 118, 119
Scottsboro Defense Committee, 119
Screen Actors Guild, 142, 161
*Scrub Me Mama with a Boogie Beat*
(cartoon; 1941), 222n46

Scurlock, Addison, 63, *64*, 86
segregation: *Birth of a Nation* and, 27; Du Bois editorials on, 93; in military, 92, 152, 171, 223n4; NAACP cultural strategy and, 95–96; NAACP interracial socializing and, 55–56; NAACP legal work against, 3, 21–22, 37, 52, 95–96, 203; NAACP stance on, 76; racism as cause of, 3; residential, 52, 56, 173–74; Supreme Court cases involving, 173–74
Selma (AL), 193
Selznick, David O., 133, 134, 135, 137, 141, 142, 144, 168, 220–21n13
Selznick International, 133
separatism, 155
"Servant, The" (F. Johnson), 91
servant stereotype, 128, 136, 157, 162, 166, 168, 191
sexuality: in *Crisis* illustrations, 81–86; interracial, 15–17; taboos, 109
sharecroppers, 86, *87*, 98
Sheen, Edwin Drummond, 86–87
*Shelley v. Kraemer,* 173–74
Sherrard-Johnson, Cherene, 76, 79
Shillady, John, 8, 22–23, 60
*Since You Went Away* (film; 1944), 157
Sinclair, Upton, 108
Sklaroff, Lauren Rebecca, 9, 120, 122, 124, 131–32, 155
slave narratives, 79
*Smith v. Allwright,* 167
"Social Life of Colored America" (photograph; Scurlock), 86
*Song of the South* (musical film; 1946), 167–68
South Carolina House of Representatives, 15–16
*Southern Holiday* (lithograph; Sternberg), 114

Soviet Union, 192
Spence, Eulalie, 69
Spencer, Kenneth, 148
Spingarn, Amy, 36, 44, 58, 69
Spingarn, Arthur, 7, 168, 171
Spingarn, Hope, 168
Spingarn, Joel E., 7, 22, 36, 50, 92, 93
Spingarn medal, 40
Spingarn (Amy) prize, 44
spirituals, 40, 41
Springfield (IL), 6
Springfield (MA), 21
Stacey, Rubin, 112
*Star of Ethiopia, The* (historical pageant; Du Bois), 29–31, 211n38
Stephens, Judith, 101, 216n8
stereotypes. *See* African Americans, racial stereotypes of
Stern, Philip Van Doren, 146
Stern, Seymour, 17
Sternberg, Harry, 114, 219n44
Sterne, Elaine, 26, 210n29
Stevens, Thaddeus, 27, 144–45, 146
St. Louis (MO), 21
Stokes, Melvyn, 11, 21, 24, 25, 30, 31, 32
Storey, Moorfield, 3, 7, 19, 28–29, 97, 99
*Stormy Weather* (film; 1943), 155
"Strange Fruit" (song; Meeropol), 124–25
Strub, Whitney, 155
*Struggle for Negro Rights* exhibition (New York, NY; 1935), 117–19, 120
St. Vincent Millay, Edna, 108
Sullivan, Patricia, 21, 37
*Sunday Morning in the South, A* (G. Johnson), 104, 106
*Survey Graphic,* 56
"Swamp Mocassin" (Matheus), 69
Sweatt, Heman, 174

*Sweatt v. Painter,* 174
Sweet, Ossian, 56
*Swing Mikado* (Federal Theater
    production), 121

Talented Tenth, 5, 59, 130–31, 199
Taylor, Prentiss, 219n38
television, 10, 154, 159, 180–86, 187–
    89, 192–93, 194. See also *Amos 'n'
    Andy* entries; *specific program*
Tennessee, 178
*Tennessee Johnson* (film; 1942),
    144–47
*Thank Your Lucky Stars* (film; 1943),
    157
*This Is Her First Lynching* (drawing;
    Marsh), 110–11, 115
*This Is the Army* (film; 1943), 157
Thomas, J. Parnell, 170
Thompson, William, 20
369th Regiment, 211n3
Thurman, Wallace, 39, 47–48, 71
Title VII (Civil Rights Act, 1964), 193
Tolnay, S. E., 219n53
Toomer, Jean, 44, 108, 218n26
Topeka (KS), 186
*To Secure These Rights* (President's
    Committee on Civil Rights), 171
Tremont Theater (Boston, MA), 20, 26
Trotter, William Monroe, 19–20, 23, 31
Truman, Harry S., 169, 171
Turner, Mary, 109–10, 218n26
Tuskegee Institute, 31, 98, 101,
    210n29
Twentieth Century Fox, 142, 144,
    147–48, 150, 155, 172, 174–75,
    178

Uncle Remus stories, 40
*Uncle Tom's Children* (Wright),
    217n22
United Artists, 168

United States Constitution, 18;
    Fifteenth Amendment, 7; First
    Amendment, 25; Fourteenth
    Amendment, 7
United States Fair Employment
    Practices Commission, 138
United States House of
    Representatives: antilynching
    legislation in, 99, 105; Census
    Committee, 60; Committee on
    Un-American Activities (HUAC),
    169–70, 224n19
United States Office of Facts and
    Figures (OFF), 138, 139–40
United States Office of War
    Information (OWI), 138–39, 151,
    153, 155, 156–57, 162, 166
United States Senate, 99, 105, 141;
    Judiciary Committee, 108
United States Supreme Court: *Brown
    v. Board of Education,* 9, 186;
    *Guinn v. the United States,* 15;
    *Miracle* case (*Burstyn v. Wilson*),
    179; *Mutual Film Corp. v.
    Industrial Commission of Ohio,*
    25; NAACP legal work at, 37;
    Parker (John) as nominee for, 127;
    *Shelley v. Kraemer,* 173–74; *Smith
    v. Allwright,* 167; *Sweatt v. Painter,*
    174
United States War Department,
    151–52, 153, 162, 199
Universal Film Manufacturing
    Company, 26–27, 142, 222n46
University of Oklahoma Graduate
    School of Education, 174
University of Texas Law School, 174
"Unquenchable Fire, The" (Bagnall),
    218n22

Vanguard (organization), 118, 119
Van Vechten, Carl, 46–48, 49, 108, 113

*Variety* magazine, 155
Vendryes, Margaret, 113, 115, 218n35
Verney, Kevern, 198
Viking Press, 53
Villard, Oswald Garrison, 7
Vincent, Ted, 92
Voting Rights Act (1965), 9, 195

Waco (TX), 112
Wagner, Robert, 99, 108
Wagner-Van Nuys-Gavagan
    antilynching bill, 105
Wald, Lillian, 7
Walling, William English, 6–7
Walsh, David, 20
Walters, Alexander, 7
*Walter White Show, The* (radio
    program), 154
Wanger, Walter, 140, 142, 144
Ward, Brian, 153, 154
Ward, William Hayes, 7
Warner, Harry, 151
Warner Brothers, 142, 150–51
Washington (DC), 30, 37, 63
Washington, Booker T., 19
Washington, Jesse, 112
*Washington Tribune,* 136
Waters, Ethel, 175, 181
Watson, J. B., 81
Watson, Steven, 70, 211n3
Watts, Jill, 158, 163
Weinberger, Stephen, 11–12
*Well, The* (film; 1951), 179
Wells, H. G., 69
Wesley, Charles, 220–21n13
West, Rebecca, 56
West Virginia, 23
*We've Come a Long, Long Way*
    (documentary film; 1944), 152
Wheeler, Laura, 68
White, Walter, 10; anti-*Birth of
    a Nation* lobbying efforts of,
23–24; antilynching activism of,
98, 107–8, 109, 111, 113, 122,
127 (see also *Art Commentary
on Lynching* exhibition (New
York, NY; 1935); Writers' League
Against Lynching (WLAL)); art
vs. propaganda debate and, 51,
96, 97; autobiography of, 111;
biography of, 211n2; on *Birth
of a Nation*'s artistic merits, 13;
congressional testimony of, 60,
108; correspondence of, 38, 52–53,
165, 168; criticism directed at,
75–76, 223n4; death of, 187, 191;
Du Bois and, 93, 223n4; Harlem
Renaissance and, 8, 36, 39, 51–54,
59, 127; as Harlem "tour guide,"
56–57; health of, 187; interracial
socializing of, 55, 127, 158, 187,
223n4; lobbying tactics of, 33, 125,
127, 142, 147; marriage of, 187; as
NAACP assistant secretary, 52, 54;
as NAACP executive secretary, 93,
128; racial violence investigated
by, 37, 109; radio program of,
154; on southern "enlightened
selfishness," 98; temperament
of, 53–54, 166; white publishers
and, 54–55, 57, 61; as WPA Five
Arts Project board member, 121;
writings of, 49, 51, 57, 58, 109,
114, 152, 160–61, 217–18n22;
WWII troop visits by, 150, 152
White, Walter, Hollywood campaign
    of: anticommunism and, 169, 170–
71; black actors and, 158, 159–62,
165, 166–67, 176, 187; cultural
strategy of, 127, 130–31, 142–44,
154–55, 158, 187, 199; *Gone with
the Wind,* 132–37; Hollywood
Bureau proposal, 162–67, 187;
lobbying tactics used in, 137–38,

White, Walter, Hollywood campaign of *(cont.)*
    142–44, 147, 184–85; post-WWII films and, 167–68, 171–73, 174–79; radio and, 154; reasons for, 127–28, 129–30; scholarship on, 131–32; successes, 147–49, 158, 187, 196, 203; television, 180–86; *Tennessee Johnson,* 144–47; weaknesses, 158, 187; WWII-era films, 147–53; WWII propaganda efforts and, 138–40, 151–53
white middle class, 133–34
white patronage, 61, 63–65, 70
white primaries, 203
white publishers, 51, 54–55, 57–58
white supremacy, 3, 13–14, 31, 100, 196, 200, 207n2
white womanhood, 100, 109
*Why We Fight* (film series), 151
Wibecan, George, 19
Widener, Daniel, 130
Wilkerson, Carmiele, 90
Wilkins, Roy, 164; as *Crisis* editor, 94; film reviews by, 136–37; motion picture industry and, 191–92; as NAACP assistant secretary, 128, 150; as NAACP executive secretary, 191; New Deal cultural projects monitored by, 121; as radio advisor, 153; radio programs reviewed by, 187; WWII propaganda efforts and, 139–40
Williams, Megan, 76
Willkie, Wendell, 131, 141–42, 147, 155, 156, 162, 179
Wilson, Dooley, 156
Wilson, Woodrow, 28

Wintz, Cary, 54
WLIB (New York, NY), 154
"Woman to the Rescue" (*Crisis* cartoon), 79
women's rights, 81
Wood, Amy Louise, 100
Woodruff, Hale, 115, 218n35
Woolworth building (New York, NY), 73–75
*Word, Image, and the New Negro* (Carroll), 66
worker solidarity, 118
Works Progress Administration (WPA), 121
World War I, 22–23, 25, 33, 92
World War II: African American cultural representation during, 195–96; African American migration during/following, 156; anticommunism following, 169; black actor employment opportunities during, 165; NAACP cultural strategy during, 33, 61, 127, 128, 131; NAACP membership growth following, 200; propaganda films during, 138–39, 142; race relations following, 159, 167; scholarship on, 9, 131
Wright, George, 216n7
Wright, Richard, 217n22
Writers' League Against Lynching (WLAL), 97, 99, 107–11, 127

Zamir, Shamoon, 90
Zangrando, Robert, 107, 124
Zanuck, Darryl, 141, 142, 143–44, 148, 172, 174–76

CIVIL RIGHTS AND THE STRUGGLE FOR BLACK EQUALITY
IN THE TWENTIETH CENTURY

SERIES EDITORS
Steven F. Lawson, Rutgers University
Cynthia Griggs Fleming, University of Tennessee

*Freedom's Main Line: The Journey of Reconciliation and the Freedom Rides*
Derek Charles Catsam

*Subversive Southerner: Anne Braden and the Struggle for Racial Justice in the Cold War South*
Catherine Fosl

*Constructing Affirmative Action: The Struggle for Equal Employment Opportunity*
David Hamilton Golland

*River of Hope: Black Politics and the Memphis Freedom Movement, 1865–1954*
Elizabeth Gritter

*Sidelined: How American Sports Challenged the Black Freedom Struggle*
Simon Henderson

*Becoming King: Martin Luther King Jr. and the Making of a National Leader*
Troy Jackson

*Civil Rights in the Gateway to the South: Louisville, Kentucky, 1945–1980*
Tracy E. K'Meyer

*In Peace and Freedom: My Journey in Selma*
Bernard LaFayette Jr. and Kathryn Lee Johnson

*Democracy Rising: South Carolina and the Fight for Black Equality since 1865*
Peter F. Lau

*Civil Rights Crossroads: Nation, Community, and the Black Freedom Struggle*
Steven F. Lawson

*Selma to Saigon: The Civil Rights Movement and the Vietnam War*
Daniel S. Lucks

*In Remembrance of Emmett Till: Regional Stories and Media Responses to the Black Freedom Struggle*
Darryl Mace

*Freedom Rights: New Perspectives on the Civil Rights Movement*
edited by Danielle L. McGuire and John Dittmer

*This Little Light of Mine: The Life of Fannie Lou Hamer*
Kay Mills

*After the Dream: Black and White Southerners since 1965*
Timothy J. Minchin and John A. Salmond

*Fighting Jim Crow in the County of Kings: The Congress of Racial Equality in Brooklyn*
Brian Purnell

*Roy Wilkins: The Quiet Revolutionary and the NAACP*
Yvonne Ryan

*Thunder of Freedom: Black Leadership and the Transformation of 1960s Mississippi*
Sue [Lorenzi] Sojourner with Cheryl Reitan

*Art for Equality: The NAACP's Cultural Campaign for Civil Rights*
Jenny Woodley

*For Jobs and Freedom: Race and Labor in America since 1865*
Robert H. Zieger

CPSIA information can be obtained at www.ICGtesting.com
Printed in the USA
BVOW05*1513090514

353029BV00003B/6/P